Primitive Passions

ALSO BY MARIANNA TORGOVNICK

Gone Primitive: Savage Intellects, Modern Lives

Crossing Ocean Parkway:
Readings by an Italian American Daughter

Primitive Passions

Men, Women, and the Quest for Ecstasy

Marianna Torgovnick

The University of Chicago Press
Chicago and London

Reprinted by arrangement with Alfred A. Knopf, Inc.

The University of Chicago Press, Chicago 60637
The University of Chicago Press, Ltd., London
Copyright © 1996 by Marianna Torgovnick
All rights reserved. Originally published 1997
University of Chicago Press Edition 1998
Printed in the United States of America

04 03 02 01 00 99 98   6 5 4 3 2 1

Library of Congress Cataloging-in-Publication Data
Torgovnick, Marianna, 1949–
Primitive passions : men, women, and the quest for ecstasy /
Marianna Torgovnick.
p.   cm.
Originally published: 1st ed. New York : Alfred A. Knopf, 1997.
Includes bibliographical references and index.
ISBN 0-226-80837-8 (pbk. : alk. paper)
1. Social structure.   2. Primitivism.   3. Man—Animal nature.
4. Sex role.   5. Spirituality.   I. Title.
[GN478.T67   1998]
305.3—dc21   98-25005   CIP

TO STUART

CONTENTS

Primitive Passions

Cross from the highway, near Nambe, New Mexico, 1963
Photographer: Todd Webb
Courtesy of Todd Webb and Olaf Olaf

INTRODUCTION

We listen to our inmost selves—
and do not know which sea we hear murmuring.
MARTIN BUBER, *Ecstatic Confessions*

W HEN THE anthropologist Bronislaw Malinowski was studying sex and trade on a South Sea island, he confessed in his private diaries to feeling by turns "ultimate mastery" and "elements of worry." Mastery flowed from collecting data and documents that would build his professional reputation. Worry arose from what Malinowski called "the atmosphere created by foreign bodies"—especially those of naked women who unselfconsciously displayed "the beauty of the body so hidden to us, whites."[1] Enthralled and confused, the ethnographer struggled to maintain his focus on work and to resist hating the Trobriand islanders as "animals" who aroused his lust and excited his fear of losing control. He guarded against the women by defining himself as a white man who could not indulge in sexual dalliances or masturbation because of "moral tenets"; and he graded himself on how well each day's thoughts and conduct measured up.

But Malinowski was less certain about how to handle another temptation, one more subtle than the lure of women but connected somehow, he sensed, with them: a feeling of "letting myself dissolve in the landscape," "moments when you merge with objective reality—true nir-vana." When these sensations came over him, Malinowksi gave himself a good shake, checked to make sure he was not developing fever, and plunged back with determination into his data and abstract theory. He wanted to get back to his intellectual work and shrugged off as a forbidden desire the impulse towards merging.

In the Western tradition, the kind of shrugging off Malinowski enacted in the Trobriands has been a frequent gesture.[2] Yet the attraction to "merging with objective reality" has also been persistent. My claim in *Primitive Passions* is that the West has tended to scant some vital human emotions and sensations of relatedness and interdependence—though it has never eliminated them. These sensations include effacement of the self and the intuition of profound connections between humans and land, humans and animals, humans and minerals, of a kind normally found in Europe and the United States only within mystical traditions. The link between such sensations and "primitive" peoples, while it is not inevitable, is, I will show, neither trivial nor incidental in the Western imagination.

The word "primitive" is sometimes used in a derogatory sense to mean "simple" or "crude," with evolutionist connotations of inferiority. That is not how I use the word, which has a rich history of alternative meanings. In its most generalized sense, "primitive" refers to a posited but ultimately unknowable original state, whether of humans or of animals, nature, tissue and cell, or of religious and social institutions. It entered the English language with special reference to the Christian church; only later, in the eighteenth century, did it come to refer to cells, nature, and indigenous peoples.[3] Today, "the primitive" often refers to specific groups living traditional lives (the Asmat in Irian Jaya, the Yanomani in Brazil, and many others)—but it also encompasses a great deal more. "The primitive" denotes the eons of prehistoric human experience; it refers as well to societies such as the Aztecs, with highly developed but now mysterious or exotic-seeming ancient histories. Most of all, "the primitive" describes a vast, generalized image, an aggregate of places, things, and experiences associated with various groups and peoples: Africa, the Amazon, or the American Southwest; communal drumming and ecstatic dancing; initiation and other rituals that express respect for the powers of nature and the supernatural.

Properly speaking, primitivism refers not just to an interest in or borrowing from indigenous groups—though that is how the term is commonly used today. In fact, this is an important, but relatively late meaning, and one that should be informed by the recognition that, contrary to the practice of many primitivists, "primitive peoples" are diverse in terms of their social systems and beliefs and typically exist today in contact with the modern world. Primitivism inhabits thinking about origins and pure states; it informs desires for known beginnings and, by extension, for predictable ends. Primitivism is the utopian desire to go back and recover irreducible features of the psyche, body, land, and community—to reinhabit core experiences. This book probes all of these meanings of the term, with special attention to connections enacted in modern lives between primitivism and spiritual emotions.

Primitive Passions widens and deepens a journey I began in *Gone Primitive*, which critiqued men's representations of Africa and the South Pacific and primitivism's damaging effects both in the West and abroad.[4] In the creations of the men that I studied there, a repressed or distorted fascination with the primitive often veered towards preoccupation with irrational frenzy and violence, expressed frequently in themes such as cannibalism, human sacrifice, and head-hunting. Typically, these themes coincided with uneasy, because unacknowledged, obsessions with male homosexuality, the working class, and women—and with the fragility and alienation of the modern human ego. Sexuality was often lurking in the male fascination with the primitive—but a sexuality that was interlaced with violent themes and that was neither recognized nor expressed in connection with more positive emotions.[5]

As I wrote *Gone Primitive*, I was tantalized by the way in which men like Malinowski repressed some of their strongest positive feelings for the primitive, what he called the nirvana impulse and other thinkers of his day called the oceanic—best defined as a dissolution of subject-object divisions so radical that one experiences the sensation of merging with the universe. I came to understand that a comprehensive psychology of the West's fascination with the primitive would require a broader consideration of male encounters with the oceanic, as well as an understanding of a variety of female responses to comparable experiences.

Fortunately, there were several odd things about how the men I had studied used motifs like human sacrifice—oddities that inspired my curiosity. Cannibalism, human sacrifice, and head-hunting apparently did not and do not really exist within most indigenous cultures or, at the very least, the extent of their practice has been wildly overstated in the West. In fact, Europeans and Americans seem to have been so obsessed with the consumption of human flesh and the hunting of heads that they described in macabre or bizarre detail practices that often either were not present or did not function in a morbid way among indigenous peoples. Indeed, when genuine cannibalism and head-hunting have been documented, they have been revealed to have specific spiritual or purgative functions and an exquisitely detailed etiquette.

Cannibalism, to cite an instance that has become a cultural cliché, was apparently never routinely used to satisfy hunger, nor did it take place amid conditions of frenzy and "horror" around the proverbial old cooking-pot; instead, it was a methodical ritual and even its victims were likely to have understood its purpose and significance.[6] Similarly, the Asmat of Irian Jaya, and other groups known to be head-hunters into the 1960s, collected heads according to specific customs and attached specific meanings to the process.[7] Although male adventurers often expressed the fear that the Asmat would head-hunt them, the Asmat actually targeted only members of rival tribes. And they treasured not just the heads of their enemies but also the heads of their own dead fathers, which they used as pillows at night, to charge their dreams with ancestral power.[8]

When, in the 1960s, the Asmat were formally converted to Christianity, controversy arose among some missionaries about whether the skulls so valued by the Asmat could be included in Christian ritual. There were uneasy compromises; photographs show priests and altar boys in full church regalia standing behind a row of human skulls.[9] One can understand why the priests felt uneasy. Yet the incorporation of skulls into Christian ritual was not really all that much of a stretch. Bones and other bodily relics of martyrs and saints have long been features of Catholicism and certain other strands of Christianity. What is more, motifs such as cannibalism, human sacrifice, and head-hunting resonate with the most basic elements of Western religious narratives, where they are associated not with sexuality, violence, horror, and alienation but with the fullest sort of communion and redemption.

In fact, the best and most important example of the double valence of motifs such as human sacrifice and cannibalism can be found in the broad contours of Christ's own history.[10] *"Take, eat; this is my body.* And he took the cup, and gave thanks, and gave it to them, saying, *Drink ye all of it; For this is my blood"*—these are Christ's words at the Last Supper.[11] Christ is the ultimate human sacrifice in the Western tradition, intended to make good what went wrong at the beginning of time in the Garden of Eden. He urged faith rather than reason as the one thing that would ensure salvation, and challenged many religious institutions. Traditions within Christianity sometimes acknowledge connections between Christ's story and other acts of human or animal sacrifice. Biblical typology, for example, customarily reads both Isaac and the lamb actually slain by Abraham as prefigurations or "types" of Christ; a standard Catholic image is the bleeding heart of Jesus, in which Christ displays to the viewer his beating heart—an image reminiscent of Aztec sacrifice and Western writing about it.

In the course of my work with religious materials and primitivist narratives, motifs such as cannibalism, human sacrifice, and the cultivation of powers counter to rationality came to seem profoundly significant. In fact, I began to see the double register of such motifs, within both primitivism and orthodox religious traditions, as a primary clue to a comprehensive psychology of Western fascination with the primitive, which can express itself in a variety of ways: negatively—for example, as fear of the primitive or as a detour into violence; and positively—as admiration for the primitive, conceived to be the conduit of spiritual emotions. The root connection between primitivism and religious traditions can be understood in this way: like the religions whose emotions it resembles and evokes, fascination with the primitive begins with the discontinuities separating human bodies, animals, and inanimate things—and seeks to bridge the gap.

From this perspective, the history of European and American encounters with "primitive" groups reads for the most part like a tragedy of errors and of opportunities missed. The West has often been described as guilty in its relationship to indigenous peoples—guilty of imperialism, racism, genocide, and almost constant exploitation and greed. That view is easy to understand given the history of imperialism and its mind-boggling effects in the past and even today, in a supposedly postcolonial age. I do not at all want to scant that devastating history, which includes—among its innumerable horrors—the enslavement of millions of Africans, the death of up to 18 million Indians in the Americas, even some of the recent troubles in countries like Rwanda.[12] While the encounters in *Primitive Passions* may seem a vivid contrast to attitudes that have been seen as typically Western, it will be my argument that they can be more accurately understood as representing different accents, a pattern of responses that is also native to the West: more openness to the Other, more surrender to perceived divine forces, and most of all more willingness to suspend the normative conditions of the Western self. The differences between the stereotypical Western response and the ones reflected in these encounters are enough to suggest the dynamic behind Western primitivism.

The West has been engaged, almost continuously, in defining itself against a series of "primitive" Others in its midst and without: from Mother-worshipping peoples in what is now Greece and central Europe; to the "barbarians" of Germania, Gaul, and Britannia; to witches and religious deviants; through Africans, Native Americans, and others. Differentiation from the Other is a response to the disruptive effects of identification with the Other. It has amounted to a rejection of certain "irrational" or "mystical" aspects of the Western self, expressed in the attempt to project them either onto groups marginalized in the West (Gypsies and women, for example) or onto primitives abroad. Fascination with the primitive thus involves a dialectic between, on the one hand, a loathing and demonizing of certain rejected parts of the Western self and, on the other, the urge to reclaim them.

My broadest claim, then, is this: the primitive is the sign and symbol of desires the West has sought to repress—desires for direct correspondences between bodies and things, direct correspondences between experience and language, direct correspondences between individual beings and the collective life force. It is the sign and symbol of desire for a full and sated sense of the universe. Such desires are complex and can lead to multiple results. They can be sentimentalized, even to the point of affectation. Or they can be denied. They can unleash or deviate into an obsession with violence and with death as a threshold experience. Or they can enhance a spiritual perception of nature and foster an intense feeling of community.

But even at its most idyllic, Western fascination with the primitive retains a dangerous edge. Perhaps because the correspondences between bodies and things are never complete or permanent, fascination with the primitive can detour, and sometimes has detoured, into violence. Perhaps because a constant awareness of death can vitiate the activities that fill daily lives, fascination with the primitive can be, and sometimes has been, misanthropic, neglectful of ordinary human communities, and even suicidal. In contact with the oceanic, Westerners often back off, intuiting that the sensation erodes the sense of selfhood necessary for mature existence in a humanistic, democratic state. The impulses behind Western fascination with the primitive are explosive and hot—but also potentially transcendent.

· · ·

THE HEART of this book is the phenomenon of merging, as it plays itself out through primitivism in contemporary life. But we cannot understand that phenomenon without looking back to the 1910s and 1920s—ancestral decades for primitivism today. During the teens and twenties, masks and sculptures from Africa and the South Pacific moved decisively out of specialized ethnographic collections and into museums and galleries via borrowings by artists from Picasso and Brancusi to Man Ray and Klee, who found in them a power previously untapped in Western art.[13] Soon, as photographs of the era show, fashionable homes often displayed an African statue or mask. In 1925, Josephine Baker dazzled Paris in La Revue Nègre, clad in a grass skirt and banana necklace. Throughout Europe, jazz was hailed for having captured an authentic primitive beat. Edgar Rice Burroughs' best-selling Tarzan novels and the numerous films based on them fed an insatiable curiosity about Africa and Africans and promulgated stereotypical images.[14]

In a similar way, during the 1920s, ethnographic studies moved out of universities and into bookstores and ordinary homes: Malinowski's *Argonauts of the Western Pacific* and *The Sexual Life of Savages* were published then, as were Margaret Mead's *Coming of Age in Samoa,* Franz Boas' *Anthropology and Modern Life,* and Marcel Mauss' *The Gift;* Ruth

Benedict's *Patterns of Culture* followed shortly.[15] Across many differences, what these books shared was the sense that primitive societies provide an illuminating model for understanding the modern industrialized
world because they are organized around patterns of experience different
from those in the West: gift-giving versus accumulation, for example; or
matriliny (descent of names and property through the mother's line) versus patriliny. Anthropological texts provided readers with vicarious experiences, much as novels do; they also served as a benchmark for
evaluating life in Europe and the United States.

Even figures who are not commonly associated with primitivism par-
took in this cultural fervor. T. S. Eliot, for example, is not usually thought
of as a primitivist. Yet he had a broadly gauged interest in, even an obsession with, anthropological texts. In 1923, Eliot wrote an essay called
"The Beating of a Drum," in which he said that modern poets must capture the rhythms of modern life, much as the drummer does in an African
tribe.[16] From 1923 through 1927, he struggled to finish a play called
Sweeney Agonistes, which explores "birth, copulation, and death" on a
"cannibal isle" and tries to reinvent ritual in modern life.[17] After 1927,
Eliot turned more and more to spiritual thinking in order to resolve the
questions about modern life that plagued him. In this movement from
the idea of the primitive to spiritual emotions, he resembles many of the
figures studied in this book—figures like Carl Jung, D. H. Lawrence, Isak
Dinesen, Beryl Markham, and Georgia O'Keeffe—who during the 1920s
were exploring Africa, Mexico, and the American Southwest, or rendering their impressions in prose or paint.

Much art and thought during the 1910s and 1920s began with the
evolutionist premise that Europeans and Americans were superior to
primitive Others.[18] But an important countervailing tendency to idealize
the primitive is noticeable as well. Underlying that tendency was a sense
of despair and anxiety caused by World War I, which made people ask the
vexed question of how and why the West had taken the wrong path.
Under the pressure of despair, many thinkers in the West began to recon-
sider the idea of the primitive.

During World War I, for example, Sigmund Freud wrote an essay in
which he lamented that "the great powers among the white nations upon
whom the leadership of the human race has fallen" had not succeeded "in

discovering another way of settling misunderstandings and conflicts of interest" different from the violence and hatred of war. He went further by extensively comparing civilized and primitive men and concluding that, in some respects, primitives fared better in the comparison: primitives, he said, are at least capable of appreciating the fact of death, of feeling remorse, and do not, like modern Europeans, hide the reality of mass death under the veils of "civilized" thinking.[19]

In 1923, the philosopher and Judaic scholar Martin Buber also compared modern Europeans to primitives in lamenting the state of the West. Buber focused on relationships of mastery—human beings over other human beings and humans over other categories of existence, such as animals and rocks—as the root cause of Western malaise.[20] "This is the exalted melancholy of our fate," he wrote, "that every *Thou* in our world must become an *It*." Buber went on to express hope for the return of what he called "I-Thou" thinking, in which every self recognizes the integrity and holiness of every other self—human, animal, or even mineral. The concept was based on his understanding of primitive groups, who still experienced, he claimed, "the true original unity, the lived relation," and so could serve as a model for the West. In fact, he said, the "power to enter into relation [is] the power in virtue of which alone man can live the life of the spirit." Buber believed that "in the beginning"—of language, of human consciousness—there existed mutual and unhierarchized "relation." If in the beginning, he asked, why not now?[21]

In his work, Buber emphasized mystical traditions within orthodox religions rather than the religions per se.[22] Many thinkers of the day shared his interest in mysticism, sometimes even criticizing institutionalized churches for curbing mystical impulses. In 1927, for example, a leading Catholic theologian and novelist in France, Romain Rolland, wrote a book whose implications staggered Sigmund Freud and shook—though fell short of shattering—Freud's belief in the inevitability and rightness of civilization. Like Buber, Rolland believed that the experience of dissolved boundaries and the interpenetration of the self with the cosmos is a universal spiritual experience. His model was the life of Ramakrishna, in which the Hindu saint describes himself several times as being like salt dissolved in the great ocean of the universe.[23] Rolland wrote to Freud urging the psychoanalyst to rethink the origin of religion since Freud had, Rolland claimed, justly criticized religious institutions in the West but had not yet understood the core religious emotion, which he believed resembled Ramakrishna's oceanic sense. Freud considered Rolland's contention for eighteen months before replying to his friend's letter; he also wrestled with it as he wrote *Civilization and Its Discontents*. In fact, in a letter to Rolland, Freud said, dramatically, that the idea of the oceanic "had left him no peace."[24]

Rolland would not have been surprised by the intensity of Freud's reaction. For in *The Life of Ramakrishna*, Rolland claimed that Europeans had "murdered sleep" by their deeds in World War I. He urged Europe to "wet its lips at the artery of immortality" (an image strikingly evocative, once again, of cannibalism). By "the artery of immortality" he meant the kind of mystical, oceanic oneness he saw in Western mystics (he names Teresa of Avila) and available still in primitive religions and in the religions of the colonized East.

Interest in the primitive recurred after the wide-scale devastation of World War II. In 1944, important intellectuals who had fled Nazi Germany, like Max Horkheimer and Theodor Adorno, blamed Enlightenment rationality and too much suppression of magical thought for the recent ills of Western civilization.[25] But this time, the idea of the primitive as a source of renovating power was complicated and problematized by its appropriation in Nazi rhetoric of the "Folk," "Blood," and "Land"—a cruel undertow that was itself a form of primitivism and oceanic thought. Nazi rituals, like the infamous rallies at Nuremberg—with their torches, chants, and wheeling configurations of bodies—seemed to represent a return to barbarism, the primitive, and the oceanic, albeit in a warped, demonic form.[26]

To some extent, the oceanic has never lost the taint of Nazism, which seemed to validate the fear that it was a phenomenon inimical to the humanist democratic spirit, one that erodes the integrity of the individual self. But in its connection with the primitive, it continued to be recommended by some as an antidote to the ills of Western life. In 1955, for example, in *Tristes Tropiques*, the famous anthropologist Claude Lévi-Strauss reflected sadly on European encounters with Amazon Indians as a sign of what had gone wrong in Western history. For him, the missteps were in the development of hierarchical thinking and technological advances that had led to "monoculture," "filth," and the projected end of "our species" by nuclear war. But Lévi-Strauss hoped against all hope that "what was done, but turned out wrong, can be done again."[27] After World War I, then, and, although with increased complexity, after World War II, primitive peoples and their cultures became common points of reference—and often an image of potential renewal and change.

I do not mean to suggest that the twentieth century was the first or only time when the West was obsessed with the primitive and attributed to it reinvigorating value. Far from it. The locus classicus of the idea of the "noble savage" living a pure life in nature is Jean-Jacques Rousseau's *Discourse on the Origins of Inequality*, published in 1755; prior to that, Montaigne had written a famous defense of "primitive" peoples in an essay called "On Cannibals."[28] In fact, since ancient times and the earliest explorations of Africa and the Americas, primitive peoples had excited fierce interest and two broad kinds of reactions in the West: fear and horror at the primitives' paganism, licentiousness, and violence; admiration for their communal life and idyllic closeness to nature.

The twentieth century did not completely revise these binary reactions: indeed, we shall see them replicated by several figures in the case studies that follow. But it did give them wider and more varied forms of expression both in intellectual milieus and in individual lives. The primitive continued to be associated with heathenism, sexuality, and excess in a way that supported the idea that primitives needed Western guidance and control—in short, the goals of imperialism and empire. But alternatively—and with increasing force up through our time—primitivism became a medium of soul-searching and self-transformation in which the idea of merging has been key, especially for people who feel ill at ease or constrained in the West.

The association of primitives with self-transformation and dissolved boundaries between people and things is not—I must be clear about this—completely factual and inevitable. Instead, it is largely the result of specific historical contexts and of metaphors used to describe primitives that acquired, in the course of time and repetition, the iron force of fact. When Europeans first encountered Africans, American Indians, and others, certain "unusual" or "magical" aspects of their lives seemed especially striking: "nakedness" and the apparent absence of work or agriculture, for example; extended or unusual kinship systems; totemism, animism, and shamanism.[29] Later, once anthropology had emerged as a discipline, these aspects came to be ascribed axiomatically and thus skewed ethnographic studies. The application of the category of "kinship," for example, actively distorted ethnographic findings by effacing social structures that were not based on notions of kinship. In the same way, the categories of "sexuality" and "magic" received disproportionate attention. As Adam Kuper puts it: "The various models of primitive societies are typically straightforward, even mechanical, transformations of their predecessors."[30]

But even if we grant that Western categories have served to limit and control Western perceptions, we still need to ask further questions: Why, for example, did these aspects of primitive life seem so striking? Why were they rather than other aspects so extensively described and studied? I believe the answer to be that, from the fifteenth through the twentieth century, as Africa and the Americas were being "discovered" or "opened" by the West, Europeans were increasingly ghettoizing and repressing at home feelings and practices comparable to what they believed they saw among primitives—including feelings of kinship with animals and with nature, and what is usually called mysticism. In Europe, these patterns of feeling and practice had sometimes been allowed into religious life, but then—when they proved (in figures like Francis of Assisi) to be allied with disruptive attitudes, such as the rejection of property—they were hounded out of institutionalized religions.[31] The patterns had fewer and fewer ways to express themselves in the West. But there was still a persistent, residual need for expression. So they were projected abroad in a complicated process by which an aspect of the self was displaced onto the Other.

Views of primitives were based on perceived, repeated oppositions between the primitive and civilization, in which the primitive was coded metaphorically as feminine, collective, and ecstatic, and civilization was coded as masculine, individualistic, and devoted to the quotidian business of the family, city, or state. In turn (in what became self-perpetuating patterns), qualities identified with the primitive, like ecstasy, collectivity, and femininity, came to acquire a double valence—both violent and spiritual—analogous to the one we previously have ascribed to cannibalism and such practices. Ecstasy, for example, has a spiritual register, of harmony and tranquillity, which involves stepping outside the self and experiencing the eternal cosmos; but it also has a commonly perceived sexual register, which can be positive (a sign of *eros* or life force) or can be imagined as a state of excess, frenzy, and potential violence.[32]

Those making policy in Europe and the United States pretty much knew what they wanted to do with Indians, Africans, and others: control or colonize them; exploit them; convert them into modern Christians, or at least into workers for the industrial state. In its demonizing, fearful mode, fascination with the primitive certainly contributed to the work of imperialism. But culture is never unified or monolithic. Alongside the desire for possession and control was the desire for access to, and the continued experience of, something different. For some people, the primitive provided an outlet and a locus for alternative impulses in which the idea of merging has been key, perhaps not so much for its inherent value as for the challenges it mounts to the values of autonomous selfhood. For if the self is not conceived as a discrete unit, cut off from other selves and the world around it, then a great many values normative in the West come into question. Ownership and hierarchy, to give two salient examples, are fully justified only in a universe conceived in terms of competing interests rather than of mutuality and interdependence.

Fascination with the primitive can, then, nurture forbidden desires to question or escape Western norms. Most of all, it can nourish intense desires to void the idea of the autonomous self and merge or connect with life sources—what primatologist Jane Goodall calls "Being-ness." Such desires are often identified in Western thinking with what Freud called the "pre-Oedipal" or "oceanic" stages of human development, by which he meant fetal, infantile, or what he saw as "regressive" states in which individuals do not perceive the boundaries of the self and the inevitability of subject-object relations. When he articulated some of society's deepest fears about this kind of pan-individual thinking, Freud saw it as connected to the "death wish," the desire of animate beings to return to "the inorganic condition from which life arose"—a condition similar to what science today calls entropy and Eastern religions call nirvana and the Tao.[33] Because he conceived of the oceanic as a form of death wish, Freud was invariably hostile towards oceanic experiences. But the oceanic can be, and has been, valued quite differently. Testimonials from many traditions, including, as we have seen, the Western religious traditions represented by Romain Rolland and Martin Buber, describe the sensation of coming out of the self and merging with outside things as the core spiritual emotion. The desire to recover this sense of coming out of the self and interdependence with the universe is the key element in the fascination with the primitive that is explored in this book.

• • •

Primitive Passions has four parts, which can be read independently but are also cumulative in effect. When they are read in sequence, they tell a compelling story about culture and gender. Through case studies, Parts One and Two demonstrate broad divergences in male and female ways of experiencing the primitive and the oceanic up to and even (in some cases) into the present. The men studied in Part One include André Gide, Carl Jung, and D. H. Lawrence; the women in Part Two, Isak Dinesen, Beryl Markham, Vivienne de Watteville, Kuki Gallmann, Dian Fossey, and Georgia O'Keeffe. Fossey and Malinowski—the anthropologist to whom I referred at the beginning of this Introduction—provide good examples of how male and female life histories have often diverged.

In the Trobriand Islands, Malinowski acutely felt and was attracted to the experience of merging with the landscape. Yet he resisted it and censored it out of his published work, preferring to dwell in the realm he called "theory" as a way of avoiding submersion in the uncharted oceanic. Malinowski's attraction and ultimate resistance to the idea of merging were not unique. Comparable patterns appear in many men's life histories (Gide's, Jung's, and Lawrence's, to name just three), and almost always in a similarly embedded or disavowed form. These men courted and embraced the oceanic—but only to a point. Then they backed away from the oceanic, perceiving it as a danger to what Jung called "the mature European self."

In contrast, Fossey exemplifies an important pattern in female experiences. Women who settled in Africa or the American Southwest often cast off (rather than protected) models of selfhood that were completely normative back home. Often, the women cultivated precisely what men like Malinowski repressed: strong attachment to, even identification with, animal life or the land. Perhaps because they had less of a stake in the norms of their culture and received less reinforcement from them, women tended to speak out loud what men only whispered: contact with the primitive can provide an "out" from Western patterns of thought and action felt to be limiting or oppressive, such as nuclear families and their obligations. It can trigger self-transformation and the experience of dissolved hierarchies and boundaries.

This gender-coded pattern of response is not, of course, absolute: some men enact, and have always enacted, patterns gendered "female," just as some women enact, and have always enacted, patterns gendered "male." In fact, within the life histories that I tell, there are counterimpulses at work that might usefully be described as the desire for movement *beyond gender.* For some people, contact with the primitive triggers experiences associated with the opposite sex and is sought for that very purpose: males court the idea of community without competition or imagine (if usually only to repress) openness and a surrender to life forces; females reject family life or enact patterns of professional or creative achievement usually open only to males.[34]

Since around 1970, under the pressure of wide-scale social change, gender differences in our culture's reactions to indigenous peoples and to the idea of the primitive have to some extent eroded.[35] As one might expect, they remain strongest in trends that are programmatically single-gender, like the mythopoetic men's movement. But today, both men and women tend to value rather than denigrate the primitive and to focus on some groups (for example, Amazon Indians or Native Americans) rather than others, often with the express desire to revive lost traditions or protect those that are endangered.[36] In addition, men today are generally more willing than men in the past to avow goals of a lapsed or transformed self: one might even say that fascination with the primitive has moved to what was once female ground. In the chapter entitled "Piercings," for example, postmodern artist and genital piercer Monte Cazazza does not fit the pattern of gender difference inscribed by Malinowski and Fossey: he flaunts, rather than represses, the urge to merge with outside things—welcoming the insertion of a metal bolt into the head of his penis, then flourishing it. What is more, his genital piercing takes place within the context of statements by male piercers which say that penis piercing imitates the female menstrual flow, envisioned as a symbol of life force.

What we are seeing in the United States today is the full-tilt exploration of patterns formed in the 1920s: fascination with the primitive as an expression of fears about what the West has wrought in the world, even of white European self-loathing—often with an accompanying utopian impetus for change. Utopian desires are emerging strongly once again at the end of the twentieth century, in movements that envision the primitive as a locus of harmony and as a shelter from the dangers and fragmentation of modern life. Part Three of *Primitive Passions* profiles the most important of these trends and movements. It probes current idealizations of Native American groups, like the Lakota Sioux (the group that adopts Kevin Costner in *Dances with Wolves*). It offers participant-observer reports on the mythopoetic men's movement and certain aspects of spirituality in the New Age. It interrogates the meanings of radical forms of body piercing, especially the now increasingly common piercing of the genitals. Although in this part of the book I use examples from U.S. culture, my hope is that readers will recognize similar patterns in other parts of the industrialized world. Body piercing and tattooing, for example, are as common in many parts of Europe as they are in the United States.

The Conclusion revisits some key questions. Do groups that have been described as primitive have a special, continuous access to the spiritual, cosmic world—or do Westerners just see it that way? What would a putative Martian say if given the opportunity to observe a variety of cultures throughout the world without Western categories in mind? Or, to move to another level of question, is the impulse to merge with outside things the core spiritual emotion, or the expression of a death wish—or some combination of both, depending on one's point of view? If merging were recognized and encouraged more in Western culture, what would be the effects upon ordinary communities, families, and lives?

There are simply no reliable sources which would allow me to decide all of these points for sure. Still, I will ultimately want to claim that the perceived "collectivity" or "spirituality" of primitives may be no greater than what has existed at different times in the West, and still does, albeit often in a displaced or distorted form. Throughout the book, my goal is to examine the circuit between the primitive and spirituality in the Western imagination; that is not the same thing as wanting to attack or deconstruct alternative world views or the idea of spirituality itself. This book wants to hear primitivism's confessions and record its hidden life. If *Primitive Passions* closes down certain possibilities—like vampiric hunger for the exotic Other—so be it. For what has been sought elsewhere may yet be found in the folds and creases of the West's own neglected traditions.

Red Willow Trees
Artist: D. H. Lawrence
Courtesy of the estate of Saki Karavas, Esq.

PART I

Men

CHAPTER ONE

"What an Ecstasy It Would Have Been!": *Gide and Jung in Africa*

IN THE EARLY decades of the twentieth century, when a man of means felt anxious about his manhood or health, or maladjusted to the modern world, one prescription dominated. Go to Africa or the South Pacific, he was advised, or to some other exotic site identified with "the primitive." "The primitive" was widely valued as a way station or spa for men suffering from cultural alienation and psychic distress. Travelling there was a method of cure pioneered by painters like Gauguin, writers like Robert Louis Stevenson and Rupert Brooke, adventurers like Richard Francis Burton and Henry M. Stanley. In the 1920s, André Gide, D. H. Lawrence, Carl Jung, Michel Leiris, Antonin Artaud, and many others made the trip. The Polish ethnographer Malinowski, for example, went to the Trobriand Islands for the climate, after a mysterious illness affecting his heart and lungs. Gide went to Africa after his novel *Corydon* (1924) was denounced for its frank discussion of homosexuality. Jung went to Africa to recover from a nervous breakdown that had left him unable to work for years. D. H. Lawrence tried to start a new life in Ceylon and Australia, and finally in Mexico and New Mexico, after having been hounded by the English police during World War I.

These men, and many others, ascribed to "primitive" places the power of possibility, of renewal and revitalization. Yet in more than one instance, the record of their encounters with the primitive reveals a surprising reaction: at some point in the experience, each of them recoils from the quest for renewal out of a perceived need for self-preservation. Seeking the primitive and submitting to it come to be recognized as threats to one's individual wholeness and well-being. In this chapter, I present two cameo histories of male encounters with the primitive, one of them being André Gide's account of his trip to the Congo and the other Carl Jung's record of his travels in North and East Africa. In each, I focus on a single aspect of the experience: a pattern by which the desire to merge gives way to a fear of merging. The next chapter will treat, in a comparable way, the late writings of D. H. Lawrence in New Mexico. My purpose is to establish not a norm—male primitivism is too complex a phenomenon for there to be a single norm—but a context to which alternative patterns of experience can be compared. This context comprises a tendency to think about the primitive, the female, and the oceanic as almost interchangeable—followed by an overwhelming fear of losing one's European male identity.

"What Joy to Find Oneself Among Negroes!":
André Gide in the Congo

In 1925, when he was fifty-five years old, André Gide experienced an intense sense of transition. He had long been torn between his austere, puritanical religious upbringing, which urged self-control and moral responsibility for others, and a desire for sexual release and self-expression, which he associated with North Africa. In 1924, Gide's persistent unease was intensified by negative reactions to *Corydon*, a more overt confession of his homosexuality than any earlier work, like *L'Immoraliste* (*The Immoralist*).[1] Since the end of World War I, Gide had been writing an autobiography, *Si le grain ne meurt* . . . (1926; *If It Die* . . .), a book of intense self-analysis, conditioned by his vexed relationships with his mother and his wife and his need for a personal ethic. But he decided he needed to do something more. In 1925, with a young companion, Marc Allegret, Gide set out for central Africa.[2] Before leaving, he had his appendix removed, ostensibly to prevent sudden death from appendicitis while travelling, but also, I think, to mark his body's readiness. In 1927 and 1928, he published his diaries of the trip, *Voyage au Congo* (*Travels in the Congo*) and *Le Retour du Tchad* (*Return from the Chad*).[3] They were dedicated to the memory of Joseph Conrad, author of *Heart of Darkness,* the strongest influence on *Voyage au Congo* and on several generations of male travellers.

Gide found Africa by turns exhilarating and exacerbating. "What joy to find oneself among Negroes!" Gide exclaimed, and it was the proximity to black men that he apparently enjoyed most. African men bore the burden of his safari and also of Gide's liberated sexual longings. He stared at their backs, finding "a joyous play of muscles; a *farouche* enthusiasm" (6). He watched them flash, "like eels," through the water. He found the blacks "excellent fellows! . . . [T]heir merriment is so charming, and their laughter so frank and open!" He developed hopes: "Their smiles are day by day becoming more confiding, more affectionate—I was almost going to say: more tender" (174). He found tam-tams (dances) by boys "admirable"; those by women "disgusting," "shameless jiggling . . . extremely painful to look at" (65). The voyager was also a voyeur: like Michel in his novel *L'Immoraliste,* Gide found hidden pleasure in the bodies of dark, exotic men.

In the Congo, Gide was outraged by the conscription of black men for the rubber trade by whites who underpaid and abused them. Upon returning to France, he would mobilize a commission to investigate conditions in the Congo and to change the ways corporations did business there.[4] In an oft-quoted dictum, Gide maintained: "The less intelligent the white man is, the more stupid he thinks the black." He prided himself on being different from most whites and on having a fine relationship with his black servant, Adoum, whom he taught at night to read.

Much as Gide dwelled upon the physical splendors of male Africans, his diaries pay equal or even greater attention to the African landscape.

Following the conventions of Western art and writers like Rider Haggard and Conrad, he ascribed to that landscape a feminine gender and regarded it with extreme suspicion.[5]

More than anything else, it was the landscape that was Gide's source of uneasiness during his trip. He felt submerged in a panorama of vast space and unlimited time. The land was so big and travel so slow that he found it a struggle to maintain his sense of himself. To cope with this disturbing feeling, he decided to organize his experience around his own body, obsessively recording every momentary turn of the wheel of his own sensations. The result is a novelistic, but also hypochondriacal, account of his own physical and psychic symptoms. Gide cast Africa as cosmic flux, himself as struggling ego.

From its first sentence, *Voyage au Congo* registers Gide's pulses: "My state is one of inexpressible languor; the hours slip by empty and indistinguishable."[6] He feels ennui, boredom, and contemplates the absurd. He notes the discomforts of travelling, with careful attention once again to how well, or how badly, he is holding up. "On the whole," he says, "I am bearing it fairly well. It is hot, thundery, damp; but I have felt worse in Paris; and I am astonished at not perspiring more" (3). Or, on a bad day: "It is frightfully hot, damp, and thundery—stifling. . . . I rose from my after-lunch siesta streaming" (25). He expresses a certain aversion to perspiration as an involuntary seepage of fluids from the body; it comes to serve as a metaphor for Africa's draining of the sense of self.

In his writing, Gide sought to establish himself as the connoisseur not only of his own body but of the overwhelming landscape as well. He felt himself acted upon by Africa and in response wanted to act on it. So Gide continually judged and gauged Africa: this is good, this is not. He was annoyed when Africa disappointed his expectations, saying: "The landscape is without nobility. I expected to find sandy shores and the desolation of the desert. But no! Quantities of medium-sized trees with their rounded clumps make a very indifferent trimming to the river banks" (136). He felt happier when "the scenery is . . . more what I expected; it is becoming *like*" (20). Most galling to Gide was how Africa failed to announce "the best" mountain or river or sunset as each presented itself: no signs or guideposts proclaimed that one feature or another was "the best" of its kind. As a result, Gide lived in a frenzy of anticipation or retrospection.

Repeatedly, Africa offended Gide's sense of aesthetic form. Everywhere he looked,

> again I see the enormousness, the formlessness, the indecision,
> the absence of direction, of design, of organization which so ex-
> cessively disturbed me during the first part of my journey, and
> which is indeed the chief characteristic of this country. (140)

He found the place a disturbing mélange, but he also found it quite fascinating:

> [T]his perplexity of nature, this wedding and welding of the
> elements, this *blending* of grey and blue, of grass and water, are
> so strange . . . that I cannot stop gazing on it. (140)

Above all, I am struck by how strongly and definitely Gide recognizes but rejects the sublime, oceanic potential of the landscape. It seems
to him undifferentiated, like the universe before creation: a "presymbolic" realm not subject to the order of language and often associated, in
the Western imagination, with the fetal state, and hence with the
mother.[7] Gide's identification of the vast landscape with the female con-
forms with earlier fictions, like Rider Haggard's *King Solomon's Mines*, in
which a chief feature of the African landscape is called "Sheba's breasts."
It follows, too, upon *Heart of Darkness*, so loved by Gide, in which
Conrad uses an African woman as the symbol of "the whole sorrowful
land," "the immense wilderness, the colossal body of the fecund and
mysterious life." In *Heart of Darkness*, the woman is "the image of
[Africa's] own tenebrous and passionate soul."[8] Gide intuitively sees it
that way too.

Gide begins chapter 6 with a lament:

> The absence of individuality, of individualization—the impossi-
> bility of differentiating—which depressed me so much at the be-
> ginning of my journey, is what I suffer from too in the
> landscape. . . . I ask myself what there is to attract me to any one
> point rather than to any other. Everything is uniform; there can
> be no possible predilection for any particular site. (111–12)

It is not, I must stress, that Gide is insensible to certain charms in the oceanic potential of Africa. The passage continues in this way:

> I stayed the whole day yesterday without the least desire to stir. . . . But how pure the air is! How beautiful the light! What a delicious feeling of warmth envelops one and fills one with pleasure! How easy to breathe! How good to live! (112)

There are many like moments of "delicious" sensations. He would breathe in and out with an unexpected enjoyment of being surrounded, filled, and pleasured.

And that, for Gide, was precisely the problem. He found oblivion in the moment far too appealing: "Assuredly, I should not have had to stay motionless many minutes for the world of nature to close over me. Everything would have been as if I had not existed and I should have forgotten my own presence and turned all vision." With part of his mind, Gide delighted in the prospect, saying, "Oh, what an ecstasy it would have been! There are few minutes of my life I would sooner live over again." Yet, in the very next sentence, Gide says that he "pressed on in the midst of this strange excitement" (157). Activity of mind and body became his defense and salvation. He had to keep going, to keep "this strange excitement" at bay. He resisted the urge to surrender by stressing the need for movement and mental "differentiation."

By the end of his voyage, the strain of singling out distinctive forms in the landscape became Gide's metaphor and model for creating the self. In fact, he said that the desirability of what he called differentiation was the central lesson of his African travels:

> This notion of differentiation, which I have acquired here, and from which proceeds the sense both of the exquisite and of the rare, is so important that it seems to me the principle thing I shall bring away from this country. (112)

Differentiation, judgment, separation, and difference make possible order and direction. They are the constitutive acts of connoisseurship and analysis—vital functions, for Gide, of secure selfhood. Only on the last day of his journey did Gide relent; now that he was about to leave Africa, it was safe to indulge in retrospective fascination: "This is the last day. Our journey is over. Perhaps I shall never see the virgin forest again. It never looked more beautiful" (302).

Conrad wrote: "Before the Congo, I was a mere animal." It was the Congo that made him a man. Conrad's heirs, like André Gide, embarked upon their travels with a similar desire for both transformation and a confirmation of selfhood. Gide came to Africa filled with confusion about his existence in France—open to change, needing it. But in Africa he both found and resisted alternative notions of being. Gide remained attached to his own pulses, pleased when he was not perspiring.

"What We Lack Is Intensity of Life": Carl Jung in Africa

Carl Gustavus Jung was forty-five when he travelled to North Africa in 1920. Four years later, he visited the Pueblo Indians in New Mexico. The year after that, he toured Kenya and Uganda. When he built a new home in Switzerland, called Bollingen, he wished it to be without the amenities of European life. He believed that the rusticity of the building would be a constant reminder of the knowledge he had acquired during his travels, one that would allow him to convert his transitory journeys into a life-long resource.[9]

Jung went to Africa in the aftermath of a profound depression that dated back to 1913.[10] In that year, he had broken decisively with Sigmund Freud after almost a decade of collaboration, during which the two had engaged in intense debate over the basis of psychic phenomena. Although he had initiated the break, Jung was emotionally debilitated by it. He became extremely withdrawn and depressed; he heard voices and had terrifying dreams; he was unable to work as an analyst, teacher, or writer, although he did keep notebooks about his experiences and dreams. His condition was exacerbated by the strain caused by an extramarital affair with Antonia Wolf, a fellow psychoanalyst, which would continue in one form or another for most of his life. (Eventually, Jung's wife would welcome Toni into their home as a kind of fictional "Aunt," thus ironically reproducing Freud's household, which included his sister-in-law, Minna Bernays, believed by some to be the love of Freud's life.)

Jung's relationship with Freud was filled with irreconcilable tensions. Freud expected Jung to be his disciple. He hoped that Jung, a Swiss Protestant who was nineteen years younger, would be in the forefront of psychoanalysis after his death and redeem it from its derogatory description as "the Jewish science." But from the beginning of their collaboration in 1907, Jung had resisted certain Freudian doctrines. The root of this resistance was that Jung valued the unconscious mind far more than Freud; in fact, he believed that many of the phenomena Freud identified as symptoms of pathology (for example, dreams or the incest wish) were symbolic codings of unconscious urges that needed to be plumbed, not eradicated.

Jung's thinking about the unconscious was rooted in personal experience. From childhood on, he had experienced states of mind in which he identified profoundly with animals or stones. In addition, he associated these states with his mother, though he was hard pressed to say why. He writes: "For me [my mother] was somehow connected with animals, trees, mountains, meadows, and running water, all of which contrasted most strangely with her Christian surface and her conventional assertions of faith."[11] He associated his mother, then, not with the stuff of Protestantism but with that of paganism and animism.

In his memoir, written in extreme old age, he describes one physical location in particular. He visited it frequently until he was ten years old, and it produced intense sensations of a oneness with nature. At this spot there was

> a stone that jutted out—my stone. Often, when I was alone, I sat down on this stone, and then began an imaginary game that went something like this: "I am sitting on top of this stone and it is underneath." But the stone also could say "I" and think: "I am lying here on this slope and he is sitting on top of me." . . . I would stand up, wondering who was what now. The answer remained totally unclear. (*Memories, Dreams, Reflections,* 20)

As a child, Jung enacted with the stone such little dramas of individuality versus merging. And for Jung, these two states of being, or urges, would remain associated with the stone well beyond the age of ten and in time would cease to seem like a game. In fact, this spot continued to exert a strong attraction when Jung returned to it "thirty years later," when he "was a married man, had children, a house, a place in the world." Revisiting the spot, he felt threatened by "the pull of that other world [which] was so strong that I had to tear myself violently from the spot in order not to lose hold of my future" (*MDR*, 20).[12] Significantly, that visit to the stone as an adult would precede his first trip to Africa. I find it quite meaningful that Jung, like Gide, associated the state of mind in which the subject identifies with the stone with a feminine principle (his mother) and that this state represented to him a danger to his "place in the world" as a husband, father, and homeowner. I will want to return to this issue later in the chapter.

In his memoir, Jung did not expressly connect this moment at the stone to his break with Freud. But he might well have. For his identification with stones and animals, like his interest in the unconscious mind, was at the root of his hostility to the older man's theories. Freud often placed Jung's ideas in what to him was a singularly derogatory category: *mysticism*. In fact, using imagery loaded with evocations of both Africans and women, Freud repeatedly warned Jung against "the black tide of mud . . . occultism."[13] But when Jung recalled emotions like those stimulated by the stone, he "became aware of how keenly I felt the difference between Freud's intellectual attitude and mine" (*MDR*, 160). Following a dream in which he descended into a womblike cave that he understood to be a feminine symbol as well as a symbol of the unconscious, he realized he would have to break with Freud:

> The deeper I went, the more alien and the darker the scene became. In the cave, I discovered remains of a primitive culture, that is, the world of the primitive man within myself—a world which can scarcely be reached or illuminated by consciousness. The primitive psyche of man borders on the life of the animal soul, just as the caves of prehistoric times were usually inhabited by animals before men laid claim to them. (*MDR*, 160)

The differences between Jung and Freud played themselves out, then, in the domain of the unconscious mind, with its shifting identifications across species and categories. Freud saw such identifications as potentially pathological; Jung valued them as clues to eternal truths. But both Freud and Jung identified this domain with the primitive.

Yet it would be wrong to see the men's disagreement over the unconscious as simply chaste and intellectual. It was also charged with a vexed eroticism. Freud freely acknowledged that his relationship with Jung resembled earlier working friendships which had ended, like love affairs, in jealousy, spite, and recrimination. His collaboration with Wilhelm Fliess, for example, ended in a bitter quarrel over the peculiar, sexualized motif of a man's bleeding nose. And there were numerous suicides and breakdowns in Freud's circle, often precipitated by the demons and displeasure of the master himself. Reportedly, Freud fainted on at least two occasions when Jung disagreed with him, adopting a "female" role in response to his intellectual "son's" rebellion; it was at these moments that he most connected Jung with Fliess.[14]

For his part, Jung had told Freud in a letter that as a youth he had been the victim of a homosexual rape by a man he "worshipped." As both men were aware that worship was precisely what Freud, the mentor, expected of Jung, the disciple, each became alert to the possibility that Jung might come to see Freud as a potential violator and try to resist him. On their joint crossing to the United States in 1909 for the famous Clark University conference, for example, Jung regaled Freud with accounts of his dreams; Freud interpreted them as evidence that Jung harbored a death wish towards him and accused Jung to that effect. I can imagine these two, trapped on shipboard, swapping confidences each morning, confidences that deeply mortified the other. The analysts turn pale, look up from their notes, challenge each other with all their doctorly authority. Freud continued to find evidence of betrayal up to and after the break in 1913.

After the break, Jung published no books until *Psychological Types* (1921). And it was not until after his second trip to Africa, in 1925, that he resumed a full professional life, publishing "The Relations Between the Ego and the Unconscious" in 1928 and beginning his long-term study of alchemy. It is not too much to say that had Jung died during World War I, he would have left very little written material to posterity, and many fewer of the ideas for which he is now famous. Almost all of Jung's major writings followed his midlife crisis, breakdown, and trips to primitive places. The renewed production points towards the healing role that his African journeys played for him. And I would further argue that they were the origin of many of his key ideas.

Unlike Gide, Jung loved the African landscape precisely because of its vastness and its evocation of an undifferentiated state. He saw Africa as the embodiment of "primordial beginnings . . . maternal mystery, this primordial darkness" (*MDR,* 269). As in Haggard, Conrad, and Gide, there is a certain reflexive identification of "Africa" with "maternal mystery." When he was alone at sunrise on an African plain, Jung said that "the cosmic meaning of consciousness became overwhelmingly clear to me" (*MDR,* 255). What became clear was this: "Human consciousness created objective existence and meaning," and thus both were the source and expression of the godhead (*MDR,* 256). It followed from this that "myths are the earliest form of science." Once he had identified the centrality of myth and its consubstantiality with the human mind and the divine, the future course of Jung's career, contra Freud's, was fully set. Freud would pursue adaptation to Western culture; Jung would pursue the mythic core of experience beneath social forms.

Africa convinced Jung, as he puts it in his memoirs, that "what we [Europeans] lack is intensity of life" (242). He said he fell "under the spell of the primitive" in Africa and believed that he had journeyed there "unconsciously" in search of a part of his personality he had lost. Jung was aware of and agreed with the Freudian insight that socialization in Western culture requires that certain aspects of the self be repressed. Yet "the sight of a child or a primitive," he wrote,

> will arouse certain longings in adult, civilized persons—longings which relate to the unfulfilled desires and needs of those parts of the personality which have been blotted out of the total picture in favor of the adapted [socialized] persona. (*MDR,* 244)

To some extent, Jung actively worked towards reclaiming those unfulfilled parts of the self. He rejected European pride in being different from Africans, asserting instead that Africans had equally valuable powers which Europeans had lost. "The predominantly rationalistic European," he wrote, "finds much that is human alien to him, and he prides himself on this without realizing that his rationality is won at the expense of his vitality" (*MDR*, 245). Yet, Jung claimed, "knowledge does not enrich us; it moves us more and more from the mythic world in which we were once at home by right of birth" (*MDR*, 252).

If Jung's perceptions often seem like a radical critique of Western norms of consciousness, in many ways they were. Jung believed, as many do today, in the constructed nature of cultural realities. He resisted a narrow emphasis on reason alone. He pursued knowledge in fields like alchemy, an endeavor embarrassing to Freud and others who thought of themselves as "men of science." He identified a female principle within each man (the anima) and a male principle within each woman (the animus), modifying conventional ideas about gender. For these and other reasons, Jungian psychology is conventionally opposed to Freud's, and his views are much in vogue today. Yet although his work embraced the "vitality" of Africa in rejection of Western rationality, Jung's memoirs record a countertendency in his encounter with Africa which ultimately prevailed and which was very much conditioned by a traditional, Western, male sense of self. Again and again in his account of his journeys, he used Africa as a conventional symbol of "dark," forbidden impulses; most of all, he came to fear what he called "going black under the skin."

During his 1920 trip to North Africa, Jung had been fascinated by the open display of male homosexuality. He had dreams that pointed back to his homosexual rape and to the traumatic relationship with Freud. In such dreams, he was attacked by a "handsome, dark Arab" who knocked him down and wrestled with him, finally pushing his head under some water. Jung responded by pushing the dark Arab's head below water as well. This violent struggle was erotic and tinged with affection, yet when it came to the water, it was also a matter of life and death. Jung said: "I [pushed his head under the water] although I felt great admiration for him; but I did not want to let myself be killed. I had no intention of killing him; I wanted only to make him unconscious and incapable of fighting" (*MDR*, 243). The dark Arab became his model for the "shadow" figure, the Jungian concept of unconscious urges that must be confronted in order to achieve psychic wholeness. Like the dark Arab in his dream, the unconscious must be respected and admired, encountered and wrestled with, but also ultimately controlled and harnessed.

If the attractive dark Arab clearly symbolizes the unconscious—and that alone is a form of racialized thinking—in conjunction with water, he also signifies potential sexual violation, loss of the self, and death. We return here, I believe, to a profound ambivalence in Jung, apparent in the earlier story of the stone that fascinated him at ten and frightened him at forty. Jung identified "Arab" and "stone" with the undifferentiated realm of the unconscious. He wanted both to join the eternal, unconscious realm and to preserve his impenetrable Western male self. Sexuality plays an uneasy mediating role in his ambivalence, which becomes even more acute in the context of his second trip to Africa, to the black, sub-Saharan part, in 1925.

In his memoir of that second trip, Jung repeatedly expressed fears of what he calls "going black under the skin" and losing his European identity. He believed that African women everywhere were freely inviting him into their bodies, and he saw sexual intercourse with African women as the threshold to "going black under the skin." Jung rarely discussed his own sexuality, and so it is hard to compare his reactions to black women with his reactions more generally. Yet it is clear that Jung was even more fearful of African females than of the dark Arab in his dream. In fact, rather than risk entrapment, he chose to refrain even from conversation: "With a single exception . . . I never spoke to a native woman. . . . The white who goes in for this not only forfeits his authority, but runs the serious risk of 'going black.' I observed several highly instructive examples of this" (*MDR*, 261–62). In a way typical of his thinking, Jung used his own emotions as the basis for generalizing outward.

"Blackness" signified for Jung the untamed unconscious; black Africans became his embodiment and symbol of "the shadow," the id forces in the human mind, the taint, if you will, of evil. For all his radicalism, Jung accepted these conventional, and some would say racist, associations. They have escaped commentary in most book-length discussions of Jung, which are almost always written by his disciples. But I am less interested here in castigating Jung for racism than in pointing out how, even for him, this radical thinker, attraction to the land gave way to fears of violation, transformation, and "going black under the skin," associated especially with women or Africans.

Although he was fascinated by Africa, by the end of his trip Jung felt "burdened by all [he] had experienced" and decided to review all the notebooks he had kept during the trek in order to clarify his impressions. He was struck by how all his dreams, save one, "stubbornly followed the tactic of ignoring Africa" (*MDR*, 272). He fixed on that singular dream as encoding the message he was most to take away from his journey. In the dream, he recalled the face of an American "Negro" in Tennessee, a barber who had done his hair. The barber "was holding a tremendous, red-hot curling iron to my head, intending to make my hair kinky—that is, to give me Negro hair. I could already feel the painful heat, and awoke with a sense of terror" (*MDR*, 272). The "red-hot iron" clearly can be sexualized, and it is charged with violence. As in the dream of the dark Arab, Jung associated blackness with the threat of violation and violation with an intolerable transformation of self.

Jung "took this dream as a warning from the unconscious; it was saying that the primitive was a danger to me. At that time I was obviously all too close to 'going black'" (*MDR*, 272). After the dream, then, near the end of his second trip to Africa, Jung realized that Africa "touched every sore spot in [his] own psychology" (*MDR*, 273). He concluded that "my European personality must under all circumstances be preserved intact" (*MDR*, 273).[15] After Africa, Jung would devote his life to what he called "individuation": the realization, through archetypes, dreams, and myths, of psychic wholeness.[16] His emphasis on the unconscious mind predisposed him to idealize Africa, which he imagined as the site of the unconscious. But like Gide's, his ultimate resource was the autonomous, rounded, European male self.

"The Primitive Was a Danger to Me":
Women and the Undifferentiated Mass

As thinkers, Gide and Jung were unusually sensitive to the issues being raised in philosophy and psychology about the nature of human selfhood. Gide's analytical moves in his autobiography testify to his acute interest in these issues;[17] for Jung, they would necessarily have been primary matters of professional concern. Yet like most people of their day, Gide and Jung shared certain blind spots. They were accustomed, for example, to thinking of the self in generic terms as "male," and they identified with the idea of the masculine self despite their complicated histories with regard to homosexuality and, especially for Jung, an awareness of the possibility of gender mixtures within individuals. What is more, Gide and Jung tended, like many men in their culture, to think of the Other as the opposite of the masculine self, and so very often as female. It would be easy to pass without comment over Gide's and Jung's "instinctive" identification of the primitive with the female, so common is it in Western thinking. But I want to focus on and defamiliarize that identification, since it is the pivot on which men frequently turn away from the oceanic back towards conventional ideas of autonomous selfhood.

It was not, of course, that Gide and Jung conceived of all Others as biologically female; indeed, they interacted especially with African men. Instead, it seems that some of the logic of imperialism worked its way into their psyches. Both European women and colonized peoples were, relative to European men, associated with the childlike, the irrational, and the dependent—and so linked. What is more, immediate precedents for gendering the land female and symbolizing Africa in female terms were available in popular writers like Rider Haggard and Joseph Conrad. In addition, the popularity and renown of historical figures like La Malinche in Mexico and Pocahontas in Virginia tended to make females into symbols of access to indigenous peoples and their land.

But ultimately, the reasons for the connection between the female and the specific sensations Africa triggered in Gide and Jung are more devious. They reach further back into Western thought. Before leaving these men, it will be worthwhile to probe, albeit briefly, some of the older stories and myths that would have impinged on them and led them "instinctively" to connect the sensations produced by Africa with mothers and females. One of their immediate sources would have been an important but now largely forgotten German-Swiss theologian named Johann Bachofen. Jung especially felt a close bond to Bachofen; as late as 1961, when Jung wrote his autobiography, he connected his home city, Basel, with Bachofen and imagined the days when Bachofen "walked its streets" (*MDR*, 111).

Although it is little read today, Johann Bachofen's *Mutterrecht und Urreligion* (*Mother Right and the Origins of Religion*), first published in

1851, was, according to the premier anthropologist Franz Boas, one of the strongest influences on anthropology as an emerging field.[18] And it remained a sourcebook of ideas well into the 1920s. Among its contributions, *Mutterrecht und Urreligion* forged some of the strongest imaginative links between the dangers of "the primitive" and women.

Bachofen believed that in the epochs before recorded history, women and Mother-centered religions dominated what became modern Europe. He described this period as one in which women were "the repository of all culture, of all benevolence, of all devotion, of all concern for the living and grief for the dead"—in short, as a period when the gods were female and when women ruled in what Bachofen posited as "primitive matriarchies." This long era in the European past, Bachofen said, was one of intense and almost unimaginable equality, in which women mated promiscuously, producing a sense of universal relatedness. "Every woman's womb," he wrote, "the mortal image of the earth mother Demeter," gave "brothers and sisters to the children of every other woman" in what Bachofen described as "the undifferentiated unity of the mass" (80). In such passages, Bachofen provided key terms that would be appropriated and transformed by Gide and Jung: within prehistoric matriarchies, he said, humans did not experience what Gide called "differentiation" and Jung called the family-bound "mature European self."

Bachofen's work is sometimes cited today for its dithyrambic description of Mother Right, yet it went on to endorse the conditions of modern European life. For Bachofen believed that the long period of Mother rule was "destined"—for women's own good—to be followed by what he called "the paternal system," with its hierarchical male-dominated religions and male control of females and of government. The new paternal system, Bachofen believed, relieved women of the strain of multiple child-bearing and placed them under the protection of individual men. Bachofen provided, then, not just the basis for Gide's idea of "differentiation" and Jung's idea of the family-bound "mature European self." He also provided a rationale for their inevitability.

Gide and Jung were also affected by Bachofen's far-reaching impact on nineteenth-century thought. For example, Friedrich Engels claimed that under patriarchal capitalism and the evolution of the family, women experienced "the world historical defeat of the female sex."[19] Bachofen's theories also informed Friedrich Nietzsche's attention to the battle of

Apollonian and Dionysian forces in Greek drama. Nietzsche believed that civilization needed to overcome what he called "the stinking pudenda"— the fetid, swamplike condition he saw in the female genitals and in chthonic nature unmediated by Apollonian form.[20] Nietzsche's readings of Greek drama supported Bachofen's theory of a transition from primitive matriarchy to modern patriarchy—and were in turn extremely influential. In fact, references to Nietzsche are common in both Gide and Jung.[21] What is more, applying Bachofen directly to Greek drama is extremely suggestive indeed.

Euripides' *The Bacchae* affords us one of the best examples. It is expressly cited by Jung and can be read in a way that prefigures Gide's and Jung's reactions to Africa. In the play, the women of Thebes have left their city to live a life of ecstasy and license on a nearby mountain where they revive "the rites of Cybele, the Mother." Their actions conform to and probably influenced Bachofen's version of what female-dominated societies were like.[22] On their mountain, the Bacchae suckle gazelles and wolves; they bring forth manna from the earth; they mate promiscuously; they whirl round and round in dance until "the beasts and all the mountain seemed wild with divinity." The older men of Thebes, like the seer Tiresias, remember the ancient forms of Mother religions and are willing to join in the women's rites. But the young ruler of Thebes, Pentheus, who represents the emerging patriarchal order, rigidly condemns the women's rites as "obscene disorder."

The play punishes Pentheus with breathtaking thoroughness. But— and this is equally important—it simultaneously signals that a reversion to primitive ways, like the women's rites of Cybele, does indeed represent acute dangers both to men and to the emerging patriarchal state.[23] Led by Pentheus' mother, Agave, the Bacchae tear Pentheus limb from limb. They are deceived by the god Dionysus into believing that Pentheus is a lion cub, not a man. Then Agave, her senses cleared in the marketplace, recognizes that she has destroyed her son and, by destroying him, has also wrecked her city.[24]

In 1912, shortly before his traumatic break with Freud, Jung published *Wandlungen und Symbole der Libido* (*Psychology of the Unconscious*). The book's last three chapters deal extensively with the figure of the "devouring" or "terrible" mother and with the sacrificed son. Jung quotes from many sources, including Nietzsche and Greek drama;

Pentheus and Agave serve as extended examples in the book's concluding chapter. After writing this book, Jung, in his own words, was "utterly incapable of reading in a scientific book" until 1921. In fact, *Psychology of the Unconscious* is the penultimate book Jung wrote before completing his travels to the primitive in Africa and the American Southwest. So it is not surprising that parts of *Psychology of the Unconscious* anticipate Jung's reactions to Africa. For example, Jung reached this summary of the relation between men and the "terrible mother":

> Man leaves the mother, the source of libido, and is driven by the eternal thirst to find her again, and to drink renewal from her; thus he completes his cycle, and returns again into the mother's womb. Every obstacle which obstructs his life's path, and threatens his ascent, wears the shadowy features of the "terrible mother," who paralyzes his energy with the consuming poison of the stealthy, retrospective longing.[25]

Reunification with the mother—Freud's incest wish, or (in a different register) "the oceanic"—can be accented as a positive symbol of rebirth in Jungian thinking, and often is in summaries of his work. But, as this quotation suggests, the mother continually presents not just the possibility of rebirth but also that of loss, danger, and engulfment. In fact, for Jung on the eve of his nervous breakdown and subsequent travels in Africa, the "terrible mother" played the same role he would later attribute to Africa and to the primitive in general: like Africa, the mother is forever an attractive, desired site of the undifferentiated; but she is also feared as the potential absorber and destroyer of the self. Intuitively, then, for men like Gide and Jung, Africa and the primitive were equivalent to the terrible or devouring mother. This kind of thinking, this kind of intuitive association, is surprisingly common in male or male-identified primitivist thinking, even when it presents itself as historical or scientific rather than as purely imaginative.

During the same years Gide and Jung journeyed in Africa, Freud took additional steps in his thinking. His new conclusions resonate with and illuminate further Gide and Jung's identification of landscape and Africans with undifferentiated nature, mothers, and the dissolution of the self. During the 1920s, Freud revisited the idea of the self and the figure of the mother, drawing on his 1920 text *Beyond the Pleasure Principle* and the concept of the death wish. By the time of *Civilization and Its Discontents*, published in 1930, Freud had connected the death wish with the phenomenon that Romain Rolland had described to him as "the oceanic," the momentary dissolution of the sense of self in the cosmos.[26] In fact, by 1930, Freud's image for the oceanic had become the nursing infant at the breast, unaware as yet of what Freud called "the reality principle" and the iron separation of the subject (the self) from the objects around it.[27] But unlike Romain Rolland, Freud saw the oceanic not as a momentary or transitory ecstatic experience but as a potentially permanent regression—and hence as a first step towards the fearful return to the inorganic that he called the death wish. For Freud, as for Jung in 1912, rejection of the mother was the first step that needed to be taken in the long and constant battle against the strong attraction of what Jung called loss of "energy" and Freud called the death wish.[28] The figure of the female was, then, linked for Freud, as for Gide and Jung, with the idea of boundary dissolution and the loss of selfhood. What is more, like them, Freud stressed the need for "differentiation" and "the mature European self."

It is abundantly clear that these linkages between the female, the oceanic, and the primitive are extremely ancient and extremely strong in Western culture. But it is important to understand that they are not in any sense factual or inevitable—nor do they represent either a proven truth or even consistently arrived at theories. Instead, the links between females, the oceanic, and the primitive were based on myths, fictions, intuitions, individual neuroses, and the wildest forms of speculation. Still, the linkage between women and the dissolution of self has been persistent and fateful in the West. Not until the 1970s, to give just one example, would psychologists propose that, contra Freud, mothers and their infants are the prototypes not of "objects" that must be rejected by "subjects" but of what has come to be called "interpersonal relations." Not until the 1970s would researchers think about mothers as subjects in their own right and consider the possibility that male and female infants interact differently with their mothers.[29]

Men like Gide and Jung—and like Lawrence in the next chapter—absorbed the links between the primitive, the female, and the oceanic freely. They imbibed them almost involuntarily, and routinely expressed them in their work. Women in Western culture would, of course, have known these myths and these connections as well, but as one might expect—and as I shall show in Part Two—they viewed them and used them differently. The knot of connections between the primitive, the female, and the oceanic in Western culture—its potential history—is vast. Yet the development of this knot has never been told *as a history,* despite its presence in the axioms or underpinnings of numerous theories of culture and gender. By uncovering the intersection of these terms and showing how it affected many lives and the culture as a whole, my aim is to make it harder for these connections to be made, as they were by Gide and Jung, "instinctively" and blindly.

CHAPTER TWO

"Something Stood Still in My Soul": D. H. Lawrence in New Mexico

I

BETWEEN 1922 AND 1925, while Jung and Gide travelled in Africa, D. H. Lawrence lived in New Mexico, occasionally venturing south. He arrived after journeys to Australia and Ceylon, where he had gone in search of a place to found an ideal community. Before that, he had wandered across mainland Italy, Sardinia, and Sicily on the same quest. Lawrence was restless and on the move following years of despair in Cornwall during World War I, when he and his German wife, Frieda, were persecuted as opponents of the war and potential agents of "the Hun." But in New Mexico, at the invitation of Mabel Dodge Luhan, who had founded an artistic colony in Taos, Lawrence found a place that seemed like home. Together, he and Frieda fixed up a simple house atop a mountain, about fourteen miles from Taos, living on the only property they would ever own. Luhan had sold Frieda the land in exchange for the manuscript of *Sons and Lovers*. This site, isolated even today, was extremely remote in the 1920s; but it offered unimpeded and glorious views westward over the Taos valley.

Lawrence was tired and ill by the time he had settled in New Mexico. The tuberculosis that would kill him within six years was already well established. Still, in New Mexico, he experienced a significant sense of renewal and lightening. In the American Southwest, Lawrence found a purity of nature he had never known in his native Nottingham, disfigured by decades of coal mining and other industry. In his new home, he wrote some of his most emotionally engaged and moving essays: "Indians and Entertainment," "Taos," and "New Mexico"; afterwards, the ideas developed in these essays figured importantly and subtly in his late fictions. In fact, New Mexico and its Indians became touchstones in Lawrence's imagination.

In an essay called "New Mexico," Lawrence addressed directly an intense experience of the land comparable to what Gide and Jung felt in Africa. "I think that New Mexico was the greatest experience from the outside world that I have ever had," Lawrence wrote. "It certainly changed me forever. . . . The moment I saw the brilliant proud morning shine high over Santa Fe, something stood still in my soul, and I started to attend."[1] The land taught Lawrence's soul a transforming lesson through the very fact of its being; reciprocally, Lawrence's reaction was quiet, even passive: his soul stood still and started to attend. There is an aura of spirituality and religious instruction in his description, and as the essay continues, it becomes clear that Lawrence fully intended both. The land, Lawrence says, provided him with direct access to the religion of the Indians who lived there. And Lawrence's description of that religion reveals a crucial impulse in his writing which has not yet received adequate attention: a strong attraction to the oceanic in nature, an attraction he both submitted to and strongly resisted. In New Mexico, he persistently displaced that attraction, though never completely or satisfactorily, onto his image of Indians. Then, in his late fiction, the experience colored his particular idea of perfect sexuality.

Lawrence's strong reactions to New Mexico were highly typical of his sensibility. He was always fascinated by dramatic, apocalyptic landscapes, like the frozen Alps of *Women in Love*: an "end of the world place," the characters call it, a place where "the mystery of creation was fathomless, infallible, inexhaustible forever." "Races came and went, species passed away, but ever new species arose," thinks Birkin, the Lawrentian spokesman in *Women in Love:* "To be man was nothing. . . . Human or inhuman mattered nothing."[2] In the Australian bush, on his way to New Mexico, Lawrence had felt himself in the presence of another such place. In a letter to Frieda's mother, Lawrence described the terrain as "terribly big and empty . . . hoary and unending. . . . It is *too* new, you see." In the biographer Brenda Maddox's words, he was "hit by such a blast of nothingness that he was frightened half to death."[3] New Mexico provided similar sensations of a primal vastness indifferent to humankind. But despite the presence of aborigines in Australia, Lawrence insisted that New Mexico was an "older" land inhabited, as Lawrence was acutely aware, by Indians before whites.

In his essays about New Mexico, Lawrence repeatedly described the land as inspiring and embodying the Indians' religion. It was "a vast old religion which once swayed the earth . . . greater than anything we [whites, Europeans] know: more starkly and nakedly religious." What Lawrence meant by this last phrase was the absence of any individuated "conception of a god." Instead, for the Indians, "all is god . . . everything was alive, not supernaturally, but naturally alive": rocks, trees, water—everything" ("New Mexico," 146). Lawrence was powerfully impressed by this religion, which he saw as entirely different from Western pantheism. Although pantheism maintains that "God is everywhere, God is in everything," it nonetheless posits a personified deity superior to His creation ("New Mexico," 146). By contrast, for the Indians, "creation is a great flood, forever flowing, in lovely and terrible waves . . . [and] God is immersed as it were, in creation, not to be separated or distinguished."[4]

The description implies a kind of religious emotion, and to experience it, Lawrence said, is to come into "direct contact with the elemental life of the cosmos, mountain-life, cloud-life, thunder-life, air-life, earth-life, sun-life. To come into immediate *felt* contact, and so derive energy, power, and a dark sort of joy." Lawrence went even further. He saw such experience as the core religious experience: "The effort into sheer naked contact, *without any intermediary or mediator,*" he wrote, "is the root meaning of religion" (Lawrence's emphasis; "New Mexico," 147).

We have seen such speculations before. In positing that unmediated contact with oceanic nature forms the core of religious experience,

Lawrence was echoing important intellectual ideas current in the 1920s. Romain Rolland and Martin Buber are two other examples cited earlier in this book. Between 1927 and 1930, as we have seen in the Introduction and Chapter One, Rolland was engaged in an important debate with Freud, each of them advancing opposing images and valuations of the experience of boundary dissolution. Rolland imaged it as the individual becoming like salt in the ocean and saw such mystical experiences as a revitalizing "artery of immortality"; by contrast, Freud imaged the experience as a nursing infant or fetus in the womb and saw it as a deathly form of regression.[5]

Lawrence would have been interested in both points of view. By temperament, he gravitated towards images similar to those used by Rolland. But even though he often disagreed with Freud on particular points, Lawrence was also saturated with Freudian models.[6] His first major novel, *Sons and Lovers*, for instance, worked with Oedipal themes, such as a son's overpowering love for his mother. In Lawrence's later fictions, he often used images of the return to the womb to signify deathly regression, as when the character of Gerald, in *Women in Love*, dies, frozen, in a fetal position. Lawrence, then, would probably have agreed with Freud and with the mainstream of European thinking on the oceanic. For while religious thinkers like Rolland and Buber were interested in restoring to modern life the sense of oceanic spirituality, Lawrence, like most of his male European counterparts, didn't think it really could, or even should be, done. In fact, despite his attraction to Indian religion and the almost overwhelming lyricism of his descriptions, Lawrence claimed that this kind of experience held dangers which ultimately kept him from embracing it.

Lawrence's ambivalence resides in his very prose. He writes that the great flood of creation is "lovely *and terrible*"; Indians feel "energy and power and *a dark sort of joy*" (my emphasis). As a defense against "terrible joy"—an unchecked and unboundaried sublime—Lawrence projected his own intuitions about and reactions to the land outward onto Indians. These feelings, he said, belong to "them"; he, Lawrence, claimed to be merely registering and recording emotions operative in others. This classic psychological tactic, by which the desired emotion is repudiated and located outside the self, is not uncommon in encounters with the primitive. In fact, Lawrence had no evidence for what Indians believed beyond the common talk of his friends in Taos and his own, very vivid impressions of the Indians' land and rituals.[7] It seems more than likely, then, that the oceanic sensations Lawrence ascribed to Indians actually existed *within himself.*

Lawrence admired Indians for retaining "some of the strange beauty and pathos of the religion [they had] brought forth." But—and this is highly significant—he also maintained that the Indians' religious sense— so direct, so intense, so cosmic—was squarely at odds with life in the modern world and prevented the Indians' adaptation and survival. The Indian's religion, Lawrence said, "is now shedding him away into oblivion" ("New Mexico," 147)—a phrase by which Lawrence meant, literally, leading to the death of the "race." Racial extinction was a concept fully consonant with the Freudian death wish, and it was much on Lawrence's mind in the aftermath of World War I.

In fact, the death wish fits importantly into the pattern of racialized thinking to which Lawrence was persistently attracted. What he says here about Indians, for example, resembles what he calls in *Women in Love* "the African way to dissolution": a highly sexualized (rather than, as with the Indians, a highly spiritualized) route to racial extinction. What African and Indian cultures shared, according to Lawrence, was a strong imbalance between the individual and what he called "the circumambient universe": both those peoples, he thought, tilted in different ways too far towards "the universe."[8] By extension, white individuals who enter similar states of mind were seen as taking a similar risk of straying too far from the self: like Indians, they too may experience "shedding away into oblivion." That is why Lawrence insists at several points in his essays on an inevitable and crucial difference between white and Indian consciousness: "The Indian way of consciousness is different from and fatal to our [white, European] way of consciousness," Lawrence said. "Our way of consciousness is different from and fatal to the Indian. The two ways, the two streams are never to be united. They are not even to be reconciled. There is no bridge, no canal of connection" ("Indians and Entertainment," 45–46).

Lawrence's reaction to the "Indian way of consciousness" is his version of the strong conflicting emotions Jung felt for his special stone and for Africa. It replicates the feeling that attraction to oceanic nature endangers the "I" and the "mature European self." It is similar, as well, to

Gide's powerful feeling in the Congo that only "differentiation" could protect his "own presence" in the midst of nature's repetitions and hugeness. Lawrence saw Indians as embodiments of the oceanic sense, much in the way that Gide and Jung saw Africa and Africans. Nature is vast and alive and threatens to swallow the "I" that observes it unless the "I" clearly marks its boundaries and borders. This, according to Lawrence, is what Indians fail to do because they experience things collectively, and not as autonomous individual beings.

When Indian men drum and chant, for example, or when they dance, Lawrence claimed that their

> experience is generic, non-individual. It is an experience of the human bloodstream, not the mind or spirit. . . . The experience is one experience, tribal, of the bloodstream. . . . There is no spectacle, no spectator. ("Indians and Entertainment," 47–48)

Group experience is registered in individual bodies, or so Lawrence thought, but in a way that was free of intellectualization and utterly spontaneous. As the Indians drum, according to Lawrence, their bodies cease to function as autonomous units, each part expressing the experience of the group:

> Strange, clapping, crowing, gurgling sounds, in an unseizable subtle rhythm, the rhythm of the heart in her throes: from a parted entranced mouth, from a chest powerful and free, from an abdomen where the great blood-stream surges in the dark, and surges in its own generic experiences. ("Indians and Entertainment," 47)

Lawrence repeats "a" and "an" in this description as though to stress what he sees as the Indians' collective, nonindividualized consciousness. Lawrence claimed that the absence of representation, spectatorship, and judgment in Indian life and ritual was a key to the difference between whites and Indians. Whites, he believed, observe the universe, represent it in art, and judge everything; Indians simply partake in essential Being-ness.[9]

In the United States today, Lawrence's rhapsodic descriptions of Indian men chanting and drumming have inspired the mythopoetic men's movement, which I shall discuss in Chapter Seven. It has adopted many of the rituals Lawrence describes, and made Lawrence himself a cult hero. Yet Lawrence had no intention of encouraging whites to imitate Indians and would, I suspect, have been appalled by the sight of white men drumming and chanting. Like many Western thinkers, Lawrence considered the faculties of individuation, distancing, and judgment essential to being European. He may have protested and ranted about what he found wrong with European society (arrogance and an overemphasis on reason, he said, and a loathing for the body). But he nonetheless accepted and lived according to European ideas of selfhood—hence, perhaps, his continual and eloquent frustration. So although Lawrence says that when Indians drum "there is no spectacle, no spectator," there is at least one spectator in the scene being described: Lawrence himself. And that, in a way, is the tender irony.

Lawrence ascribed to the Indians the fullest experience of the blood, like the land itself the very image of pure life force. He described this experience as offering unmediated access to creation and to Being-ness— the core religious emotion. But he imagined a different fate entirely for whites, and specifically for white men. The white man's burden—but also his fate and glory—is the individuated self. As Gide and Jung found, for Lawrence too, what exists in the primitive is unimaginably rich, a form of knowledge that is delectable, but also deadly and threatening. The rhythm of attraction and repression Lawrence enacted in his essays about New Mexico informs the fictions he wrote after 1925. These fictions draw on Lawrence's views of Indian religion and rework those views—especially with regard to women.

II

After New Mexico, Lawrence wrote an important short story, "The Woman Who Rode Away" (1924); two novels, *The Plumed Serpent* (1926) and *Lady Chatterley's Lover* (1928); and a major novella, *The Escaped Cock* (published in the United States as *The Man Who Died,*

1929).[10] The two fictions he wrote while he was still in North America—
The Plumed Serpent and "The Woman Who Rode Away"—reflect very
directly Lawrence's theories about Indian religion, wedding them to his
theories of sexuality. Because Lawrence's views of Indian religion were so
complex, and sometimes even contradictory, the plots of the stories are,
to put it mildly, unusual and striking.

"The Woman Who Rode Away" is one of Lawrence's most shocking,
and even offensive, tales. In it, a wealthy European woman wanders off
into the wilderness and encounters a group of Yaqui Indians. At first, she
fears she will be raped; but instead, the Indians bathe and feed her, dress
her in flowing robes, and give her peyote. After a while, she learns that
they have special plans for her. Because of her sky blue eyes, she is to be
their annual sacrifice to the sun. The woman and a male Indian talk back
and forth about the meaning of what is to come, with the Indian repeatedly urging her submission. In fact, the "Indian" speaks in a way very
similar to Lawrence's Gypsies, miners, and other "dark men." He is the
spokesman for Lawrence's theories about women, theories laced with a
fear of female power consistent, as we have seen in Chapter One, with
many Western traditions. The Indian in "The Woman Who Rode Away"
turns out to be fully persuasive. At the conclusion of the tale, the woman
acquiesces, agreeing to be a human sacrifice. The story ends as the dark
Indian plunges his knife into her chest before the ritual extraction of her
steaming heart, with which he will greet the sunrise.

The Plumed Serpent elaborates similar themes. In this peculiar novel,
a Mexican Indian named Cipriano, an important general, is leading a rebellion in an isolated rural province seeking to break away from the
nation-state of Mexico and return to ancient Indian ways. Cipriano has
absolute power over his followers and calls himself Huitzilopochtli, the
Aztec god of life and death. From time to time, he dresses up as that
Aztec god in order to slay with impunity those he has judged to be trai-
tors. Cipriano justifies his actions to his European wife, Kate (who is appalled by the murders), by appealing to ideas reminiscent of Lawrence's
views of Indian religion: *"The blood,"* he tells Kate, *"is one blood"*
(Lawrence's emphasis).[11] From this point of view, the individual death is
irrelevant. In the novel's highly idiosyncratic Lawrentian logic, Kate's acceptance of this truth is linked with the necessity of relinquishing her

"female will," a phrase often equivalent in Lawrence's writings, as it clearly is here, to the drive for orgasm. The novel ends ambiguously, with Kate half determined to leave Cipriano and half determined to stay.

Given what Lawrence says in his essays, it is fascinating to see how he represents, or rather uses, Indians in his fictions. In his essays, Lawrence insists that the gulf between Indian and white consciousness is unbridgeable, with "no connection between them." What is more, in his essays he does not even suggest that Indians have any particular views on either female will or the proper form of sexuality. Yet in "The Woman Who Rode Away" and *The Plumed Serpent,* Indian men give ample voice to Lawrence's own long-term obsession: the need for females to relinquish "the will." In "The Woman Who Rode Away," the woman relinquishes through death; in *Serpent,* by following the man's lead during intercourse and not actively seeking orgasm. Orgasm and death are frequently linked in the Western literary tradition, where orgasm is *la petite mort* (the little death), an expenditure or "spending" of life force. But in a weird reversal of the tradition, Lawrence equates death with forgoing orgasm, not orgasm itself. What's more, Lawrence often confines the issue of orgasm to women.

There is a second important difference between the essays and fictions. In his essays, Lawrence does not see violence as a special part of Indian religion: violence, he says, must be accepted insofar as it is part of creation, but it is in no way a central feature of Indian life or ritual. Yet both "The Woman Who Rode Away" and *The Plumed Serpent* emphasize human sacrifice and the loosing of the "blood" which is "one blood." Macabre though it may seem, Lawrence's emphasis on human sacrifice is just one instance of an image of Indian culture quite persistent among men of his day. Antonin Artaud in Mexico fantasized a theatre of cruelty and violence; Georges Bataille was fascinated by Aztec rituals of human sacrifice—hearts ripped out, heads rolling, bodies tossed down the sides of pyramids—and, along with other intellectuals in the Collège de Sociologie, wanted to enact a ritual human sacrifice in Paris as an instrument of cultural renewal.[12]

In the male imagination of human sacrifice, the body is projected as open to death and as fodder for the universe. Therein lies the thrill, the pleasure, of writing about the act. Yet the writerly male self remains intact and autonomous and continuously aware of himself. He chooses to identify most with the executioner, not the victim—to fill the active ("masculine") role, not the passive one. The thrill of reversal—in which the executioner can become the next victim—is always present, but it is also always safely forestalled. This model of male writing about human sacrifice, in which writing allows safe access to extremes of experience, applies almost exactly to "The Woman Who Rode Away" and *The Plumed Serpent*.

. . .

LAWRENCE'S two other late fictions—*Lady Chatterley's Lover* and *The Man Who Died*—continue and expand Lawrence's meditation on the primitive. They are not set, in any obvious way, in "primitive" places. Nor do they feature Indians as important characters. Yet they allow Lawrence to gain more direct, though still only partial, access to the feelings the land inspired in him in New Mexico. The primitive, as a category, is still allied in these fictions with the power of sexuality. But it is no longer directly connected with violence and human sacrifice.

In *Lady Chatterley's Lover*, Lawrence's notorious novel about a love affair between an aristocratic Englishwoman and the gamekeeper on her husband's estate, manor houses and technology belong to the deadened upper class, but the woods belong to the lovers. Connie first realizes Mellors' attractiveness when she sees him showering outdoors. Then Connie and Mellors learn more about each other through conversations about chicks and other animals. Finally, they mate outdoors in the rain or in a hut that is described as being close to nature.

Mellors, the gamekeeper, is a working-class male with dark coloring. All his life, Lawrence had tended to see such men as representative of bodily, underground, id forces. (Lawrence's father, an uneducated coal miner, is likely to have been the most immediate source of these ideas, though they were also present in the culture at large.) After New Mexico, the dark working-class male merged to some extent in Lawrence's imagination with the "primitive" Indian. Like the Indian in "The Woman Who Rode Away," like Cipriano in *The Plumed Serpent*, Mellors instructs his lover in the true, "essential" nature of womanhood, including the obligatory Lawrentian doctrine that a woman must receive orgasms from a man without doing anything to aid the process. Mellors speaks the English of the educated class; but he deliberately lapses into heavy dialect when he is imaged as a "primitive" force of nature. Despite being set in England after World War I, then, the story reflects Lawrence's fascination with the primitive.

In fact, Lawrence's experience of Indian religion shows up quite directly in the extensive sex scenes that made *Lady Chatterley* a landmark in discussions of pornography and art and delayed its publication in the United Kingdom and the United States for many years. Because of its history of censorship, the novel is usually read as advocating what Mellors bluntly calls "fucking." But given that conventional reading, it's remarkable how reluctant Mellors is to engage in sex, and how much he prefers a state of quiet, nonsexual contact with Connie. "She nestled up to him, feeling small and enfolded, and they both went to sleep at once, fast in one sleep," reads a typical moment, which then blends into brief but vivid descriptions of birds, light, and woods.[13] It would not be going too far to say that, in *Lady Chatterley's Lover,* what sex is best for is what comes afterwards—the warmth, but especially the feeling of oneness with each other and with nature. In a sense, the novel is a broad reexamination of the terms of sexuality, redefining the sexual as far more than genital contact. It is not hard to imagine at least one biographical motivation: Lawrence must have welcomed such a redefinition, indeed required it, at this late point in his life, when he was almost certainly impotent and yet married to the sexually adventurous Frieda.

More important and mostly unnoticed about *Lady Chatterley's Lover* is how Lawrence experiments with a language for female orgasm. In Lawrence's earlier fiction, orgasm (male but more often female) had been imaged in negative terms drawn in part from the Italian artists who called themselves Futurists: movement towards orgasm is "frictional," "corrosive," and "burning"; it is "like a harpy's beak" that makes a man's heart "fuse, like a bead"; or (on the male side) it is like "electricity," the tolling of a bell, the pouring of semen "darkly, like death." But in *Lady Chatterley,* the metaphors describing female orgasm are oceanic in a way that recalls Lawrence's description of Indian religions, in which there is communication with the "great flood of creation, forever flowing in lovely and terrible waves."

Here, for example, is a typical description from *Lady Chatterley:*

It seemed she was like the sea, nothing but dark waves rising and heaving, heaving with a great swell, so that slowly her whole darkness was in motion, and she was ocean rolling its dark, dumb mass. . . . [F]urther and further rolled the waves of herself away from herself, leaving her, till suddenly, in a soft, shuddering convulsion, the quick of all her plasm was touched . . . the consummation was upon her, and she was gone. (163)

In passages like this, female sexual climax occurs as an overflow, a dissolution of boundaries—an oceanic experience. Lawrence's prose is admittedly clumsy and would be criticized today: for being overwritten, for example, and for rendering the woman in objectifying terms as "dark" and "dumb" (speechless). Many readers would also find fault with Lawrence's insistence that Connie's orgasms must be timed to Mellors' and occur solely by penetration. But it is important to remember that this description was written at a time when few novelists, male or female, dared to mention female orgasm in their fiction, much less to describe it. When the subject was broached, it was often in reference to black women (another image of "the primitive"), as in Gertrude Stein's "Melanctha" (in *Three Lives*). Even then, it was typically coded in a vocabulary of phenomenological or biblical "knowing" rather than located in the body.

In *Lady Chatterley,* the association of female sexuality with the oceanic seems to be a mostly positive one: we are, after all, asked to believe that sex with Mellors has rescued Connie from the deadness of modern life. But, as we have seen in the discussion of Lawrence's view of Indian religion, he linked the oceanic to both delight and danger. Since Lawrence understood sexuality and spirituality to be continuous impulses that could be expressed in similar language and imagery, it comes as no surprise that his linkage of female orgasm with the oceanic is likewise fraught with a mixture of fascination and fear. The fascination is plain; and it is curious, given that Lawrence was a male writer, how much more often and more fully he describes female, as opposed to male, orgasmic experience. The emphasis on women recalls for me how, in earlier fictions by Lawrence, male characters (like Tom Brangwen in *The Rainbow*) experience strong envy of pregnant females and women in childbirth. They imagine women as having experiences that open them to the universe and the forces of nature, ones that men can only guess at or experience vicariously.

But the fear is evident as well. Such extreme experience is for Lawrence as dangerous as it is desirable. Women, like Indians, know the cosmos but also presumably run the risk of what Lawrence called "shedding into oblivion." Hence, I believe, the continuous slippage between death and female orgasm in "The Woman Who Rode Away" and *The Plumed Serpent.*

Ultimately, there is something almost transparently fearful about all of Lawrence's views of the oceanic. This is true whether it resides in the land and in Indians (as in the essays) or in women's bodies (as in the late fictions). Like identification with the land or what Jung called "going black under the skin" (experiencing things as "natives" do), the woman's sexual response is fascinating, but potentially vast and overwhelming to the male. Lawrence would, I think, agree with Camille Paglia's statement that "every penis is made less in every vagina, just as mankind, male and female, is devoured by mother nature."[14] For thinkers like him, female orgasm elides into fear of loss of self and fear of death. To retain control, a man must deploy every resource of his body, psyche, and art. That is why Lawrence insisted throughout his writing that women allow men to give them orgasms. Lawrence's ambivalence about orgasm suggests a new way to regard his insistence that male-male love supplement heterosexual experience, even though such love is never to be sexually consummated or acknowledged as erotic. Free of orgasm, such love is, for Lawrence, cleansed of the taint of death. In this realm, and on these terms, the man's identity and control are never critically jeopardized.

The continuity of coition and oceanic feeling, sexual and spiritual experience, crucially informs—I am tempted to say, determines—Lawrence's obsession with sexuality. Yet perhaps because he regarded the oceanic as an essentially female form of experience, Lawrence only rarely explored that continuity, in positive terms, in his male characters. But one rare instance occurs in his daring last novella, *The Man Who Died,* published the year before his death. *The Man Who Died* is clearly a primitivist narrative, but in a different register than we have seen so far, one more directly tied to "the primitive" as having to do with the "original church" (see the Introduction). The novella is set in the year of Jesus' death, at the dawn of Christian time: it goes back to the origins of Christianity and offers a reimagination of the Resurrection story. The Man Who Died (who both is and is not Jesus Christ) does not ascend, body and soul, into heaven. Instead, he journeys to Egypt and reluctantly mates there with a priestess of Isis, for, like Mellors, he is afraid of sex. In *The Man Who Died*, as in *Lady Chatterley*, nature figures importantly in the lovers' eventual sexual union. It is both the setting for sexuality and the source of metaphors for orgasmic and postorgasmic experience.

In the novella, as in the novel, actual sex is arguably less rhapsodic than what takes place afterwards. Coition is tersely described by the biblical "So he knew her and was one with her." But then, after he mates with the priestess, the Man Who Died goes out into the night and experiences an epiphany of Being-ness that might be considered the real climax of the story:

> The man looked at the vivid stars before dawn, as they rained down to the sea. . . . And he thought: "How plastic it is, how full of curves and folds like an invisible rose of dark-petalled openness. . . . How it leans around me, and I am part of it, the great rose of Space. I am like a grain of its perfume, and the woman is a grain of its beauty. Now the world is one flower of many petalled darknesses, and I am in its perfume as in a touch."[15]

The path to ecstasy is routed through sexuality as the threshold experience. The Man Who Died has to enter the female before he can enter the cosmos. The movement is out of the body and into a vitalist, cosmic emotion in which the landscape is experienced as an unfolding rose, an image linked through long literary traditions both to female sexuality and to the experience of the divine. In a passage like this, Lawrence comes as close as he ever will to expressing his own feelings for nature inspired by the experience of New Mexico. The cosmic emotion registers in the body, as the speaker reaches beyond the "I." But the iteration of the "I" also suggests a resistance at last to losing oneself in the experience. Although awash in ecstatic sensual metaphor, the "I" routinely reasserts itself as though to preserve a centered, discrete sense of self. Surely, Lawrence's attraction to the oceanic is manifest in all of the prose I have quoted. But finally Lawrence returns to his commitment to Western individualism, conceived as something masculine that must stand as fully as possible against the oceanic—pun fully intended.

Lawrence said that New Mexico was "the greatest experience from the outside world that I have ever had. . . . [S]omething stood still in my soul, and I started to attend." He refers to precisely the same sense of intense awe and wonder that Gide and Jung felt in Africa. And like Gide and Jung, he develops elaborate theories and strategies to rein it in. Even in the sentence from "New Mexico" with which I began, Lawrence hedges the oceanic emotion. New Mexico is vital and active, but it is defined as a force from *"the outside world"* acting on an "I" firmly boundaried as an observer, an "I" to which the sentence punctually returns, as it does in *The Man Who Died*. Lawrence had strong affinities for oceanic nature, conceived as the site of eternity, the site of the oblivion of the autonomous self. His expression of those affinities is part of his greatness; his sublimation of them in sexuality is typical of his gender and his time.

Twilight Canyon, Lake Powell, 1964
Photographer: Todd Webb
Courtesy of Todd Webb and the Museum of Fine Arts,
Museum of New Mexico, Todd Webb Study Collection

PART II

Women

CHAPTER THREE

Loving Africa:
Memoirs by European Women

I

I HAD A FARM IN AFRICA," Isak Dinesen mournfully intones at the beginning of *Out of Africa* (1937), a title steeped in bereavement and loss. One hears the words as coated with the raspiness of age and the timbre of desire as snow drifts outside the window where the author writes the memoir of her farm in Kenya.[1] Dinesen desires Africa's majestic hills and plains as she sits and writes in Denmark, in her mother's house, in the bedroom she had occupied as a child. Her forced return, one might say exile, to this house ironically completes the circle of Dinesen's life. For she had gone to Africa as an answer to the men who had disappointed her: her father—a traveller who lived for a time among Indians, who cultivated her talents and gave her a taste for the exotic, but hung himself when she was nine;[2] and her first love, Hans Blixen, who spurned her. In 1913, she followed Hans' twin brother, Bror, to British East Africa, where they married and became partners in a coffee farm. In

1921, she divorced Bror and continued to run the farm on her own, with intermittent visits from Denys Finch-Hatton, an adventurer who was her truest love. Then, in 1931, the coffee market collapsed and Dinesen was forced to sell her farm; that same year, Finch-Hatton died in a plane crash shortly before Dinesen had to leave Africa and return to Denmark. She writes the book to commemorate the life she created in Africa—a mostly solitary life and yet an active one. Dinesen wrested from loss—the loss of these men, of Africa itself—the book that now assures her immortality.

Alone and bereft in Denmark, Dinesen still has the power to evoke, in words, the feeling of being on hills in Africa, the feeling "of having lived for a time up in the air . . . drawing in a vital assurance and lightness of heart," of waking up and thinking, "Here I am, where I ought to be" (4). This feeling can confirm and buoy the "I," like the male imperative discussed in Part One, though it is evoked now only in words, and no longer experienced with every waking, with each breath. But what is most striking in Dinesen's perceptions of the land, at least compared with the men considered in Part One, is how little concern she expresses at times for preserving the integrity of individual identity. For example, when Dinesen is alone with Finch-Hatton at night on an African plain, she feels "infinitely small," part of "a unity" that neither she nor Finch-Hatton spoils by using words (245, 247). At its most radical, this kind of feeling leads to the imagination of death, as when Dinesen muses on the Gikuyu custom of leaving bodies in the bush rather than burying them, saying, "I thought that it would be a pleasant thing to be laid out to the sun and the stars, and to be so promptly, neatly and openly picked and cleansed; to be made one with Nature and become a common component of a landscape" (352).

This oceanic view of the self in relation to nature turns up with enormous frequency in women's writing about Africa. It contrasts strongly with Gide's and Jung's experience of Africa as dangerous to a sense of self and a writer's art. Women writers typically saw Africa as an opportunity to escape the limitations of women's domestic lives at home and actively sought there a vocation and self-fulfillment. Although their memoirs necessarily memorialize the experiences and feelings of the writerly self, the women often consider themselves atypical Europeans, feeling and reporting a special rapport with African peoples and their nonindividualistic, animistic beliefs. More important, the women feel an openness towards oceanic experience, a willingness to "become a common component of a landscape" that is utterly at odds with the way male writers in the early twentieth century tended to feel about the land and rendered those feelings. The women want to merge with the land, and perceive their identities in and through it. But unlike their male contemporaries, they do not gender the land as feminine, which perhaps accounts for why the land poses no threat to their identities and indeed sustains their mature vocations. Women, of course, were familiar with those prevailing myths and ideas about the primitive that impinged on men, but often they imagined and used them quite differently.

Dinesen is the best-known European woman writer on the subject of Africa. But the pattern of a loss recouped in Africa, often followed by further loss, typifies patterns found in many memoirs by European women including Mary Kingsley, Vivienne de Watteville, Beryl Markham, and Kuki Gallmann—the subjects of this chapter. So too does a love affair with the land and animals of the continent as an alternative or supplement to family attachments. These women's tales of Africa are often predicated on a loss that ends in a vocation, or spiritual triumph, or both. As in Dinesen's history, the founding condition is typically the women's adoration of a father or some other male relative—brother, husband, or son: the fantasies he engendered about Africa or exotic places, the money he lost, his death. The result is the women's attachment to Africa—a love of the land that replaces love of the father or amatory partner.

These women travel or (much better) live there, carving out a life that is unconventional, for a female of their time or even of ours. Losing the father or husband, they find a vocation, a mission to center their lives. The one substitutes directly for the other: indeed, had death and devastation not entered their lives, these women might have remained under a man's shadow. Often, the women find new masculine loves, but these do not last, sometimes because the women do not really seem to want them. Finally, these women are alone with the experience or memory of Africa, writing about it for us, the readers. As for Dinesen, the writing is regarded with a certain ambivalence: it is all she's got—and very good indeed—but is still perceived as a compensation, in some ways not as good as what is lost. The women discussed in this chapter are solitary, austere, grand—terrifying and yet impressive in their bereavement—rather like certain females in Greek myth and drama. In fact, I will ultimately want to claim that these women, like the men examined in Part One, began with complex symbolic linkages between the primitive and the oceanic, but appropriated and transformed them quite differently from the way their male counterparts did.

One of the strongest themes in these books is a full-blooded assertion of oneness with animal life and with the land: a powerfully articulated oceanic sensibility, which amounts to a symbolic claim to a continuity of Being-ness with the material of Africa.[3] The women's narratives do not always constitute, in any obvious way, a continuous tradition.[4] Yet their ideas and episodes, their prose and ethos, differ decisively from the ideas and ethos found in similar male narratives from the same period. In this chapter, I want to discuss several twentieth-century European women's narratives of Africa, both famous and obscure, which illuminate the patterns I've described. All involve an intelligent woman's desire to escape the limitations of middle- and upper-class European life, which dictated that women define themselves through family, not work; all express the joy of vocation and of action. All involve a man's influence on a woman's choice of Africa and the fruition of the woman's work through the loss or discarding of male influence. All express a direct relationship with the land and, sometimes, beyond the land, to spirit, that compensates for human losses. Finally, all are about the act of writing about loss and the land.

II

Mary Kingsley published the record of her journeys through Africa, *Travels in West Africa* (1897) and *West African Studies* (1899), close to the time of major European explorations. Her voyages followed Sir Richard Francis Burton and William Speke's expedition to find the source of the Nile by roughly forty years, Henry M. Stanley's to find Livingstone by only twenty. But the motifs of her work are highly consistent with those in the best-known women's memoirs of Africa that came later, in the 1920s and in the decades leading up to and following World War II. Kingsley came from a literary and scientific family that appears to have

been highly eccentric. Her father was a doctor and an amateur anthropologist who travelled extensively in Asia, the South Pacific, and the
Americas. Two of her uncles were novelists who wrote fictionalized accounts of English exploration that glorified the vigor of the Anglo-Saxon
race (for example, Charles Kingsley's *Westward Ho!*). Had her parents
lived long lives, Mary Kingsley would probably have been the angel in
their house, the unmarried daughter who tended them in old age. After
they died in 1892, she decided to use her inheritance to travel, ostensibly
to do scientific studies, most notably in West Africa, collecting fish specimens for British museums. By some accounts, including her own at some
points, Kingsley saw herself as directly continuing her father's work. Her
uncle Charles introduced his niece to scientists who eased her way.[5]

But the scientific pretext of her travels often seems the thinnest of
veils over more profound desires. For example, Kingsley devotes one of
her longest and weightiest chapters to the subject of African spiritual beliefs, not fishes. What is more, towards the end of her second trip
through West Africa, Kingsley could not resist the challenge of climbing
Mount Mungo Mah Lobeh (Mount Cameroon), although she knew that
this was not the most likely site for collecting saltwater aquatic samples.

Mary Kingsley's story leaves much to the imagination. For here was
this plain blond spinster, in full Victorian women's garb, negotiating with
Fan tribesmen to take her over trade routes obscure and dangerous, even
for the Africans themselves. She traversed forests and swamps, often
thanking her voluminous skirts for keeping her comically afloat during
mishaps and warding off the bites of the region's voracious mosquitoes.
Her voice is wry and witty—as unconventional as her deeds. She says she
began by knowing nothing of West Africa beyond the oft-repeated cliché
that it was "the white man's grave." She ended by knowing a great deal
which did not necessarily contradict the clichés but which construed
them differently.

Here, for example, is Mary Kingsley's sly list of the information to be
found in her book, *Travels in West Africa*. She presents it, in her preface,
as a joking, but also parodic, table of contents:

The dangers of West Africa.
The disagreeables of West Africa.
The diseases of West Africa.

The things you must take to West Africa.
The things you find most handy in West Africa.
The worst possible things you can do in West Africa.[6]

Anyone who has read Henry M. Stanley, André Gide, or similar male accounts of journeys will recognize, in this pithy list, the essential matter of their tomes on African travels. The dangers, disagreeables, and diseases of Africa—along with the narrator's heroic account of his deeds and castigation of his black servants—are the essential matter of many male travel narratives. Sometimes, especially in the French tradition, meditations on the traveller's psychic and physical condition are also standard, as well as on sundry Western texts (often Conrad) brought along as reading material. Compare, for example, the perceptions in André Gide's *Voyage au Congo* (discussed in Chapter One), which is typical of male narratives.

In contrast, Kingsley gives her list of African woes with her tongue firmly in cheek. She suffers from malaria and other fevers along the way—of course, doesn't everyone? But she dismisses these incidents in a brief phrase or two. She has uncomfortable nights in African villages, but also some that are downright cozy. She meets the odd hostile tribe and eludes it, but more often she records the habits of the groups she encounters as a goal in and of itself.

Henry M. Stanley and other men came to Africa with different and more specific goals: to find Livingstone, to rescue the Emir of Equatoria, to map the sources of the Nile, to find geographical markers for European maps. Fame was at stake, and glory and reputation—as well as the money that would follow. Gide travelled to work out a psychological crisis at home, connected with coming out as a homosexual. Other men of his time, like Carl Jung, came to Africa in the wake of nervous breakdowns, seeking there renewed psychological health.

Perhaps because she was a woman, Kingsley had no heroic or even geographical mission. She had relatively little to gain back home by her ventures in Africa. She was seeking no cure, just an escape from a woman's confinement.[7] She was an open-minded, curious traveller, nominally collecting fishes. But the journey itself became her goal and her glory. No specific reports or accomplishments were expected back home, so she took the time to enjoy the experience. If Africa for Stanley was a chore to be completed, for Kingsley it was a respite from the dullness of life as a Victorian spinster. Kingsley's tone is modest and unheroic, often mock-heroic. Her focus is on the land and its peoples, not on her own valor or psychic state, so that the overall balance and style of her narrative differs greatly from Gide's or Jung's.

In fact, while for many travellers Africa reinforced clichés and stereo-types, Kingsley describes how Africa ran counter to her preconceptions. She says:

> I went out with my mind full of the deductions of every book on Ethnology, German or English, that I had read during fifteen years—and being a good Cambridge person, I was particularly confident that from Mr. Frazer's book, *The Golden Bough*, I had got a semi-universal key to the underlying idea of native custom and belief. But I soon found that this was very far from the case. (435)

While she stops short of advising "Do not read Ethnography," Kingsley urges travellers to run the written theories along with firsthand experiences through "the mill of your mind" (436). This was, in fact, the method she employed during her own travels:

> One by one I took my old ideas derived from books and thought based on imperfect knowledge and weighed them against the real life around me, and found them either worthless or wanting. (6)

She describes herself and Africa as having "gradually educated each other," and concludes, "I had the best of the affair" (6).

What she comes to want most in Africa is an understanding of the ways in which Africans think about "great phenomena," by which Kings-ley clearly means religion. No universalist or semiuniversalist, she distinguishes between groups and tribes on these matters. She rejects the theory that religion originates in dreams or taboos, and other ideas that would later be pursued, with variations, by Sigmund Freud, Lévi-Strauss, and others. She also rejects the view (epitomized by Lucien Lévy-Bruhl) that primitives are incapable of rational thought. In fact, she concludes that the West African belief in spirits and their multiple influences arises in a manner that is "natural and easy"—logical on its own terms and neither better nor worse than Western explanations. In this careful, respectful relativism, Kingsley anticipates the findings of ethnographers still many decades into the future.

Kingsley was not an exemplary figure, free of prejudice and flaws. She shared, for example, the common European belief of her time that blacks were, by and large, lazier and dirtier than whites. She was not an entirely atypical specimen of white traveller: how could she be, really, in a culture that largely imagined imperialism as inevitable and natural?[8] But Kingsley brought to her journey an openness and curiosity that distinguished her from most people of her day. She was, for example, quite contemptuous of the missionaries' role in Africa (despite her liking for certain individual missionaries). She was also quite skeptical about the worth of the civilizing mission:

> Nothing strikes one so much, in studying the degeneration of these native tribes, as the direct effect that civilisation and reformation has upon hastening it. The worst enemy to the African tribe is the one who comes to it and says: Now you must civilise, and come to school, and leave off all those awful goings-on of yours, and settle down quietly. (404)

Kingsley regretted how missionaries "wrote their reports not to tell you how the country they resided in was, but how it was getting on towards being what it ought to be" (3). She would have preferred to see Africans left alone to develop their cultures as they pleased, even though she would also have liked to see them brought into European systems of trade and provided with a "technical" education. Although she was no postcolonial saint,[9] Mary Kingsley showed many traits that distinguished a surprising number of European women in Africa, above all a skepticism about European superiority and an openness to African spiritual beliefs.

Like all the women discussed in this chapter, Kingsley associated African spirituality with landscape. But she did not sense any danger of what Jung called "going black under the skin" because she related so strongly and so directly to the land. Given her natural caustic wit, although Kingsley describes the landscape abundantly, she always does so with some self-irony. She says, for example, that she does not want to sound like a Romantic poet as she records feelings of rapture and transcendence in Africa. In fact, she does not sound anything like a Wordsworth or a Keats, because she records a sensation of willingly and fully lapsing out of the self which the Romantics tended to regard as a temptation that must ultimately be resisted.[10] In one remarkable passage, she even tells us that avoiding rhapsodies on the landscape is her very goal. But she ends this quotation with a confession that strikes me as quite astonishing:

> In the darkness round me flitted thousands of fireflies and out beyond this pool of utter night flew by unceasingly the white foam of the rapids; sound there was none save their thunder. The majesty and beauty of the scene fascinated me, and I stood leaning with my back against a rock pinnacle watching it. Do not imagine it gave rise, in what I am pleased to call my mind, to those complicated, poetical reflections natural beauty seems to bring out in other people's minds. It never works that way with me; I just lose all sense of human individuality, all memory of human life, with its grief and worry and doubt, and become part of the atmosphere. (178)

This brisk, commonsense woman notes here, quite casually, a habitual surrender of identity and blending with the atmosphere. It is reminiscent of Dinesen's wish to be picked clean and merge with nature. It is an expression of ecstatic emotion and will prove to be one of the most typical assertions of European women writing about Africa.

III

When Vivienne de Watteville was in her early twenties, she accompanied her father, Brovard ("Brovie") to Africa on a specimen-collecting safari. He was mauled by a lion and died on the trip. Four years later, she returned to Africa to revisit and make peace with the landscape she had so loved on her first visit. Her project was ambitious and audacious. She wanted to track elephants and lions, without guns, using only her naked eye and the camera lens. Armed with cameras, not guns, she exorcised her father's death, but also trumped his cards: he had brought guns and found death; she would bring cameras and find peace.

Once she was back in Africa, de Watteville decided to camp for several months on a mountaintop just below the daunting Mount Kenya. Although de Watteville repeatedly refers to her condition on the mountain as one of profound "solitude," she was not technically alone. For the first part of her project, numerous African porters and guides accompanied her; for the sojourn on the mountain, two of her African retainers remained nearby as almost constant companions. I point this out for accuracy's sake, rather than to undercut the unusualness of de Watteville's goals and tenacity. For make no mistake: her safari in 1928–29 was an ambitious and adventuresome undertaking for a pretty and sensitive young Englishwoman who, aside from writing about her adventures twelve years later, seems to have settled afterwards, very decently, into life as a British wife and mother.

In *Speak to the Earth: Wanderings and Reflections Among Elephants and Mountains,* Africa and de Watteville's relationship to it are the paramount subjects. And what a relationship it is! Expressed in pink-purple prose, it embraces ecstatic states of mind and moments of authentic communion. De Watteville possesses from the beginning of her narrative, perhaps practically from the day she was born, a keen visual sensibility wedded to extreme lability of self. She painstakingly records the color, feel, and texture of things; more, she attempts always to enter into relations of understanding with them that end up becoming relations of identity. De Watteville's narrative begins at a high oceanic pitch and progresses from there.

This, for example, is what she says of a favorite spot:

I loved this place that no one knew, and often kept tryst there; for what I craved for (having come so far to seek it) was to make friends with all that world about me, to come near to its spirit. Alone in the listening silence and the beauty of that solitude, I sometimes came near to the fringes of it. Lying with my heart pressed against the red earth and my forehead upon the stones was not physical nearness only; for as I lay there thinking how I, too, was composed of that same earth I touched and loved, and of the same elements that go to make the rocks and trees and stars as well as the birds and beasts, I felt myself merged into this deep love and unity with the earth, and found that it was at the same time unity with the spirit. The grey and silver thorn tree, soft-coloured in the dusk as the light of doves' wings, gathered me beneath its shadows; and all over, like a healing stream, lay the spell of absolute and perfect quietness.[11]

Her body presses against the earth. Her eyes caress "the velvet depths of space," "sapphire depths and fiery constellations," and "the fond curve of the mountain black against the stars" (161). A great many occasions and visual stimuli bring her to the state of "melting into all things and belonging to them," being "transported out of yourself in the sheer love of things" (161).

Like Mary Kingsley, de Watteville had read Romantic poetry. I feel the pressure here of Blake's "For every thing that lives is Holy," or Wordsworth's evocation of the child's sensation of "splendour in the grass" and "the life of things." But these are no mere abstractions or poetic principles for de Watteville, and above all no evocation of childhood. Instead, they are the result of disciplined months on the mountain, stripping the self down emotionally to achieve an openness to nature.

De Watteville's state of mind in Africa leads her to reject "the error of thinking of myself, because I happened to be a human being, as something higher" (175). Her emotions are, on the one hand, specifically Judeo-Christian, since de Watteville sometimes alludes both to the Bible and to the figure of God. But more often her emotions are guided by an animistic spirit, a kind of archetypal oceanic that she frequently cultivates, experiences, and records. When she realizes, for example, that she has approached the elephants as "a very ordinary predatory human," without displaying "the power of the spirit," she decides to follow the examples of Buddha and Francis of Assisi. She wants to purge herself on a mountaintop and to escape there, once and for all, the arrogance of being human (204).

The mountain gives her, in almost unbearably pure form, the shape of nature:

> In Nature, you learn to know yourself as the thing nearest at hand with whom you must live and work, after which you can forget your very existence in the million beautiful and interesting things around you. And it is the supreme test, because in Nature nothing false can exist. All that is superficial you must shed like a husk, for it has no place there. (274)

For de Watteville, closeness to nature is Africa's chief gift; it makes her feelings real and inescapable.

On the mountain, de Watteville achieves a balance between accepting herself and seeing herself as part of the cosmos:

> Looking up into the sky, I thought that each of us is revolving like one of those spheres in space, moving at his own speed, carrying with him the atmosphere of his own thoughts and individuality. Things from without filter through, but not without in some measure taking the colour of this atmosphere or being distorted by it. To hear, see and feel them truly, it is necessary to project a part of oneself outside the mist and the hum of these revolutions, into the utter stillness of space. (288)

In de Watteville's evocation of the eternal and cosmic, the self is preserved—it would have to be in order to be able to record these sensations; yet the self projects beyond itself, into the "colour of this atmosphere," and is changed by it. Metaphors of breathing in and out, of incorporation are embraced here as in Dinesen—something once again very different from what is found in male writers like Gide.

De Watteville's language resembles nothing so much as the language of meditation and mysticism. The passage I've just cited, for example, shows a strong affinity to Dante's vision in the *Paradiso;* elsewhere, as I have said, de Watteville alludes to Buddha and Francis of Assisi. In fact, there may even be a direct experiential connection between the experiences of mystics and those of de Watteville in Africa. Accounts by mystics often cite a parent or spouse's death as the motivation for devoting the self to the spirit. In addition, throughout history, mystics have found a special resource in mountains. De Watteville's mission to Africa had the hoped-for spiritual result—and something more. She not only put to rest the memory of her father's death but claimed a state of mind in which that death faded into insignificance.

De Watteville's prose is lush, almost embarrassingly so—hyperbolic and explosive. It strikes me sometimes as overwritten or even as badly written—perhaps the best she could do, given the difficulty of capturing the sublime in words. For de Watteville worked, painstakingly, towards the state of mind she believed necessary for Africa: a state of oneness between human, animal, and plant life, between flesh and matter. Other women of European origins, born or raised in Africa, claimed the sensations de Watteville arduously pursued as their earliest and most profound inheritance.

IV

Imagine that you are a little girl whose earliest and happiest memories are of being out, barefoot, on a hunt with African males, including Kibbii, an uninitiated boy who is your friend and playmate. With your father's blessing, you range over your large and isolated farm, with a keen sense of the land and filled with awe for its creatures. That father is a ne'er-do-well, a will-o'-the-wisp, but you love him. You've been brought to Africa to escape his debts; your mother picked up her son and left—leaving you behind with your father—and Africa.[12] His very laxity makes possible a freedom few females enjoy. You grow up with zebras and other animals and believe the birth of a foal to be a miracle in which you are privileged to participate. You know African Nandi and Gikuyu, and Asian Indians, remember them, describe them, and record their words. You believe that the Africans' life is "much greater than our own." More, you believe that Europeans are interlopers in Africa, parasites on the land, its people, and its animal life—even as you know that you belong here, and nowhere else. The end point of this childhood idyll is World War I—a "white man's war"—which conscripts the African men who guided the hunt. You are sixteen at the end of the war, and your ties to the land are being severed. Your father leaves for a new farm in Peru, and now you are a displaced person, a woman adrift in Africa as the tide of modernity washes in. Ironically, these disruptions furnish you with the chance for self-fulfillment—first training and riding racehorses and then becoming the first female pilot to cross the Atlantic on a solo flight.

The "you" is Beryl Markham, and the situation is one she describes in *West with the Night* (1942). She writes from a much later perspective, but not (as in Dinesen's *Out of Africa*) from the perspective of desolation and exile. Markham writes as if she were still in Africa; in fact, she returned there after World War II. Her writing suggests that she found, in her career as an aviator, an emotional equivalent to the barefoot hunt, her companions now, instead of Nandi warriors, legendary white adventurers like Denys Finch-Hatton and Bror Blixen (who were also, respectively, Isak Dinesen's lover and husband). In fact, all the stages of Markham's life—as horse trainer and racer, as aviator—were attempts to capture the purity and unselfconscious certainty of her movements during the hunts of her youth. She evolved an ethos of speed and courage that provided the standard against which to judge everything, including herself: the perfect horse, the perfect African, the perfect man, the perfect airplane. She ordered the world according to merit and without regard to the conventional oppositions of animal and human, animate and inanimate.

In her journey from her father's farm to becoming a pilot, some of Markham's African friends came with her. Kibbii, renamed Arab Ruta after attaining manhood, is her all-purpose servant and maintenance man. He is also her companion, even though he addresses her now as "Memsahib," his female master.[13] She presents his employment as "a pretext" designed to make him available for the real business of conversation—"thinking, talking, dreaming." And she regards him as a seer and sage, possessing uncommon wisdom, intelligence, and intuition—a man who treats an airplane like a horse. Beryl Markham is of the European world, and not; of the African world, and not.

Although Markham earns a living finding herds of elephant from the air to make the work of the hunters less grueling, she looks upon the tourists she is helping with indifference bordering on contempt. She rescues her clients from mistakes when possible, but on one occasion she records with cool irony the smell of burning flesh when one of them is cremated after a fatal error she could not prevent. The dead man had been mauled by an enraged wounded lion as he foolishly attempted to photograph the death throes of his prey. Men like this hunter lack what she and Bror Blixen possess—what she calls a real "feel" for the animals. Once, when she and Blixen are cornered by a massive bull elephant, she is understandably terrified when the beast begins to charge: "A single biscuit tin, I judged, would do for both of us—cremation would be superfluous" (217). But she also expresses respect for the elephant's intelligence, for his wit (trapped in an unwieldy body), which she firmly believes rivals that of human beings.

Markham was a celebrity in her own time. She was feted in 1936 as the first woman flier to cross the Atlantic, and then again in 1942 as the author of *West with the Night,* a book whose fame was too quickly eclipsed by World War II until its reissue in 1983. She remains legendary as a pioneer of Kenya: tough-living and tough-loving, strong, promiscuous, and proud, she got rich and went broke several times, and loved and married often. Unlike the white men who were her companions, she lived to extreme old age, supported by the contributions of friends and admirers who saw in Markham the essence of old Kenya—and something more, something that flickers throughout *West with the Night.*[14]

That something is an aesthetic of silence and solitude. It is not unlike de Watteville's cultivated meditations upon the mountain, though it is born through action, not stasis. Running with the wind on the hunt, hunkered down in her airplane far above the dark Atlantic for hours upon hours, Markham attuned herself to what was around her. Every nerve in her body was taut, alive, vibrant. Immersed in silence, she lived intensely in her mind even as her body performed the actions necessary to complete the hunt, to glide the plane over the Atlantic: action became a form of meditation. There is no overt religious sense in Markham's writing and her life was far from saintly. But, as with the other women discussed in this chapter, animism and spiritual emotion infuse her writing. The energy of action is rapturously absorbed as the body is risked, allowed to float in pure speed by which motion transcends itself, achieving silence and stillness.

Certain passages in *West with the Night* seem suspended in a Zen moment—as here, in this description of flight in which time and space are collapsed:

> Watch the fence. Watch the flares. I watch both and take off into the night.
>
> Ahead of me lies land that is unknown to the rest of the world and only vaguely known to the African—a strange mixture of grasslands, scrub, desert sand like the long waves of the southern ocean. Forest, still water, and age-old mountains, stark and grim like mountains of the moon. Salt lakes and rivers that have no water. Swamps. Badlands. Land without life. Land teeming with life—all of the dusty past, all of the future.
>
> The air takes me into its realm. Night envelops me entirely, leaving me out of touch with the earth, leaving me with this small moving world of my own, living in space with the stars. (15)

Perhaps such passages quite literally are suspended in a Zen moment: Eastern religious texts were being translated and circulated during the first decades of the twentieth century—for example, by Romain Rolland, Martin Buber, and the Theosophists. They were popular among Markham's contemporaries and (just as Romantic poetry did for de Watteville) may have provided a rudimentary guide for the book. There may be another source of the actual words as well: after their divorce, Markham's third husband, Raoul Schumacher, claimed authorship of *West with the Night*, an assertion accepted by some, though it is unlikely ever to be confirmed or refuted.[15] But whoever furnished the words, the blood of the book is ecstatic feeling: the feeling of the childhood hunt and of flight, the sensation of harmony with nature. These are, without question, Markham's own.

V

In the late 1960s, when Kuki Gallmann was still in her twenties, she was in a devastating automobile accident with two friends, Paolo Gallmann and his wife, Mariangela.[16] Mariangela was killed. Paolo and Kuki each suffered multiple injuries. For a period of almost four years, Kuki, who was crippled, struggled to walk normally again—which she did after a series of operations. Then she married Paolo. In 1972, they went to live in Kenya, a land of dreams Kuki had inhabited mentally since girlhood. As a child, she had explored prehistory with her father, an archeologist; in her imagination, Africa had come to represent the epitome of "how it [life] all began" (*I Dreamed of Africa*, 7). The bond with her father was decisive: "When people ask me why I decided to come to Africa," she says, "the answer lies in the days of my childhood."

In Kenya, Kuki and Paolo bought a ranch on the edge of the Rift Valley, northwest of Nairobi. It was among the largest and wildest locations available—a natural preserve of elephants, rhinos, and leopards. Living conditions resembled those in the early years of colonial Kenya: no telephone, just radio contact, precarious roads, a household airstrip for flights to the city. Day-to-day life followed the patterns described in various memoirs of those early years: Isak Dinesen's *Out of Africa*, Beryl Markham's *West with the Night*, Elspeth Huxley's *The Flame Trees of Thika*. The cast of characters bears comparison too: Kuki to Dinesen and Markham; her children, Emanuele and Sveva, to the young Elspeth Huxley, who adopted and befriended many animals; Paolo to Bror Blixen and Denys Finch-Hatton. On many occasions, Gallmann herself makes the comparisons.

Gallmann found in Africa all the elements of the childhood dreams engendered by her father. Dreams of essence and origin. Miles and miles of natural beauty so intense that walking through it seemed sacramental. Lions, rhinos, and elephants. Turkana and Nandi tribesmen of dignity and grace who had stayed close to ancient ways—many of whom Gallmann considered close to her family. It was her express hope that her children would experience Africa and learn those ways—as they did, each developing a special affinity for the continent.

As her story unfolds, Gallmann is not always a likable figure. Like Dinesen and Markham, she casts herself as a steward of the land, a redeemer of its people, though of course no one invited her. Gallmann writes:

I considered the future of Africa with its growing population of people, children of today in whose hands the destiny of Kenya will soon lie. Children brought up on the outskirts of the towns, where nothing wild had been left, their minds confused and polluted by alien religions, by poverty and lack of worthy goals. These children had never seen and been taught to appreciate the beauty of their country. The average urban African has never seen an elephant. . . . The only solution was education. (251)

Gallmann never blinks at the irony that she, an Italian socialite, should speak for Africa. She never considers how Europeans are largely to blame for some of the very conditions she deplores. Yet her account of Africa is heady, intoxicating stuff, animated by Gallmann's devotion to the land even when she is faced with devastating experiences.

In fact, Gallmann's narrative authority—like de Watteville's and Dinesen's—depends on the degree to which the dream of Africa encased a nightmare. Like Africans she knows, Gallmann believes she can tell when certain places will bring bad luck: on vacation with Paolo, she refuses to camp at one such spot where she senses "a grey cloud of doom." But Paolo confesses that he has taken her to the spot because he had previously camped there. Bad luck does strike, in the form of numerous deaths and near deaths: a friend, Chiara, killed in another automobile accident; Paolo's brother, badly gored by an elephant. Then Paolo is kidnapped by some African car thieves and only narrowly escapes. Thereafter, Paolo, convinced he would die soon, becomes obsessed, for the first time in their ten-year marriage, with Kuki's bearing his child. He is killed in yet another automobile accident on his way to fetch a crib for the expected baby. Kuki's son by her first marriage, Emanuele, finds consolation after Paolo's death in building a collection of snakes that becomes known throughout white Africa. The coup de grâce: Emanuele, at seventeen, is the victim of his longtime hobby and obsession when he is bitten by a puff adder.

Called from her daily shower, Gallmann found Emanuele

rigid, legs spread out on the green cement, facing the window. . . . From his open mouth, green saliva dribbled in ugly bubbles. The skin was grey, the eyes staring and glassy. . . . He was blind. . . . [T]he poison had reached his heart. His blood was coagulating. (196)

On the long, futile drive to get help, Gallmann heard

> a voice, unrecognizable . . . wailing loudly: who was it? I moved
> my head to look at Emanuele in the mirror and I stared at my
> face with an open mouth: I was screaming. (198)

The story is sad and filled with grief. It is poignantly expressed. In fact, it is almost enough to forestall criticism of Gallmann: her claim on Africa is staked by the bones of her loved ones.

Kuki tells us several times that despite its tragedies, her life has been filled with joy and that she has never experienced boredom. She passes on her father's advice, given when she was nine or ten: "The most important thing you can ever learn in life, Kuki, is to be able to be alone. Sooner or later the time will come when you will be alone with yourself. You must be able to cope and face your own company" (243). She undergoes a process of separation and shedding, like a snake leaving behind parts of itself as it enters into a new life. She tells of the joy of love remembered, love that is felt to transcend the grave. There are hints at several points in the narrative that, like the other women I have discussed in this chapter, Gallmann finds a rapturous solitariness born of grief.

Like Dinesen, Gallmann tells of funereal and memorial rituals touching in their simplicity and elegance. The sensibility expressed is often profoundly animistic. It is the oceanic feeling associated with Africa unbound. These kinds of emotions structure a poem, for example, written in Italian by Kuki at the time of Paolo's death:

> *Your eyes were the colour of water:*
> *Yes, you are water.*
>
> *They had transparencies of air:*
> *Yes, you are this sky now.*
>
> *Your skin was baked by the sun*
> *like Kenya's earth:*
> *Yes, you are this red dry dust.*

Forever, forever, forever, Paolo,
you have become everything.
(128)

They recur in the poem she wrote for Emanuele's funeral:

You were but seventeen
but wise beyond your age,
and now you know already
the answer to all questions.

I am asking: where are you really
as this is but your body?
are you now the hot sun of Africa?
are you the clouds and the rain?
are you this wind, Emanuele,
or are you the sky overhead?
(213–14)

Most notably, she tells of an intense and consolatory feeling for nature experienced sometime after Emanuele's death:

In the beginning, my senses numbed by grief, I walked as if in a vacuum. I never spoke, my mind was full of thoughts and memories, voices and screams, and it groped through the tortuous labyrinth of my unresolved questions. Then, gradually, a silence descended and my mind became quiet and relaxed: the outer sounds and the essence of nature reached it once again, and I became more alert and perceptive than I had ever been. . . .

From sunrise to sunset, I trekked up the majestic hills and down the steep valleys. Untouched landscapes are demanding and in them all pretensions and all acting cease. Nothing was expected of me by the ancient silence of the mountains and of the mysterious gorges. In their unjudging, harmonious existence I found again my own identity, and my place. (228–29)

Gallmann begins by revealing the full extent of her devastation. She describes losing herself in the grandeur of the land but then affirms that her sense of self has been strengthened, and not destroyed, by her experiences. Once again, one feels a certain ambiguity: Does Gallmann describe emotional displacement and consolation? Or does she find socially illicit ecstasy in being alone in Africa?

As a reader, I honor the healing role that writing played in Gallmann's life. As it did for Dinesen and for de Watteville, writing for Gallmann functioned both as a way of dealing with loss and as a pressing, ubiquitous theme of her narrative. Paolo and Kuki exchanged letters every day, even though they lived in the same house. Shortly before his death, Paolo suspended a secret message, encased in an eggshell, above their bed; Gallmann decided to bury the egg with Emanuele, unopened, its message forever unread. Emanuele had kept both a personal diary and a scientific journal recording his experiments with snakes. Gallmann read both after his death, and quotes extensively from the journal. We learn as she does that Emanuele had been bitten by snakes many times, so that every descent into his snake pit was an invitation to death. Gallmann writes throughout the night before her husband's and her son's funerals in order to produce something to read at the assembly the next day. Writing had been an obsession with the family, and writing sees her through crisis. Like *Out of Africa* and *Speak to the Earth*, Gallmann's *I Dreamed of Africa* is clearly a work of healing as well as a record of the healing process.

Gallmann's book made me cry and repeatedly knock on wood. Yet there is a troubling aspect to it, even beyond the sadness of the events recounted. At times, the writing bares so much: emotions at a husband's grave, and a son's. But at other times, the writing leaves loose threads or raises unsettling questions. For example, little is said about Paolo's daughters by his first marriage, although the girls sometimes seem to live with Kuki. Similarly, Gallmann passes quickly over the unusual fact that her first husband, Mario, later married one of her stepdaughters, saying only that it has been a good match.

The aestheticization of emotions is always a danger in autobiographical writing. At moments in this narration, aesthetic perceptions undercut emotional truth. When I read the poems Gallmann wrote for her husband's and son's funerals, for example, I found it hard to imagine that such poems—whose effect is to transform one kind of emotion (grief) into another (oceanic)—could be written the night before such wrenching events. They seemed to be pat formulations of the consolations Gallmann claims to have found only later, walking her land, after the death of her men. Something about the ready-made, to-hand quality of the emotion made me wonder about the role of writing in Gallmann's narrative, especially in relation to expressing the oceanic sense. Writing always suggests control and shaping, rather than emotion and spontaneity. But the oceanic is constitutively an overwhelming, irresistible sensation. In her narrative, Gallmann seems too ready at times to make the stylized gesture, to arrange her experiences aesthetically. In fact, her writing raises pressing questions about the nature of "oceanic" writing practiced by the authors discussed in this chapter.

VI

Since the film *Out of Africa*, Dinesen, Markham, and the other Kenya pioneers have become icons of popular culture. There have been new editions of their work, major biographies, and, sometimes, the publication of letters and books of criticism. Fashion alludes freely to the Kenya style—in everything from Safari perfume to home decor. The attraction is obvious. Most generally, the Kenya revival has fed a cultural nostalgia, evoking a simpler day when Africa was "young" and wildlife abundant, when Europeans could live lives of adventure and glamour in rapport (they claimed) with black Africans. Viewed in the context of contemporary gender politics, Kenya also provides strong, androgynous models for feminism today: women who were free-loving, free-living, talented, and bold—masters, if I may say so, of their own fate.

I feel some danger of adding to the effect that popular culture has had on the Kenya pioneers, with not altogether benign results: romanticizing them, scanting their egoism and indifference to such minor facts as inconvenient men, or children, or Africans who just happen to be living on "their" land. In fact, although each claims a special exemption, all of my subjects share or benefit from the privileges conferred upon white Europeans in a colonial setting. They are relatively admiring of the Africans they encounter and relatively sensitive to the customs and beliefs of groups of Africans; but they are far from paradigms of conduct by any enlightened standard.

In fact, with the partial exception of Kingsley, all of these women were connoisseurs of Africa. They viewed it through an aestheticizing, aristocratic lens. Animals and humans rise or fall in the author's hierarchy according to the degree to which they conform to her conception of what is noble, swift, and beautiful—that is, like the author herself. The reader of the memoir is, of course, invited to identify with the author and her values, thereby entering this aristocracy. But if one resists, as I found myself doing, particularly in Gallmann's case, the narrative's charm falters.

The assessment of these women only becomes harsher when we focus on specific points—for example, their tendency to present "natives" as props or adjuncts of their relationship to the land. Postcolonial analysis is certainly far enough along in its evolution that it is possible to criticize almost any Westerner with regard to Africa. But I find it more fruitful—more likely to produce new insights—to focus on what it means for these women to identify so strongly with an impersonal, cosmic landscape, especially in relation to the death of their men. So I want to put more generalized critique aside, so as to think further about the complex of issues I have raised: women, the self, mortality, loss, vocation, and the land.

In these narratives, the role of language is complicated and ambiguous. Language records sensation—the way life was, the feeling of "being there." But it also betrays the gap between experience and memory, immediacy and recollection. This double-edged effect of language is to some extent endemic to the genre of memoir. Memoir converts time lost into gain, and in these narratives it converts bereavement into vocation. But language comes into conflict with the aims of these writers, even as it is their only means of accomplishing their work. For example, each author represents, in words, nature's sublimity. In fact, she represents more than sublimity; she renders the feeling of actually blending with the cosmic and ceasing at some level to be herself. Both phenomena are normally considered apart from, and even inimical to, words. Generally, they are something words can only hint at or approximate.

Through words, the memoirist inevitably constructs a sense of the self. Yet these writers assert their power to blend with things—to efface, at least temporarily, the sense of selfhood. Then they come back and write about what the experience was like. When talking about the male Romantic poets and the sublime, Neil Hertz suggests that a writer's evocation of "difficulty" or "blockage" in putting sublime experiences into words is a necessary defense against the pre-Oedipal state—what I call the oceanic—a defense that confirms, even while it seems to threaten, the integrity and unity of the self.[17] But his model is only partially applicable to these women. For unlike most Romantic poets, they do not express difficulty or blockage in portraying sublime emotions. Instead, they portray them with lavish ease. The "difficulty" inheres only in the price these women paid for access to their feelings—the number of conventional roles (daughter, wife, mother) they sacrificed or had stripped from them before achieving their vocations. It is only the *maimed* self, the survivor of loss, who can write these texts.

In fact, these female writers do not conform to most available models of the relationship between oceanic experience and language. They do not repress or move away from the pre-Oedipal or oceanic plot, as in much Romantic poetry. Nor does the male father or father figure prohibit that plot, as in Jacques Lacan's model of the presymbolic. Indeed, their "fathers" set the oceanic plot in motion. At first glance, the women's writing may seem to conform to Hélène Cixous' and Luce Irigaray's concept of *l'écriture féminine* insofar as these writers are female and express a rapturous sense of oneness.[18] Yet feminist revisers of Freud, like Hélène Cixous, Luce Irigaray, and Julia Kristeva, accept the Freudian identification of the oceanic with the mother's body, even though (unlike Freud) they exalt it as a female sublime.[19] For the most part, in these women's memoirs of Africa, landscape is not identified with the female body. Some critics (especially of Dinesen) read the land as gendered female in this work, but they are, quite simply, wrong; they see what they expect, or want, to see.[20] In these women's writing, the land is not gendered female. Instead, it is beyond gender—a simulacrum of spiritual emotions.

I am tempted to call the patterns I have found in their work "the father-based oceanic," to distinguish it from Freud's oceanic, which is mother-based and expressly disconnected from spiritual emotions. The term would be useful to underscore how identification with the father, like identification with the land, was these women's point of entry into creative life. But the label would only be useful to a point. In these texts, the positive value attached to "the oceanic" may originate in the facts of gender, much as the negative value of the oceanic does in the male narratives examined earlier. But it also, and more crucially, involves a state beyond gender.

Still, there is an unanswered question hovering around these issues. I must raise that question, even though what answers I can propose are multiple and open-ended. Reading Dinesen, Kingsley, de Watteville, Markham, and Gallmann together, one wonders: Where did their ideas come from? Or, why is there so much similarity among these female writers and their view of nature? It is not impossible to think of literary sources, especially in poetry: William Blake ("For every thing that lives is Holy"), William Wordsworth (seeing "into the life of things"), Emily Brontë ("When I am not and none besides . . . "), Walt Whitman ("I contain multitudes"). It is not hard to think of philosophical sources: in Romanticism, or American Transcendentalism, or late nineteenth-century spiritualism. It is not hard to think of religious sources, in nature as "the book of God," and in the popularized versions of Eastern religions that dazzled the Transcendentalists and, later, the Theosophists and Modernists as something exotic and new. But such influences are, finally, not fully satisfying as an explanation, in part because they are impossible to prove for at least some of these women.

In answering the question "Where does the similarity of their ideas come from?" I want to resist two overly simple explanations: the first having to do with their female commonality and some "natural" identification between women and landscape; the second pointing to Africa, long the site of origins, of the wild and natural in the Western imagination. Indeed, I have critiqued both of those associations in earlier chapters. But rejecting these explanations is not the same thing as saying that reasonable explanations cannot be found by thinking about "being female" and "being in Africa" as cultural realities.

For these women, their men were motivators. But their men were also in the way, ultimately, of their greatest achievements, which depended on losing the men or being left by them. These women's grandest deeds were solo, against the grain, outside the norms of female activity. Their inspiration, even if originally it was written literature, philosophy, and religion, indisputably became Africa itself. The choice of

Africa may have been the choice of difference. For on this continent, so vast and so varied, it was possible for women to escape the nets of convention. Perhaps the loss of the men was inevitable, when it was not (as it was for Dinesen) partly manipulated. For only on their own would these women come fully into their own, test the limits of their being—in Africa, the place of possibility.

In colonial thinking, the white woman occupies a special position: she is considered superior to both male and female "natives," and hence enjoys a level of superiority usually afforded only to men.[21] In isolated locales or remote households, the women could avoid communities whose conventions demanded domesticity and mildness in females. At the same time, because they were women and not men, they did not have a place in the imperial, governmental, or bureaucratic structures (corporations, armies) that absorb or reward men. They had no "careers" in the usual sense to pursue in Africa, no promotions or newspaper contracts or missions to fulfill, no bosses to answer to in Europe. They were free to establish relationships to the land and its people outside the norms, to select the Africans they admired. By and large, they were sympathetic to Africans' points of view—often sharing, for example, a belief in the spirit world that characterizes many African religions. Most of all, these women were less obsessed than many of their male contemporaries with prevailing stereotypes of "Africans."

In fact, it is significant that these women chose the landscape as the focal point for their feelings, rather than the Africans themselves. It is also significant that, contrary to most existing Western traditions, they did not feminize the land, but rather perceived it as beyond sex and gender, as a sign of the sacred, as a sublime portent of cosmic unities. As I have shown, conventionally (which is to say, in most men's writing about Africa), women are associated with the landscape—in Conrad, for example, or in Gide. Freud, as we have seen, imagined the undifferentiated "pre-Oedipal" domain as continuous with the death wish; he identified it with female sexuality, which he described as a "Dark Continent," a common epithet for Africa in his time.[22] In a similar spirit, Gide hated the "formlessness" of Africa, its lack of "differentiation," and saw the imposition of aesthetic control upon the landscape as the only way to certify his selfhood (see Chapter One). That the spirit of Africa is female was a colonial trope, enabling mastery. The women discussed here both used and transformed the trope. They saw the landscape as majestically impersonal. Then, by claiming the merging of the self with the landscape, they came to share its august impersonality. Identification with the landscape conceived in these terms, then, may be the logical expression of the way these women cast off men and conventional female roles in the process of becoming their writerly selves.

Conventional women are daughters, sisters, aunts, wives, mothers—domestic, family roles. Each of these women sprang from such roles, left behind as husks of the self, lovingly remembered but never regained. These women were adventurers, explorers, writers, entrepreneurs—impressive in their unconventionality, but perhaps ill-suited to life as a mother, wife, friend, or neighbor. In fact, viewed in the harshest light, these women resemble Agave in Euripides' *The Bacchae*. Agave, we might recall from Chapter One, "returns to the rites of Cybele, the Mother," and thereby attains a feeling of oneness with nature in which "all the mountain seems wild with divinity." She exults in moving beyond conventional female roles—"leaving the shuttle" to lead a community and be a mighty hunter. But, almost as a penalty, she is unwittingly made to behead her own son.

But the connection between these women and Agave needs one more, concluding turn.[23] Through Africa, the women I discuss identified with nature, transcended the perceived limitations of their gender, cast off or learned to live without family ties, and converted loss into gain. They knew that the loss would be permanent unto death, but that the gain transcended even the facts of death. These women were themselves mythic figures—with an attractiveness and a fearsomeness worthy of goddesses. If they resemble Agave, they represent all the more something new in Western literature: Agave, written in her own voice.

CHAPTER FOUR

Dian Fossey Among the Animals

I

THREE IMAGES of Dian Fossey are reproduced in almost every piece of writing or footage about her. In the first, a young Fossey, hair flowing and face radiant, sprawls on the ground in her work clothes, one arm flung out towards a gorilla named Peanuts. The gorilla reaches towards her as well, nestling its hand in hers—the first recorded touch between a live mountain gorilla and a human being. It is an image of contact, communication, warmth, affection. Hands reaching across species, animal hand reposing in human palm calmly, in a spirit of trust. Michelangelo's God with Adam, transposed to a Rwandan mountain, with "God" a woman. It is a seductive image, so seductive that one is disappointed to learn that the photograph which originally inspired the image records the instants *after* the actual touch, the shutter having snapped just seconds too late to record the moment itself.

The second image is very different. Fossey is alone in a thick forest, dressed in work gear that is saturated, like the foliage around her, with rain.[1] She sits in a fetal position, looking both defensive and deranged. Nestled against the wet greenery, her face looks tense, unfocused, drunk or drugged. Her eyes stare at the ground, apparently at nothing. In one photo, her arms are discernible but, like her hands, are drawn inward, hidden beneath the folds of her rain-soaked jacket. The theme of the image is nothingness: no gorillas, no purpose, no contact, no awareness of the photographer. Nothing. At this stage, Fossey has taken the solitude and impersonality cultivated by women in Africa and pushed it over the edge, into misanthropy, into the void.

There is another kind of image that is sometimes substituted for this one. In a whole series of photographs, Fossey stands with some of her African workers who are restraining a captured poacher—sometimes a man, sometimes a boy. The poacher is held above the wrecked bodies of slain gorillas, nose practically rubbed in the detritus of the once-living beings. Fossey scowls with fierce disapproval. Her expression is tight; her posture full of suppressed rage. Although the poacher is the logical object of these emotions, the pictures suggest a detachment akin to the image of Fossey, in a fetal position, alone in the forest. The hatred in Fossey's face seems directed at the viewer, at humans quite generally. Fossey seems to be opting out of humanity to identify instead with the gorillas or even, via dead gorillas, with inorganic matter itself.

The third image has been reproduced only in words, never to my knowledge in any published photograph. Three of the most recent studies of Fossey either begin or end with this image and describe it graphically.[2] Crumpled near her bed now, not in the forest, Fossey lies, face up, one arm flung outward, the other beneath her. Her face is split nearly in two by a pamba, a machete, that had once hung decoratively in her room. With one such blow, death must have come instantly. But the blow evidently did not fall until Fossey had scrambled around the room trying to grab a gun and cartridges. Her final efforts were fierce but futile: the cartridges were the wrong size to fit the gun; she was found clutching both. In all its horror, the image completes the triptych, the dark obverse of the idyllic first picture: indoors, not out, a gaping hole in the wall through which the murderer entered; hands clutching weapons, not gorilla or self; body prone on the floor, not in the forest; face grisly and bloodied, no longer a fit sight for human eyes.

Three linked images that progress in time: from youth to middle age to death. Three images that tell a story of decline and decay: from buoyant discovery, to solipsistic isolation, to the most terrifying of moments, violent destruction at the hands of an enemy. Three images in a story that has excited feverish interest in Fossey, interest fueled by articles, books, and television specials during her life and by books and films since her death. Why does Fossey continue to be such a source of fascination?

Her violent murder in 1985—which remains unsolved—is one key element. Few things exert such a hold on the popular imagination as unsolved crimes. Left open with killers at large, such cases are subject to endless reexamination of the evidence and conjecture: the Lindbergh kidnapping; the Kennedy assassination; the murders of Nicole Brown Simpson and Ronald Goldman. Fossey's case is a cocktail of particularly nasty thrills. The murderer's identity and motive have been publicly proclaimed in the Rwandan courts: the authorities alleged that her graduate assistant, Wayne McGuire (who found the body), did it to steal her notes. But no one in or out of Rwanda seems to believe this, and McGuire was allowed to leave the country before his trial and conviction in absentia. Other guesses have been made: a fired or otherwise disgruntled worker at Karisoke, her home base in Rwanda (a tracker named Rwelekana was arrested and reportedly hanged himself in prison); a government employee on the take and disgusted with Fossey's interference. Many guesses implicate the poachers against whom Fossey had waged a decade of ugly war, especially one man who was released from prison shortly before the murder and has disappeared since.

No one really knows who killed Dian Fossey, nor, I would suggest, do that many people really care. The Fossey case, like other murders in the public eye, needs its tantalizing blend of the known and the unknown—the almost, but not-quite, truth. Its famous victim gives the case a "how the mighty are fallen" tragic aura. Since the victim was female, the case has a special, erotic thrill, with an added racial charge in that the victim was a white female and the killer potentially a black male. Because the setting was Africa, the crime feeds ideas of African dangers, African deadliness, "African madness" (this last the title of Alex Shoumatoff's book). The ending to Fossey's story was almost guaranteed to generate interest. It was also, in a curious way, consistent with the whole.

In her life, Fossey enacted an identification with the gorillas that required an even more extreme form of casting off than is typical of the other women in Africa I have discussed. In fact, Fossey eventually cast off everything: family, nation, friends, lovers, Rwandans, health, self-interest, professional reputation, and finally life itself. I have described the double edge of the primitive—as a potential source of transcendence, but also one of danger and death. As suggested in the last chapter, female fascination with the primitive courts the oceanic as a way of transcending the limitations of gender, even the limitations of mortality and other loss. Fossey's story exemplifies a more perilous course. It can be told as a cautionary tale or as an inspirational one—but neither extreme, taken alone, would be entirely true. In fact, the story of Dian Fossey remains fundamentally ambiguous—far more so, for example, than that of Georgia O'Keeffe, who is the subject of the next chapter. After probing Fossey's ambiguous life and O'Keeffe's triumphant career, Parts One and Two of this book will have mapped out a range of possibilities with regard to fascination with the primitive earlier in the century, setting the stage for my exploration of developments today.

The end of Fossey's life was admittedly grim. I begin there in order to get it out into the open, to exorcise the story of this most unsettling fact. Even so, the end to Fossey's life is something she might well have made up for herself: almost as good, in terms of fixing her image and spreading her fame, as being killed by a poacher while defending a baby gorilla in the open air. Almost.

II

Fossey's life is the stuff of legend. The paleontologist Louis Leakey plucked her from obscurity and placed her in Africa to study the mountain gorilla, previously studied (and then only briefly) by George Schaller. Leakey and his wife, Mary, had dedicated their careers to finding skeletal remnants of the earliest human beings in Africa. The greatest triumph of their careers was the discovery of Zinj in 1959, perhaps the most outstanding skeletal discovery until 1974, when Donald Johanson found "Lucy."[3] The discovery of Lucy proved that human life had existed on earth longer than had previously been thought and consolidated a belief Leakey himself had long held: that Africa had been the cradle and origin of human life. Leakey wanted to learn more about apes in order to find out how early humans lived, and so he chose Fossey and set her up in Africa. The National Geographic Society funded most of Fossey's work and made her famous.

For most of the nineteenth and twentieth centuries, primatology and paleontology were saturated with evolutionist thinking. They conceived of themselves as investigating earlier or less complex forms of life ("primitive" tribes or ape "families") as clues to human development and modern social organization. Although they dealt with animals and skeletal remains, primatology and paleontology constitute a part of primitivism, broadly conceived as the quest for origins.

Experts now agree that the evolutionist premises upon which these disciplines were founded were wrong. Modern society did not, they say, evolve in any simple way from "primitive" societies, nor did humans descend from apes. Instead, most now believe, multiple lines of evolution led, on the one hand, to certain ape species, and, on the other, to *Homo habilis, Homo erectus,* and then *Homo sapiens.*[4] In the same way, "civilized" groups did not uniformly evolve from "primitive" ones: there were parallel evolutions, some leading to forms of social organization now called "primitive," others to forms now called "modern." Yet the popular imagination, saturated with notions of single-stemmed evolution, uses the more complicated model reluctantly—whether applied to human groups or to animals.[5]

National Geographic tried to make Fossey's life and work conform to primatology's founding premises. The Dian Fossey segment of the famous video *Search for the Great Apes* (1975), for example, begins with long shots of tall, lanky Fossey striding through the forest. As she crests a hill and is foregrounded against the horizon, the voice-over announces that she is a specialist in human development, a scholar come to study gorillas in order to learn something about human origins and human nature. This is stirring, but wrong. Fossey was *not* a specialist in human development when she went to Africa in 1967: she was a physical therapist who had made her living working with mentally handicapped children, and she was obsessed with Africa. In 1963, she had scraped together funds for a trip to Africa; one stop on her journey was Leakey's research camp, where she went to tell him about her fascination with apes. Three years later, she approached him again when he gave a lecture in the United States. Impressed by her persistence, Leakey decided that Fossey could succeed with the gorillas and urged her (with him making the necessary arrangements) to earn a doctorate in the comparative study of animal life. She completed her degree only in 1976, almost ten years into her odyssey among the gorillas. Even then she refused to follow the statistical methods preferred by academic ethologists.[6]

As Fossey perceived it, writing up her experiences and getting her degree were necessary but annoying formalities. She was a reluctant Ph.D. who left her isolated center, Karisoke, only under financial pressure. Years later, she wrote *Gorillas in the Mist* in an effort to secure funds during a teaching stint at Cornell University. But she hated this period, her longest enforced absence from her African home base.[7] *National Geographic* suggested something very different. In 1971, a photo showed Fossey, by lamplight in Africa, hard at work on the materials that would eventually yield her the necessary Ph.D. *National Geographic*'s emphasis was always on Fossey as a trained scientist with a scientific mission.

Yet from the beginning, Fossey's goals diverged from those of the scientific establishment. She didn't study primates in order to find clues about the earliest human social evolution. Her interest was always ape conservation, not human beings.[8] She studied gorillas in order to learn about them, and particularly about the conditions they will need to survive. Indeed, it is not too much to say that Fossey took the primitivist basis of primatology (the linking of apes and humans) and moved it in a different direction. She developed a radical identification with animals as profound symbols of Being-ness.

To understand Fossey's approach, it's helpful to compare her work to that of George Schaller, her predecessor in studying mountain gorillas. Schaller says, conventionally enough, that his research suits "an age when man more than ever before is wondering about his origins and worrying about his behavior."[9] He occasionally displays a rhapsodic interest in the gorillas similar to Fossey's, but his actual encounters with gorillas in the wild were minimal. In fact, he came into contact most often with traces of gorilla life, such as nests filled with dung, and published a scientific book containing notations he made on the subject of gorilla nesting habits. His popular account of his research, *The Year of the Gorilla,* is filled not with material about gorillas but with information about geography and the conditions of African social life. It includes as many photographs of African villagers and villages as it does of gorillas and gorilla groups.[10]

Fossey all but ignored these factors in her more exclusive focus on the gorillas. In her first major publication (the 1970 *National Geographic* piece), Fossey boasted, "I know the gorillas as individuals, each with his own traits and personality," and said that gorilla groups "accept my presence almost as a member." In her own words, her mission was to "save the mountain gorilla" by "learning more about it."[11] Clearly, the emphasis has changed from Schaller to Fossey: from gorillas in the context of African geography and, most of all, modern African life, to gorillas pure and simple. Only rarely did Fossey display much concern for human beings or human culture.

In fact, it would be possible to characterize Fossey's history as one of blindness towards Africans—in her case, ultimately quite dangerous. Rwanda is a very small, densely populated country with intense rivalries between two different groups, the Tutsi and the Hutu. Overpopulation puts intense pressure on land and the food supply. The extent of Rwanda's plight only came home to the West in 1994, when conditions led to murders by the thousands, littering the country with corpses; but the desperation and potential for violence was present even in the 1970s, when Fossey lived there. For poachers, selling a baby gorilla or gorilla trophies (hands made into ashtrays, for example) could mean the difference between poverty and wealth, food and privation. Fossey's indifference to the Africans' needs may have doomed her. She stubbornly refused to think about gorillas from the Rwandans' point of view, and this blindness, or willfulness, may have cost her her life.

But while acknowledging that view, I want to press further. Fossey's obsession with the gorillas led to her eventual indifference to everything else. Perhaps only so single-minded a fixation could have kept Fossey in Africa so long, living in conditions so different from those normal for an American of her class and background. Karisoke is on Mount Visoke, where it rains heavily for much of the year: an unhealthy climate for someone afflicted, as Fossey was, by emphysema. Her absolute devotion to the apes made her cross the line from what *National Geographic* considered responsible science to what it considered gorilla-fanaticism.

During her long stay in Africa, Fossey wrote three articles for *Na-*

tional Geographic that galvanized the public's interest in her project: "Making Friends with Mountain Gorillas" (1970), "More Years with Mountain Gorillas" (1971), and "The Imperiled Mountain Gorilla: A Grim Struggle for Survival" (1981).[12] During these years, and especially after 1971, Fossey was engaged in grim struggles of her own. She battled with the poachers impinging on the gorillas' scanty reserve. She experienced depression and alcoholism, especially after the end of her affair with photographer Robert Campbell (her collaborator on the two earlier pieces). She quarrelled with the National Geographic Society itself, beset by reports from Rwandans and students who worked with her that her methods for preserving the gorillas might, by abusing Africans, result in the gorillas' destruction for revenge. Only the first of these struggles was made public during her lifetime. Each article mentions the struggle with poachers, but in accordance with *National Geographic's* upbeat tone, none mentions Fossey's personal difficulties or the Society's own reservations about her methods. *National Geographic* was, it appears, determined to put on a happy, animal-loving face that would mask from its reading public the power struggles and ruptures behind the scenes.

In each piece, Fossey ends with several paragraphs about the poachers. As her hope diminishes, her note of concern and alarm grows. And so does her misanthropy. In 1970, Fossey seeks help: "Money alone will not solve the problem. Conservation groups and political authority must join in concerted programs if this three-nation area and its wildlife are to be saved from human trespassers. Such help is overdue. I only hope that Rafiki, Uncle Bert, and Icarus [some favorites among the gorillas] can survive until it comes" (67). In 1971, Fossey ends with a description of five gorilla corpses that "had been mauled by dogs, pierced by spears, and battered by stones, apparently just for the excitement of the hunt." Fossey then personalizes the same concern expressed at the end of the 1970 piece, but with a less hopeful slant: "I think of the gorillas I have written about, whom I have come to regard as friends, and I wonder—will some of them be next?" (585). By 1981, Fossey depends not on humans at all but on the gorillas' own inventiveness: "Perhaps we will find—we may hope at least—that the gorillas' own strategies of group growth and maintenance will circumvent group disintegration caused by man's encroachment" (522).

The progression here mirrors that in the sequence of images of Dian

Fossey from youth to death with which I began: looking out and invoking human aid in 1970, bemoaning the conditions alone in 1971, looking to the gorillas for help and seeing all human "encroachment" as dangerous in 1981. Bleak, bleaker, bleakest; seeking human contact, going it alone, rejecting human contact. This progression underscores what is hinted at in the progression of *National Geographic* titles from 1970 to 1981: from the upbeat "making friends," to the static "more years," ending with the pessimism of the "Imperiled" title, and its subtitle, "Grim Struggle for Survival."

To its credit, *National Geographic* does not appear to have altered the text of Fossey's articles in order to achieve the emphasis it desired. But it did feel free to caption photographs in a way that emphasized its version of Fossey's mission. The long captions repeatedly suggested that Fossey's work was not simply about gorillas but was finally about the grand entity called Man. In the 1970 piece, the caption for a photo of Rafiki began with the words, "Bridging the gap between man and animal, the author and a 400-pound gorilla named Rafiki take each other's measure" (52). A later caption proclaimed (significantly, without quotation marks) that Fossey feels her work "can help man protect the species, and even increase his understanding of himself" (67). The captions propagated the impression that Fossey's work would tell us as much—if not more—about humans as about gorillas. Almost obsessively, they repeated those terms generally applied to human families which Fossey herself used to describe gorilla groups.

One photo is described as a "family portrait." Group members "huddle around a regal patriarch" (1970; 66). We hear about the "burdens of motherhood," "impromptu nurseries" of branches (1975; 583), and so on. By 1981, the metaphor of the human family is in full swing: "Safe and secure in Puck's arms, five-month-old Cantsbee enjoys the tranquillity of a midday rest with her mother" (512). In fact, "young gorillas rarely leave their mother's touch" (513). Fossey "spoils" a young gorilla she must raise after it is saved from poachers. Yet the family metaphor, as *National Geographic* used it, functioned quite differently from the way that Fossey employed it.

Although Fossey used family metaphors in her work, she never connected the family metaphor to the quest for human origins stressed by *National Geographic*. In fact, I believe that Fossey's use of family metaphors began as a mental convenience, since family and friendship are easy images for humans to bring to the interaction of other species. The family metaphor, for example, enabled Fossey to create empathy for the gorillas among human audiences: "Safe and secure in Puck's arms, five-month-old Cantsbee" is a more winning object than gorilla #54 in dorsal contact with gorilla #32—and more likely to generate contributions for gorilla conservation. But ultimately, the metaphors served Fossey's personal, idiosyncratic psychological needs. The image of tender family life among the apes allowed Fossey to replay her own family history. Initially, what she found among the gorillas must have seemed wonderful; later, as she discovered among the gorillas infanticide and other forms of aggression against the weak, the information proved traumatic.

III

Fossey was an only child whose father drank and got into trouble with the law. Her parents divorced when she was six years old, and her contact with her natural father was minimal after he left the family.[13] In 1939, a year after the divorce, Fossey's mother remarried and her stepfather became the special villain in Fossey's tale. All of Fossey's biographers stress the deprivations of her early youth. Her stepfather banned her from the family dinner table and ignored her throughout her childhood; then, when she was an adult, he tried to stop her from going to Africa. After Fossey's murder, he successfully challenged her will. Instead of going to the Digit Fund (a memorial Fossey had established and named for her favorite gorilla) for antipoacher patrols, as she had wished, her money went to him and her mother. How Fossey must have hated him. How she would have hated his taking money from her gorillas.

So what did Fossey find in Africa? Gorilla bands organized patriarchally, a dignified silverback (a mature older male) in charge, a younger silverback often doing sentry duty as protector of the band (this was her beloved Digit's role). Females would go from band to band, often to enhance their own status or the likelihood of reproductive access to males, but their devotion to their infants ceased only with the infants' death. Yet infants often died when leadership changed or when a new mother switched groups. Fossey noted this phenomenon initially with puzzlement; it seemed like a discordant element in the gorilla's idyllic family life. Her bafflement turned to distress once she recognized a pattern of deliberate infanticide.

The first observed instance of infanticide occurred in 1972, when a primiparous (first-time) mother named Bravado gave birth to an infant named Curry. Bravado's group was invaded by a rival silverback shortly after Curry's birth. After the invasion, the infant was found with "ten bite wounds of varying severity. One bite had severed the infant's femur and a second had ruptured the gut, causing peritonitis and instant death."[14]

In the days following Curry's death, Bravado lived up to her name by displaying exuberance and high spirits. In *Gorillas in the Mist,* Fossey records her bewilderment:

> I had been deeply saddened by Curry's unexpected death and subjectively expected Bravado to show some sign of distress. I was yet to learn that nearly all primiparous mothers, those giving birth for the first time, upon losing their offspring by infanticide, will react exactly as did Bravado. This type of behavior might be a method by which a female seeks to strengthen her social bonds with other group members following the trauma of having her infant killed. (71)

One expects, in proper sequence (i.e., once Fossey has confirmed the practice of infanticide and learned more about it), a fuller discussion. Yet *Gorillas* mentions infanticide only seven more times, each scantily, and usually only to express Fossey's "deepest sorrow" (220). The silverbacks turn out to have horrifying mechanisms for infant death. The discovery is at odds with the dominant image of the silverbacks as gentle giants.

Males as instruments of death to infants; mothers as collaborators or, at least, as accepting lookers-on. The trauma caused by this discovery coincided with Fossey's work on her dissertation and a hiatus in her *National Geographic* pieces.[15] Fossey had come to the gorillas with a gentle, idealized image of their lives as marked by primitive harmony: it was to be a kind of Eden, translated to the animal world. So Fossey had trouble accommodating facts that reeked of death and ashes. In fact, when Fossey wrote with the knowledge of infanticide behind her, the challenge was to stress the patriarchal warmth of the male gorilla, especially towards infants and children, in light of her new findings. Fossey could only accommodate the existence of infanticide by treating it as a regrettable requirement of the larger gorilla family structure.

According to the theory Fossey developed to explain infanticide, the act was necessary to ensure a silverback's reproductive prerogative. She strongly hints that the pattern may be a late development, under the pressure of human encroachment, to assure species survival. In *Gorillas in the Mist*, her fullest treatment of the subject of infanticide ends by blaming poachers more than the gorillas:

> Twenty-two days after Uncle Bert's killing [by poachers], Beetsme succeeded in killing fifty-four-day-old Frito even with the unfailing efforts of Tiger and other Group 4 members to defend the mother and infant. Flossie [the mother] carried Frito's corpse for two days before being forced to drop it in self-defense during another attack by Beetsme. The tiny body was buried next to that of her father in the graveyard in front of my cabin. Frito's death provided more evidence, however indirect, of the devastation poachers create by killing the leader of a gorilla group. (218)

Shortly after Frito's death, Flossie offers herself to Beetsme for breeding, although he is still an immature male, unable to sire infants; Fossey sees this as an attempt to preserve group solidarity and peace, similar to Bravado's earlier actions. Flossie then deserts the group at the earliest opportunity—an action Fossey cannot help but approve, though it removes Flossie from Fossey's direct sphere of observation.

In her 1981 *National Geographic* piece, Fossey takes on a more difficult task. She discusses an infanticide prompted by a silverback's natural death, rather than at the hands of poachers. Although the article as a whole suggests that the pattern may be part of the gorillas' response to species endangerment, Fossey here gives her fullest explanation of the mechanisms involved:

I now believe infanticide is the means by which a male instinctively seeks to perpetuate his own lineage by killing another male's progeny in order to breed with the victim's mother. In some cases, the stratagem seems necessary to maintain a healthy degree of exogamy, or outbreeding. (512)

The logic behind this conclusion runs as follows. A female gorilla nurses her infant for roughly three and a half years, during which she is unavailable for breeding with the dominant silverback, protector of the group. If the infant is that of the dominant silverback, or another gorilla tolerated by the silverback, the group dynamic proceeds peacefully. But when male gorillas become rivals for leadership, trouble results. The mother of a murdered infant enters estrus soon after the infant's death; typically, she then mates with the new silverback, ensuring the survival of the strongest genes and her continued membership in the group. Hence the routine slaying of a dead male's infant by the new silverback: it is potentially useful in species survival. The argument sounds logical, though many reservations and questions remain. In her *National Geographic* piece, Fossey could only hope that infanticide was indeed a mechanism that would help assure the growth of the gorilla population, even though it paralleled the poachers' victimization of baby gorillas.

For Fossey, the question of infanticide was extremely difficult. We can understand why by imagining what her theory must have meant to someone with Fossey's family history. Fossey was a young child at the time of her mother's remarriage; as such, she would have been the likely victim of the new "silverback" (her stepfather). Like Flossie's infant, Fossey depended on her mother's support and protection. And like Flossie, Dian's mother failed, in her daughter's eyes, to protect her young and (even more gallingly) chose to remain with the new silverback. No wonder that this twist in the gorilla family romance was so upsetting to Fossey and that it had to be contextualized as a necessary thing. For not only would this fact have undermined Fossey's major claim for the gorillas' preservation (these are gentle beings, sentient like us; we must treat them with respect, save them, not simply because they teach us about ourselves but because they *are* us); it would also have threatened the re-created, re-designed family model she had evolved during her years with the gorillas. And make no mistake: Fossey had to have that gorilla family as a surrogate structure. She never married; she chose only married or otherwise engaged men as lovers; she was repeatedly deserted by these men. For her, only the gorillas deserved lasting affection. So the gorillas had to be made to last; everything else—including scientific research and her own health—had a lower priority.

There is a rare and particular heroism in Fossey's singular energy and drive that inevitably commands admiration. While we may become vegetarians or contribute to Greenpeace, Fossey staked and lost all in her devotion to the gorillas' survival. There's a pleasure in seeing someone— someone else—self-immolate in a worthy conservationist cause. Precisely at the point where Fossey crossed the line from normal to deviant, "scientist" to fanatic, public interest in her story became inevitable. But it also acquired an aura different from that which originally surrounded the figure of the female primatologist. Fossey's experience moved, I will argue, from the gentle images with which it began to the razor edge of ecstasy.

IV

In the popular imagination, Fossey existed not alone but as one of a trio of women chosen and tutored by Louis Leakey. Jane Goodall studied the chimpanzee in Tanganyika; Biruté Galdikas, the orangutan in Indonesia; and Dian Fossey, the mountain gorilla in Zaire and Rwanda. Their findings about ape life (including Goodall's discovery that chimps use tools) astonished the world. Each became famous. And yet each moved, over the course of her career, further and further away from Leakey's original mission. Each identified more and more with apes; each became less and less interested in scientific research that might illuminate human origins. Each of the other two replicated Fossey's pattern, though in different ways.

From the beginning, the public and the scientific establishment perceived these women as quite different from one another. Blond, English, and reserved, Goodall fit best (especially at first) the image that Donna Haraway calls "the virgin in the forest," of the young beauty studying beasts in the abstract interests of science and human understanding.[16] She began her work at Gombe, her research center, in 1960, when she was in her mid-twenties, assisted (and chaperoned) at first by her mother. In 1964, she married Hugo van Lawick, a photographer Leakey sent to photograph Goodall's work who he hoped might become her mate. The matchmaking worked. Goodall married Hugo and they spent the next years working together at Gombe. Their son, Hugo Eric Louis, called "Grub," was raised among the chimpanzees until he was sent to school in England.

Raising a child at Gombe was far from easy. The difficulty was compounded by certain discoveries similar to Fossey's among the gorillas. Just as Fossey had discovered infanticide, Goodall discovered positive proof that chimps would kill and eat young baboons or human infants. It became necessary to lock her son in a wire cage, inside her house, which was also secured with screen doors and windows, so that he would be safe from intruding chimps. But the photographs released for public consumption did not stress these rather grim expedients. Instead, the photos and their captions stressed the similarity between Goodall's handling of her infant and the chimps of theirs, or between the way Hugo held the baby's hand and the way he held an infant chimp's.[17] The public's perception of Goodall's family life was colored by its obsessive desire to see chimp families as analogous to human ones—so that cannibalism as a theme had no place. Cannibalism among chimps was like infanticide in the story of the mountain gorillas. It was a disruptive element in the narrative of idyllic animal life that the primatologist wanted to tell and the public, at least at first, wanted to hear.

The public's focus on Goodall's private life ended, significantly I think, when she divorced Hugo. It has all but vanished since Goodall has become an activist for animal rights, seeking better conditions for chimpanzees used for medical research.[18] While Goodall lived a "normal" heterosexual life—as virgin in the forest or Hugo's wife—the public's level of comfort with her and her image was high. Since her life has changed, the public's interest in her has markedly diminished.

Goodall's own early writings contained the images the public wanted. Her best-known book, *In the Shadow of Man,* records the early years of her stay among the chimps and was published during her marriage to Hugo.[19] The book begins with Goodall's early contacts with the chimps and her determination to become an accepted physical object in their world, for which she waits quietly, persistently, and unaggressively. Her early history includes some remarkable evocations of her feeling for the landscape during this solitary period in Africa. These feelings are extremely similar to those we have seen in women's memoirs of Africa:

> I accepted aloneness as a way of life and I was no longer lonely. . . . In fact, had I been alone for longer than a year I might have become a rather strange person, for inanimate objects began to develop their own identities: I found myself saying "Good morning" to my little hut on the Peak, "Hello" to the stream where I collected my water. And I became immensely aware of trees . . . the pulsing sap within. I longed to be able to swing through the treetops. . . . In particular, I loved to sit in a forest when it was raining. (64–65)

Goodall was, however, not destined to become "a rather strange person." Although she invoked this remarkable state of mind, she was aware of its dangers. Hugo's arrival two chapters later ends her aloneness and openness to nature. Rather coyly, Goodall followed the chapter that introduced her love for Hugo with a chapter called "Flo's Sex Life," Flo being her favorite female chimp. It was a hint of something that we will see played out less adorably in Fossey's story: a connection between the primatologist's sexuality and that of the apes she studied.

As I have said, of the three female primatologists, Goodall was the one who most approximated the image of the all-American girl or British maiden. She was cast as Cinderella, elevated to her position at Gombe by Leakey. In fact, Goodall signed her letters to him "Foster Child," and addressed him as "Fairy Godfather," perhaps as part of a successful strategy to avoid Leakey's romantic interest (Leakey was a notorious womanizer). This variation of the father theme so prominent for Fossey strikes me as significant, even though it is scantily developed in Goodall's life. But overall, in relation to Fossey, Goodall functions as the conventional light-haired heroine to Fossey's dark-haired counterpart: *Gone with the Wind*'s Melanie to Scarlett—both of whom have their "fans" among readers.

Goodall's life has been even-keeled, although not always happy and at times even tragic. But she is basically a compromiser, someone who does not actively court disaster, as did the more problematic Fossey.

Biruté Galdikas, the third of Leakey's "ape ladies," embarked on her research with a husband, Ron Brindamour, who was shown with her in the National Geographic Society video that made celebrities of all three women. At the start, she was a long-haired, lovely, voluptuous figure, whose sensuality was perhaps held in acceptable bounds by the presence of the husband. Like Goodall, Galdikas had a son during her first marriage; like Goodall's, her first marriage ended after the man said he wanted a life away from apes. The breakup of this marriage and her surrender of her son were, however, more flamboyant and scandalous than Goodall's divorce (Ron fell in love with an Indonesian woman employed by Galdikas). The events were hard to reconcile with the early image of Biruté and her husband as dedicated parents and coworkers; subsequent attention to Galdikas' personal life dropped off.

Early in her career, Galdikas published work favorably received by the scientific community. Of the three "ape ladies," she was the most respected by scholars. She soon ceased publishing scientific work, however, choosing instead to dedicate herself to the individual orangutan's welfare—quietly, in her camp in Indonesia. Perhaps because she has confined herself to Indonesia (with yearly teaching stints in Canada), the public's focus on Galdikas has blurred over the years. But another reason may be Galdikas' second marriage—to a Dayak tribesman, by whom she has had two additional children. Gone native, gone orangutan, Galdikas no longer suits the Western public's image of the lady scientist. Like Goodall to some extent, and Fossey even more, she hasn't really wanted to.

In the best-known study of primatology to date, Donna Haraway speculates that in enacting the image of the "virgin in the forest," the young female primatologist serves unwittingly as a symbol mediating between nature and culture as large social constructs. That reading seems to me wrong in its initial premises. For women like Fossey, Goodall, and Galdikas, the choice to be a primatologist involved fighting the establishment, living alone or reshuffling the demands of domestic life, becoming the heads of major research establishments, handling publicity, becoming famous, and using their fame for their own goals. This does not sound like passive femininity, a kind of Miss America contest in the jungle. Haraway concentrates on early publicity and surface image. The aspects I have highlighted support a different reading. If these women began by being perceived as "virgins in the forest," chastely mediating between culture and nature, each in her own way became incompatible with that narrative. Especially in middle age, they used their fame for purposes decidedly their own; they identified, more radically than their culture approved, with the apes. Of the three, Fossey changed the script most spectacularly and in ways that, after her death, simply could not be ignored.

From the beginning of Fossey's career, and more and more after her death, there has been obsessive speculation about Fossey's sex life and proclivities (it's a lurid word, but the only one to use). The speculations simply do not fit the Haraway thesis. Early images of Fossey stressed her unusual height for a woman and often showed her in male clothing: jeans, flannel shirt, hair untidily pushed back or bound. Fossey was as large as a man and notoriously flat-chested. Because she was unmarried, her male lovers are absent from all the official versions of her story during her lifetime. Although she was a strikingly attractive woman, her image is not feminine and always more androgynous than female.

A tall figure striding in the jungle, living alone on a mountaintop with African workers, running the show at Karisoke, Fossey was a woman living like a man. And that, I think, was part of the fascination from the start. What the public did not initially know about Fossey—her chain-smoking, her heavy drinking, her bossiness, her violence, her abuse of African poachers, and her sexual freedom—could only have strengthened the perception of her as a warrior-woman, a manlike woman, since these are all conventional attributes of the male white hunter or adventurer.

Many theories about Fossey's life are based, outright, on speculations about her sexuality. In the first full biography published after her death, *Woman in the Mists,* Farley Mowat stressed her unhappy love affairs with photographer Bob Campbell and an unnamed black African doctor. Both men were already attached to other women, to whom they eventually returned (Campbell was married to a fellow European; the African doctor to an African common-law wife with whom he had children). Harold Hayes' claim to newness in *The Dark Romance of Dian Fossey* was based on extensive interviews with Fossey's lover Bob Campbell. From these interviews, it was clear that Campbell regarded sex with Fossey as a mutual convenience to pass the time at Karisoke, hardly as the impassioned love featured in the film *Gorillas in the Mist*. In the film, Campbell wants to marry Fossey and leaves only after she refuses a reasonable compromise that would allow them both to have careers; in real life, marriage was apparently never an issue and Campbell left with no reluctance. Hayes also claimed that Fossey underwent several abortions during these affairs—information that remains unconfirmed elsewhere.

Alex Shoumatoff's portrait of Fossey in *African Madness* similarly focused on her sexuality. But he dwelled much less on her affair with Campbell and did not mention the African doctor. Shoumatoff's theory of Fossey's behavior centered instead on her early experiences in Zaire, when she was ejected from her first research camp just a few months after her arrival and held captive by Congolese rebels during the 1967 civil war. This standard plot element in Fossey's legend has always had a risqué element, insofar as it is widely believed that Fossey was being held in order to be offered as a sexual tidbit to a Congolese general; her daring escape to Rwanda, the story goes, was in fact an escape from concubinage with the general. Shoumatoff does not believe the story of her escape. He claims instead—and quotes others as having heard as much from Fossey—that she was raped repeatedly by Africans during her captivity. That experience, he believed, explained her vehement hatred for the African poachers and the fantastic vengeful scenes she enacted against them. (It does not explain her apparent comfort in being alone with black male African workers at her camp, but Shoumatoff is silent on that point.)

It seems clear, at this date, that it would be impossible to verify or deny any of these hypotheses about Fossey's sexual history, which have almost nothing in common. Having returned to his wife, Campbell has every reason to downplay his affair with Fossey, especially fifteen years after the fact. The rape and the abortions, which are certainly possible, can neither be proved nor disproved except on the basis of hearsay evidence; the same is true of details concerning the affair with the African doctor. Fossey exists in a web of rumors and counterrumors, and the effort to prove or dispel them seems, finally, unrewarding. The more interesting question seems to me why people continue to care about Fossey's sex life.

The answer requires that we recognize how female primatologists have been seen as specimens of femininity. Their lives have been scrutinized for clues about the "essential" nature of female sexuality. In other words, a curious shift has occurred in which all of these women, but especially Fossey, have been "gorilla-ized." That is, they have been seen as offering clues to some essential truth about human, specifically female, sexuality. In the popular imagination, they were initially cast as lady scientists dutifully studying their subjects. But since her death, Fossey has been treated as though she herself were the subject of research whose habits would reveal the truth about female human nature. Female primatologists, as well as their apes, have been watched with prurient eyes.

Perhaps because of her murder, and certainly because she is already dead, fantasies have erupted about Fossey. Among those fantasies are, perhaps, at least some of the speculations in recent biographies. More covertly, there exist hints of symbolic bestiality (itself often a conceptual stand-in for interracial sex) in the discussion of Fossey's love for her favorite gorilla, the young male Digit. Digit is portrayed as Fossey's "lover" in pictures and captions; she herself referred to him in print as "my beloved Digit." Several of her friends and associates say, in so many words, that Digit was the greatest love of Fossey's life. Biographies repeatedly assert that Digit's murder (more than Campbell's desertion or any other human fact) motivated Fossey's escalating assaults on African poachers. Since she is thought to have been murdered by a poacher, the suggestion then becomes that Fossey died for love, Digit's love, much in the way a woman does when she commits suicide after her husband's death; suitably, Fossey was buried by Digit's side.

The film *Gorillas in the Mist* (1988) makes these assertions quite clearly in the way it juxtaposes shots. It repeatedly cuts from images of Fossey with her lover Campbell to images of either Digit or Fossey's chief black male worker[20] looking at the two white lovers. The cuts establish a visual symmetry between Digit and the worker—gorilla and black African male. Both are voyeurs and onlookers during Fossey's affair with Campbell. Both are, by visual proximity, substitutable for Campbell. Part of Fossey fever continues to depend on the public's intense interest in "taboo" subjects like interracial sex, bestiality, and "unbridled" female sexuality. These subjects also appear in popular narratives of West-primitive encounters, like *The Last of the Mohicans* (discussed in Chapter Six). Fossey fascinates the Western imagination because she resembles Conrad's Kurtz—and is a woman, to boot. She was a renegade with "unsound methods" and transgressive emotions, dead in "the heart of darkness."

V

My fascination with Fossey and my version of her may suffer from some of the very flaws I have denounced: prurience and a fascination with violence, a psychologizing of Fossey and her public that verges upon "gorilla-izing." I am aware of that and concerned about how it falsifies the original source of my interest in Fossey. For I was initially drawn to her story because I was intrigued by the first of the images with which I began: the image of the young and beautiful woman, hand out to the gorilla, open and receptive to other forms of life—caring for them passionately and doing something about ensuring their survival. It's an overly romantic image, to be sure. But as with most romantic images, there are grains of truth beneath its glittery surface.

In a recent study of Goodall, Galdikas, and Fossey, Sy Montgomery claims that the three chose to enter the animals' world with typically female generosity and to be receptive to it. She says that the women's refusal to follow "scientific" methods requiring distance and nonintervention in the animals' lives guaranteed their outsider status in the scientific community and the lack of respect accorded their popular work. These women, Montgomery says, resemble not so much scientists as shamans, adopting animals as totems, at times *becoming* the animal.

Montgomery's view depends on an essentialist idea of female conduct that I must reject. She maintains purely and simply that these women's openness to ape life was typically female, part of the "boundary permeability" that Nancy Chodorow and others have theorized as a component of female nature in our culture.[21] I cannot entirely support Montgomery's idealized image, in part because these women dealt with the modern world. They did not simply exist in a spiritual-mystical relationship with the apes. Yet it remains true, at some inner level, that their dedication to animals depended upon their living apart from the modern human world, in quest of some essential primitive, defined as life force as embodied in apes. That, I believe, is the ultimate reason why Fossey's story continues to exert such a hold on the imagination.

The analogy between the shaman and the devoted female primatologist has only a metaphoric validity. Metaphor is different from identity, in both intention and method. But metaphor is no small thing. It controls and structures much of the human imagination and human language. In fact, there is often a certain slippage from metaphor to fact. And that, I believe, is what has happened in Fossey's history. Many details in her life have a certain affinity with shamanism. In turn, that affinity has allowed her story to serve needs also served by the idea of shamanism. Fossey's life speaks to feelings that are displaced and sometimes inchoate in our culture, when they are not trivialized or sentimentalized: most saliently, the desire for ecstatic contact with animals.

Fossey herself encouraged Africans to think of her as a shaman or witch doctor. She adopted the Africans' name for her, Nyiramachabelli— the woman who lives alone on the mountain. Legend has it that she wore masks and stressed the fiery red color of her hair, a sign of an African witch, when she interrogated captured poachers. But something else is at work in Fossey's history beyond such surface tricks. Her life fits certain "deep structures" in shamanism: for example, intimacy with mountains, and, most of all, friendship with animals and access to the language of the beasts.[22] Indeed, Fossey's entire strategy for studying the gorillas depended upon establishing physical proximity and then physical contact by learning and imitating the gorillas' "language" of gestures and sounds.

In fact, the metaphor of Fossey as shaman points to something at the heart of this book. The primitive can be a channel for spirituality outside of organized religion; the primitive can be one route in the quest for ecstatic contact with the essence of life. For some specific ideal of godhead or Being-ness, Fossey substituted the gorillas. She was a modern woman with impulses that might, in other contexts, have become religious. She was bound to come into conflict with the modern world since it made available to her no organizations or systems of belief to support or accommodate her aspirations.[23]

So now I need to turn on my own arguments. I need to end with a more sympathetic understanding of Fossey and her aspirations as ecstatic in impulse and structure. Fossey's sordid history and the inconsistencies in her work that I have described are real enough; they undercut any simple idealization of her history. But I need to end by approaching her in the sympathetic way in which I came to her. It is, I believe, no less (though certainly no more) true than the debunking views I have given. I need to tell the tale of her love for the gorillas, stripping it down to what it was: a love of life-essence, as embodied in the gorillas, so intense that it did not, could not, hesitate to court isolation and even her own death. In this sense, the image of Fossey touching the gorilla's hand (with which I began) can be said to include the later images of isolation, misanthropy, and even the invitation to murder. In the mountains of Rwanda, Fossey played out the drama that Freud and others have labelled the death wish. Yet for her it may have had another meaning entirely.

VI

Dian Fossey loved her gorillas so much that when she woke up one morning awash in a sea of warm diarrhetic dung, she was overjoyed. She had expected to find the baby gorilla she had taken to bed, like a sick child, dead of a lingering illness. The warm dung showed that the gorilla was still alive, and likely to recover. Fossey hardly noticed the dung. It was the baby's wellness that counted above all. Psychoanalysis tells us that the abject (often symbolized by excrement) is a displaced symbol of the transcendent.[24] But something more radical was at work without any complex conceptual apparatus in Fossey. Fossey gained access to the joy of life through the baby gorilla's diarrhetic dung which signified, for her, renewed health and vigor.

Ten years later, as Fossey wrote *Gorillas in the Mist,* she recorded that that gorilla, Coco, died in a zoo in Cologne, where she was imprisoned with another young gorilla named Pucker. Fossey tells us that she never got over the deaths—and I believe her. For *Gorillas in the Mist* is remarkable testimony by someone who clearly experienced gorillas as beings who must be protected as the containers of life.

Every bit of the book, including the packaging, insists that we regard the gorillas as characters—that is, as stand-ins for people in the ongoing drama of life. In my edition, the endpapers feature sketches of the gorillas most often named in the narrative. Fossey points out that every gorilla has a noseprint as unique as the human fingerprint. And lo and behold— the faces do not look at all alike.

Fossey wrote *Gorillas in the Mist* as a series of vignettes or stories: Coco and Pucker, destined to die in a zoo; pets she had other than gorillas; her most beloved object of study, Digit. The section that hooked me most into the narrative was a generational novel in miniature: the story of three generations in a group Fossey called Group 4. The gorillas— Beethoven and Effie, Marchessa and Patsy, Icarus and Ziz—age, mate, change, and die. As I read their life histories, something remarkable happened. I began to care about the gorillas as though they were people and to read the narrative as though it were a novel tantalizing me with the question "What happens next?"[25] In fact, I found myself looking for pictures of the "characters" in the interpolated sections of photographs. Like many readers, I had browsed the photographs already, shortly after I had begun to read. When I first looked, I saw gorillas. Now I saw Effie or Beethoven or Digit and was disappointed in some profound way when it turned out (as it often did) that the photograph had been taken by someone other than Fossey and so did not identify the gorilla pictured by name.

My reactions were not, I think, just idiosyncratic. Instead, they were prompted by a remarkable quality in Fossey's story. On the wooded slopes where the mountain gorilla survives, Dian Fossey observed, initiating change as little as possible. Yet she repeatedly, and with thematic insistence, engaged in the godlike practice of naming and creating the story of gorilla life. No gorilla escaped the naming and narrativizing process. When a gorilla previously thought to be male suddenly gave birth, the newborn ape received as its name the first words uttered by Fossey: "Can't be," or "Cantsbee." Her utterances were that powerful, that godlike. To see was to name, and the name, once uttered, altered the gorilla, made the gorilla enter a network of relationships with his fellow gorillas and with Fossey herself. The naming motif may at first seem to be one of domination (human over animal). It may well betray too much confidence in the correspondence between names and things. But it is still very powerful. Indeed, in certain mystical traditions, "the fact of giving names or changing them plays a similarly important part in eschatological pronouncements. . . . [It] brings about a moral conversion of humanity, and even a transformation of the animals . . . which characterizes the world fresh from the hand of God."[26] Fresh from the hand of God. In touch with and renewed by the life force.

In this symbolic sense, Fossey's act of rendering or perceiving gorillas as characters or people was only an intermediate step, necessary to accommodate what otherwise could not be said. The gorillas were not really being anthropomorphized—or they were being anthropomorphized only as much as is inevitable given the perceived closeness of humans and apes. As containers of Being-ness, they were rendered identical in value to the "human." They were placed in a group and a family, with genes and bloodlines, parenting roles, innate dispositions, random circumstances, and a complex fate that would include eventual extinction. Like humans; like Fossey herself. Which is to say, aspiring to something inhuman, something sublime that Fossey found even smeared with the diarrhetic dung of a baby gorilla.

CHAPTER FIVE

"The Bones and the Blue":
Georgia O'Keeffe and the Female Primitive

I

N AKED ON BROADWAY": that was how Mabel Dodge Luhan, leader of the artists' colony in Taos, described Georgia O'Keeffe. She was referring both to the elemental, exposed quality of O'Keeffe's art and to the ambiance surrounding her affair with Alfred Stieglitz.[1] Stieglitz made hundreds of images of O'Keeffe, beginning soon after they met, and exhibited them freely.[2] Even today, these close-up, intimate photographs shock the eye and the imagination.

In one series of photographs, O'Keeffe's pubic mound fills the frame. There it is: firm, round, black, hairy, outlined by slim, bony hips. The same image occurs over and over, in tonalities that vary with the processes Stieglitz used to develop his negatives. In another series, O'Keeffe's breasts hang surprisingly full on a thin body—heavy, with large dark nipples, sometimes smooth, sometimes taut or textured. In another, her hands turn this way and that—like flowers, arabesques, pure forms. In another, her ankles become the obsessive subject of the camera's eye. The images focus tightly on one body part or another, rarely showing her entire form.[3]

In many of the photos, O'Keeffe's face stares boldly at the camera—strong brows, stark expression, hair pulled back, sometimes topped by a man's bowler hat. In some, the face is tired and anguished or masked by a coat or hands; others suggest postcoital photography, the woman's hands clutching a flimsy jacket, her hair hanging loose. Some poses must have been uncomfortable to hold. A neck twists around and upward, its strain visible in tendons forming a tight V; arms lift in a perfect parabola, held with perfect stillness.

From the very beginning of O'Keeffe's career, the replication of her face and body parts turned her into an icon. With their repetition of breasts and pubic mound, hands or feet, naked torso, the photographs of the body or its parts became symbols of the sexual female—soft and round, or hard and angular, yielding or withholding. With their somber shadows and ageless depths, the photographs of the face remained more ambiguous, even androgynous.

Every inch of O'Keeffe was naked on Broadway, in images that could not help but arouse sexual speculation. O'Keeffe's relationship to Stieglitz, and his famous photographs, gave a special and undeniable edge to showings of her paintings in his galleries, which were bastions of American Modernism. From the beginning, O'Keeffe's work was on view and admired. But when people looked at her art, they also saw the work of Stieglitz' lover, a woman naked on Broadway.

In 1929, Mabel Dodge Luhan invited Georgia O'Keeffe to Taos to live at her artists' colony. It was O'Keeffe's first chance since getting involved with Stieglitz to leave New York for a sustained period, and she seized it. New Mexico gave O'Keeffe some of her most powerful, suggestive, and characteristic imagery: bones, especially skulls and pelvises, against the sky; snail or clam shells against red hills; rugged, jagged mountains raked by crevices and gullies. These images crystallized tendencies always present in O'Keeffe's art. Indeed, her work came to be identified with them and they are crucial to understanding her immense popular appeal. These images render natural forms or simple man-made shapes in startling scales and from unusual angles that cause objects to lose their familiarity and become strange.[4] Although they represent objects that are recognizable from the sensory world, her paintings treat the largest possible subjects: sexuality and energy, life and death, nature and spirit, the temporal and the eternal—what she would later call "the Bones and the Blue." O'Keeffe's art is infused with an instinct for the oceanic, an instinct quickened and intensified by her love affair with New Mexico.

It is essential to O'Keeffe's legend that she eventually settled in New Mexico, first near Taos, then at Ghost Ranch, then alone in her own house in an isolated, tumbledown village called Abiquiu. For people in the United States, she remained a familiar face and figure, much photographed and frequently exhibited. But she was no longer "naked on Broadway." In New Mexico, O'Keeffe became herself, sans Stieglitz in her adopted spiritual home, clad in black or white, advancing from middle through extreme old age. The transition from one state to the other demanded the ability—which O'Keeffe cultivated—to seize control of and shape her public image. Stieglitz' photographs remained a constant point of reference for her. But she gradually transformed their meaning and suggestiveness. Brilliantly, O'Keeffe manipulated categories that the art world dubs "male" or "female" and associates with the "artistic" or "primitive." The labels "female" and "primitive" had dogged and troubled O'Keeffe from the very beginning of her career. Late in life, she successfully transformed them both, providing a final example—a triumphant one—of women's encounters with the primitive. O'Keeffe owed the labels "female" and "primitive," like everything else, to Alfred Stieglitz.

II

Admired, resented, and loved, O'Keeffe's mentor and lover Stieglitz was the ghost figure in her psyche. Largely because of her connection with Stieglitz, O'Keeffe was never a neglected artist. Part of the O'Keeffe legend is that, soon after her training at Columbia Teachers College, a friend showed her work to the famous Stieglitz, who exhibited O'Keeffe's art in 1916 without asking her permission. She protested. He invited her to lunch. She went and lingered for thirty years.[5] It was the perfect debut for someone of O'Keeffe's ambitious but private temperament. Without ever having put herself forward, she was able to have her talent and achievements recognized. In a brief time, she moved from being a provincial unknown to a mainstay of one of the foremost avant-garde galleries in New York, hung in the same rooms in which Picasso, Matisse, and African sculpture were displayed in the United States.[6]

Stieglitz cultivated her fame, handled her business negotiations, and mediated between her and the art establishment—as she put it, "made [her] world for [her]" (*Letters*, 244). In the first decades of her career, O'Keeffe exhibited almost exclusively in the prestigious spaces of Stieglitz' "291," Intimate, and American Place galleries. Reviews of her shows appeared in prominent places, almost always written by Stieglitz' friends and associates. The exhibitions and reviews charted O'Keeffe's development in the 1920s and 1930s: from charcoal line drawings to experimentation with color, shape, and mood in landscapes and evocations of music in paint; from the suggestive "female" imagery of the flower paintings through a brief excursion into the "male" imagery of New York skyscrapers.

O'Keeffe enjoyed her growing fame and financial success. At first, it must have seemed like a dream: sex, love, art, fame, and power—all available through the same brilliant and devoted man. But as their union progressed into the twenties, there must have been years of reckoning as O'Keeffe learned how Stieglitz would limit her life.

The photographer, who was twenty-three years older than O'Keeffe, never varied his routines. He refused to travel, except to his family summer house at Lake George, New York—which O'Keeffe hated, feeling "smothered in green" and mired in the extended Stieglitz clan. Shuttled between Manhattan and Lake George, surrounded by Stieglitz' circle, O'Keeffe began to see the meaning of having someone else "make [her] world." More and more, she felt the need to produce a vision and an art that could not be subsumed—à la Svengali—under the powerful influence of Stieglitz, a vision and art unlike (as she put it) "anything anyone had ever taught [her]." O'Keeffe felt oppressed by perceptions that she "was born and taught to walk" by Stieglitz, a notably maternal metaphor for his role, which points to another vexed issue in the couple's life (*Letters*, 236). Around 1920, as O'Keeffe approached her mid-thirties, she wanted to have the child Stieglitz had promised her. But Stieglitz was in his late fifties and already a father. He was also estranged from his adult daughter, who had sided with her mother during Stieglitz' affair with O'Keeffe and the divorce that followed. And when his daughter became mentally ill during an extended postpartum recovery, he became immovably opposed to the idea of O'Keeffe bearing his child. He put the alternatives starkly before O'Keeffe: stay with him and be a great artist, or leave and perhaps have a child with another man, but risk damaging her career.[7] She chose to stay, and in later years they called her paintings "children" and placed them with parental care. But the events distilled a drop of poison into their relationship.[8]

As the twenties progressed, flirtations and infidelities accumulated. The summer after the decision to remain childless, O'Keeffe became severely depressed. Feeling neglected and annoyed, Stieglitz began to flirt outrageously with a mutual friend, Rebecca Strand, whose husband, Paul, was executing (not so coincidentally) a series of photographs of Rebecca that imitated Stieglitz' photographic portrait of O'Keeffe. Strand had asked Stieglitz to develop the prints. Stieglitz found himself stimulated. He wrote to Beck Strand repeatedly, in this vein: "For an hour or more I have been tickling up your rear into the most perfect state of delight" (quoted in Eisner, *O'Keeffe and Stieglitz*, 302). Beck Strand visited Stieglitz' country house at Lake George; O'Keeffe abruptly and atypically departed. Then Stieglitz behaved so badly (complaining about O'Keeffe's absence, pursuing other women) that even Beck lost interest.

That same year, 1924, Stieglitz and O'Keeffe married. He would soon turn sixty; she had just turned thirty-seven. They had been together for more than seven years, and the desire for legal marriage appears to have been mostly his. The marriage followed the incidents with Beck Strand and a joint exhibition that marked a growing professional rivalry over the relative place of photography and painting in the artistic hierarchy and the issue of realism. O'Keeffe became so anxious about this exhibition of his photographs and her art that she fell ill—a pattern that would recur over the next two decades. Both O'Keeffe and Stieglitz would periodically become invalids; one suspects they often used illness to command each other's attention or to justify their own conduct.

Meanwhile, the relationship continued to develop complications. By

1928, Stieglitz had begun a long affair with Dorothy Norman—a young, newly wed socialite who managed the American Place gallery. The Jewish-American Norman may have represented for Stieglitz a return to his roots after his union with O'Keeffe, a daughter of the solidly Protestant Midwest. Shy, pliant, and adoring, reminding him of what his wealthy first wife and his estranged daughter might have been like (Eisner, *O'Keeffe and Stieglitz,* 361–62), Norman received the aging Stieglitz' attentions—and at a time when O'Keeffe was undergoing several operations to remove benign growths from her breasts. In a way that must have been infuriating, Stieglitz idealized Norman's youth and her maternity. With his typically reckless indiscretion, Stieglitz posed Norman in a series of photographs unmistakably based on his early portraits of O'Keeffe. Stieglitz' passion for O'Keeffe had led him to photograph her obsessively; now he used the medium of photography to reveal his new amours—a tactic O'Keeffe herself would soon adopt.

O'Keeffe was humiliated by Stieglitz' affair with Norman—and she struck back. When she went to Taos in 1929, she took Beck Strand with her and lived there for four months in what may have been a romantic relationship, according to numerous accounts of nude sunbathing and photographs of O'Keeffe in men's shirts with her arm protectively around the feminine Beck's shoulders (Eisner, *O'Keeffe and Stieglitz,* 395, 380). O'Keeffe also became close to Tony, Mabel Dodge Luhan's Pueblo Indian husband, which excited Mabel's jealousy. Other reports link her over the next few years with Paul Strand and Mabel herself. Later on, she chose the attractive black male writer Jean Toomer as intimate friend and, most likely, lover. Beyond that, she allowed a new photographer to record her beauty—Ansel Adams, who captured a smiling, radiant O'Keeffe, less austere than the woman photographed by Stieglitz. For the rest of her life, O'Keeffe would choose photographers with care, knowing the power of the photographic image, which had played so intimate and surprising a role in her life. When she posed for Stieglitz after 1929, she always posed with a symbol of her new life: her Ford automobile, an Indian blanket, New Mexico's flowers or skulls.[9]

By 1930, O'Keeffe's fame was secure and her income steady. She could have simply left Stieglitz and may have wanted to. But she owed everything to him—and she knew it. More, she loved him, in a complicated and competitive way that must have seemed, even to her, unhealthy. By the time O'Keeffe went to Taos for the first time in 1929, the power dynamic in their relationship had shifted decisively. But at first, she couldn't admit that, and the guilt took its toll on her body. As the twenties drew to an end, O'Keeffe repeatedly experienced acute bouts of influenza and fatigue. In 1933, while painting a doomed urban mural of "male" skyscrapers for Radio City Music Hall (for O'Keeffe, a difficult regression in subject matter after Taos), she had a full-blown nervous breakdown that left her a semi-invalid for months. After that, she probably felt that she had earned the right to make her yearly escape to Taos. In a pattern that echoes women's memoirs of Africa, Alfred Stieglitz became the man O'Keeffe cast off for New Mexico.

New Mexico and New York divided O'Keeffe's loyalties for the next two decades. After 1929, with a few exceptions made on account of her health or Stieglitz' (he suffered a number of heart attacks after 1928), she spent part of every year in New Mexico. In 1946 (after Stieglitz' death), she moved there permanently.

On her own, O'Keeffe would go far in the West, but she would never absolutely escape from Stieglitz. When she was interviewed for the 1977 Perry Miller Adato documentary on her life (called simply *Georgia O'Keeffe*), she was asked how she got along with the men in Stieglitz' circle. O'Keeffe said she got along fine, but then added, with a wicked gleam in her eye: "Of course I got along with them. I did all the hard work. . . . I was a useful citizen." The interviewer, wanting to know more about her relationship with Stieglitz, asked why, way back in 1916, when O'Keeffe had wanted to remove her art from Stieglitz' gallery, she had not challenged his refusal. O'Keeffe looked at the camera, every wrinkle on her craggy face alert and amused. She said, in her gravelly voice: "Listen, *you* try arguing with him and see where *you* get." Roughly sixty years after the offending moment, O'Keeffe's answer, cast in the present tense, conveyed affection and resentment in equal parts.[10] Still, in New Mexico, O'Keeffe used the resources of middle and old age to take control of her life and perceptions of her work. She became Galatea perfecting Pygmalion's art.

III

Stieglitz' was the most powerful male voice in O'Keeffe's ears. But Stieglitz' friends, especially during the pivotal late 1920s and early 1930s, were also O'Keeffe's critics—and profoundly influential in constructing the public figure called Georgia O'Keeffe. In pieces published about her in the twenties, the overwhelming tendency was to treat O'Keeffe first and foremost as a woman artist whose subjects were female biology and interests. Stieglitz himself is said to have initiated this tendency in criticism of the artist's work when he pronounced, upon first seeing her paintings, "At last, a woman on paper"—by which he meant the essential female temperament, expressed for all time in art.

Stieglitz' cronies took up this line in reviews that verged on self-parody. O'Keeffe was described as a "priestess of eternal womanhood,"[11] an avatar of a pagan past. Critics saw allusions to genitalia everywhere in her work and used Freud's theory of "penis envy" to interpret them: O'Keeffe, it seems, could not help but express female grievance at lacking the desirable male appendage.[12] In 1925, the influential critic Marsden Hartley (also a Stieglitz crony) invoked the deep-seated identification of nature with women when he maintained that O'Keeffe came by her relation to "the true force of nature" through distinctly "female" properties of mind. She "lays no claim to intellectualism," Hartley wrote. "She frets herself in no way with philosophical and esthetic theories—it is hardly likely she knew one premise from another."[13] For Hartley and most critics through the thirties, O'Keeffe was "a highly developed intuitive." While men (as the critic Alan Burroughs suggested) get answers by "a lifetime in careful consideration of questions," O'Keeffe followed a woman's path, getting answers "by guesswork." In 1932, Vernon Hunter compared her to "the little Amherst witch," Emily Dickinson—an earlier incarnation of miraculous, untrained female talent.[14]

Hartley and other critics of his generation matured in a climate in which primitivism had loomed large in the art world, ever since Picasso and others had begun to use and imitate African masks and sculpture in their work.[15] Male artists saw themselves, and were seen by critics, as self-consciously tapping into "the primitive" as a source of artistic power.[16] They saw themselves and were seen as recognizing strong qualities of form and expression of which the "primitives" producing the art were thought to be unaware. They saw themselves and were seen as plumbing, by controlled experimentation, the psychological depths (the hearts of darkness) suggested by African and South Pacific art.

But for women like O'Keeffe, association with "the primitive" worked differently. Women were seen as trapped in their instincts and limited in intellect by the very structure of their minds and bodies. For them, the label "primitive" was not a special source of power but a marker of naïveté (think Grandma Moses) or of the same preponderance of instinct, lack of control, chthonic nature, and sexuality that male Europeans and Americans often saw in Africans themselves. In fact, critics used terms to describe O'Keeffe as a female artist that corresponded to derogatory cultural clichés about Africans and other so-called primitives:[17] intuitive, not skilled, sexual and emotional, not rational—this was praise for lucky fools, possessing against all odds the ineffable, transcendent quality of the true artist, the quality that in white males would have been called greatness.

Early in her career, O'Keeffe seemed truly ambivalent about dividing the art world into male and female domains. Sometimes she seemed to view her art as distinctively female and encouraged others to view it alongside other women's.[18] At other times, she bristled with resentment at the fact that women, whatever their wealth or status, constituted an underclass in U.S. culture.[19] Her remarks on women as an underclass remind me of Virginia Woolf's tough-minded comments in *Three Guineas* (1938), in which she maintains that women of the upper and middle classes cannot and should not honor the class loyalties felt by men. Like Woolf, O'Keeffe perceived acutely both her privilege and her privation. It was, then, eminently natural that O'Keeffe came to feel uneasy about discussions of her work as "female art."[20]

Writing in 1975, feminist artist Judy Chicago described how male teachers often denigrate women's art when it contains forms suggestive of female anatomy by labelling it "intuitive" or "primitive." In her own career, Chicago responded to the denigration by reversing the value judgments attached to these terms. When she began to teach women artists, for example: "I . . . tried . . . to help my students realize themselves through their lives and feelings as women—to be themselves, even if that meant revealing their primitivism."[21] For Chicago, the word "primitivism" means honesty and fidelity to biological life, imagined as positive alternatives to modernity. She embraced the label "primitive" willingly. Supported by seventies-style feminism, she conceived of herself as oppositional, struggling, defiant. In her best-known composition, *The Dinner Party*, for example, a large table (an actual table surrounded by actual chairs) is set with a feast of menstrual pads and tampons streaked with red paint. The assemblage, a massive hymn to menstruation, recalls famous Italian frescoes of the Last Supper, with stained female paraphernalia replacing Christian bread and wine. The work embodies what we might call a "menstrual primitive" that links women to primal essence, which continues today to be both celebrated (as it is by Chicago) and denigrated.[22]

Chicago's allusions to the "primitiveness" of women artists would not have surprised O'Keeffe, but the view of it as such a positive quality probably would have. During the twenties and thirties, several exemplary works of Modernist art, by artists exhibited in Stieglitz' galleries, made negative associations between the female and the primitive, and these had become customary in Europe and the United States. Picasso's *Les Demoiselles d'Avignon*, for example, showed whores with faces like African masks—in other words, female sexuality with a "primitive" face. But the most directly relevant examples, with respect to O'Keeffe's history, are Man Ray's photographs of Alice Prin (called Kiki) with an African mask. The most famous of these is *Noire et blanche*, sometimes now also called *Kiki*.

Noire et blanche is part of a series of shots Man Ray executed of Kiki, reminiscent of Stieglitz' series on O'Keeffe. As in the photos of O'Keeffe, the subject is Kiki's head, or her body, but rarely the two together. In *Noire et blanche*, two disembodied heads—an African mask and the white Kiki's—rest perpendicular to each other and cast symmetrical shadows. Both are perfect ovals, and Kiki has been styled so that she precisely resembles the mask, with her hair slicked back, her eyebrows tweezed, her eyes closed, and her nose and mouth smoothly shadowed. Until I did some research, I assumed (as most viewers would) that *Noire et blanche* had been inspired by the uncanny resemblance between the model and the mask. But in fact, the historical Kiki was a famous celebrity whose trademarks were her bangs, her big round face, and her toothsome smile. Her best-known features are effaced in the Man Ray photograph, perhaps as a deliberate joke meant for friends and insiders. Also effaced are her other claims to celebrity: Kiki was an artist in her own right who had a successful show in 1927; she was also the owner of a nightclub, appeared in early Surrealist films, and wrote a best-selling memoir about Paris in the 1920s.[23] She was a well-known public figure, a symbol of artistic Montparnasse. Yet these facts about her rarely get mentioned; she is usually identified simply as Man Ray's model and mistress. The labels are deceptive, given her independent fame and finances.

Like Kiki, O'Keeffe was arranged and presented by Stieglitz as a representative of "woman." In the 1990s, knowing that O'Keeffe was a great and famous painter, it may seem shocking to think of her as a potential Kiki. But in the teens and twenties, in many ways, that is precisely what she was. O'Keeffe might have ended up as a footnote in books about Stieglitz—a prop used and put aside, like an African mask. To avoid this fate, O'Keeffe needed to take charge, to become an active participant in constructing and promulgating her image. She needed, in effect, to take control of the association between the female and the primitive. Over time, and under the influence of New Mexico, she manipulated and transformed the clichés in a way that nourished her art. But first she had to identify herself as something other than a "female" artist and an "intuitive" primitive.

Appraisals of O'Keeffe in terms of formal and technical mastery were a secondary theme of reviews from the 1920s. O'Keeffe gradually came to the conclusion that this was the theme she should stress. In a review from 1927, Henry McBride noted a "French" influence on O'Keeffe and read her works as being *about* color and light, "planned . . . out in her mind," much as the Impressionists' art had been. In a letter, O'Keeffe thanked him and cultivated his favor. In *Time Exposures,* Waldo Frank expressed doubt as to whether the New York art scene would be able truly to appreciate O'Keeffe, whose art, he maintained, strives after an astonishing formal "purity" and, far from being thoughtless, is infused with thought much as a tree is infused with life. Once again, O'Keeffe believed that she had found a friend and ally.[24] In these views and in her espousal of them, O'Keeffe was cast, and cast herself, as a latter-day Flaubert: an artist of technical vision, dedicated to style and form, who is persistently misread, in Freudian terms, as female and (in her flower paintings, for example) deemed almost pornographic.

In his early canonizing history of modern art, Samuel Kootz applauded a change he saw in O'Keeffe's work after 1930. He described the change as "formal order getting the upper hand over unchained exuberance," the triumph of "intelligence" and the "basic laws of organization" over "emotion." Kootz praised the new "raw, brutal splashes" in O'Keeffe's paintings as male, describing the quality of her earlier art as "female."[25] What was a woman to do? Present a "female" temperament and thereby limit herself as an artist? Or enter instead the "raw, brutal" male world of formal power? Despite periodic gestures towards affirming the female against the misunderstanding and misrepresentation of male critics, O'Keeffe appears to have chosen the second option in written statements about her art, though not, I think, in the art itself.

O'Keeffe's letters to male friends who were also critics (especially at mid-career) suggest an effort to present herself as a strict formalist. She spoke of wishing to capture colors, to create shapes, to compose the whole—in accord with her "vision," to be sure, but in a "careful" way. She fended off, though in highly ambiguous terms, the sexual readings of her early flower paintings.[26] Even late in life, she declined to be shown in some exhibitions of women's art and refused to allow her flower paintings to appear in books on women. Respectful of artistic intentions, critics in the formalist 1960s through 1980s tended to accept O'Keeffe's pronouncements as definitive. The view of O'Keeffe as neuter formalist became the party line, barring attention to her femaleness—most notably in the famous Whitney Museum exhibition of 1973, the important centenary exhibit of 1987–88, and in the influential catalogues produced in conjunction with them.

Yet all the while, O'Keeffe was harboring and acting upon an alternative definition of form as experiential and spiritual—one that would increasingly fall out of favor with critics during the twentieth century but was still alive and viable for artists like O'Keeffe. In a letter to a friend, the writer Sherwood Anderson, written in 1923, O'Keeffe defined "real living form" as "the natural result of the individual's effort to create the living thing out of the adventure of his spirit into the unknown." She defined form as emotion, as feeling, as (in D. H. Lawrence's very similar terms) "relation between man and his circumambient universe, at the living moment."[27] Such views were continuous with nineteenth-century movements such as vitalism and spiritualism. They had been articulated in influential books such as *The Art of Spiritual Harmony* (1914), written by the German Expressionist Wassily Kandinsky, and they initially motivated what has been called this century's most typical movement, Abstractionism.[28] In addition, a kind of experiential and spiritual form was ascribed to "primitive" art (for example, African sculpture), which was believed to have been spontaneously rather than painstakingly produced, whatever degree of technical mastery it might display.[29]

Yet during the teens and twenties, a different meaning of "form" was repeatedly advanced by critics, who used the word to designate technical mastery—line, color, pattern, and shape intentionally produced. At its most aggressive, this definition of form was conceived as requiring (as one influential aesthetician, Clive Bell, put it) "nothing from life, no knowledge of its ideas and affairs, no familiarity with its emotions."[30] O'Keeffe's letter to Anderson suggests a keen awareness of the difference between artists like herself and most critics on this point:

You and I dont know whether our vision is clear in relation to our time or not—No matter what failure or success we may have—we will not know—But we can keep our own integrity— according to our own sense of balance with the world, and that creates our form—

What others have called form has nothing to do with our form—I want to create my own I cant do anything else—if I stop to think of what others—authorities or the public—or anyone— would say of my form I'd not be able to do anything. (O'Keeffe's punctuation; *Letters,* 175).

"If I stop to think of what others . . . would say of my form I'd not be able to do anything": so extreme a statement suggests that O'Keeffe knew that her definition of form was particularly dangerous for a woman to espouse without reinscribing derogatory clichés and stereotypes—including the association of women and "primitives." In addition, O'Keeffe apparently was aware of—and accepted as inevitable—the fact that aesthetic appreciation was becoming the province of critics and academics within the art world as much as, if not more than, of artists. Talking in public about form as "the adventure of the spirit" was likely to seem unsophisticated and naïve; why, O'Keeffe seems to have thought, make an issue of it? O'Keeffe's dilemma is a snapshot of large-scale cultural developments: as the public marketplace for art expanded, as consumers of art increasingly looked to "experts" for advice, the role of the critics would continue to grow.

Ideas about form similar to O'Keeffe's did circulate after 1920. But as the twentieth century progressed, definitions of form as pattern, structure, and the technical handling of materials displaced, and finally effaced, the more experiential or spiritual definition. Indeed, by the 1980s, the experiential and spiritual definition of form was all but forgotten, so that today it may seem startling to the critical imagination—a "fossil," as one critic recently called it.[31] But it is crucial that, for O'Keeffe, form happens out of the process of living, of being, as she put it, "in balance with the world." Critics tend to see the kind of "form" life confers as being cheap and effortless. But audiences, I believe, continue to respond to O'Keeffe's idea of form when they admire her art, and that is one reason why O'Keeffe's life history has become legendary. O'Keeffe knew that form was the hard work of each and every day. "I was terrified all the time," O'Keeffe once said. "But I never let that stop me."[32] O'Keeffe found the ideal place to explore her notion of form in New Mexico. Its landscape allowed her to express the vision that kept her going.

IV

O'Keeffe's New Mexico paintings contrast with those of most Taos artists, whose literalist work depicted Native Americans as they interacted with the cowboy West. Joseph Henry Sharp, Victor Higgins, Oscar E. Berninghaus, Dorothy Brett, and E. Martin Hennings, as well as others, all painted Native Americans at work or dancing, dressed in traditional or modern garb. Although she chose to live and work in New Mexico, O'Keeffe rarely painted Native American subjects or artifacts directly. She did some paintings of Indian kachina dolls and an abstract painting called *At the Rodeo*, but, by and large, she showed relatively little explicit interest in Native American life.[33]

Nevertheless, O'Keeffe was aware—how could anyone in or near Taos not be?—of the Indian heritage of the land. North of the town, and a celebrated destination, lay the Taos Pueblo—a thousand years old, its adobe forms magnificent against Taos Mountain, the center of the Indians' spiritual life. Nearby lay other pueblos, their culture a part of New Mexican life. Much as O'Keeffe's paintings avoided any literalized representation of this life, there is a quality to their aesthetics that suggests an assimilation of the Pueblo Indians' fundamental precepts.[34] In accord with her personalized definition of form, O'Keeffe expressed in her paintings her feelings about the earth and, beyond the earth, the cosmos—feelings that seem distinctly outside what we have become accustomed to thinking of as European and American norms. She conveyed a sense of connectedness between humans and the earth more consistent with what we have been taught to think of as Native American spirituality. O'Keeffe's paintings place in mutual, unhierarchical relation nature with humans, the cosmos with the self, death with life.

O'Keeffe's celebrated skull and pelvis paintings suggest a relationship to death that is neither necrophobic nor necrophilic. It is equally accepting of the animate and inanimate, the living and the dead, as part of a total picture, mutually framing, harmonic, simply coexisting.[35] Her art shows an awareness that life is valuable but can end abruptly; that the body is destined to return to matter, is even continuous with matter. And so she insisted that the bones she painted didn't symbolize death but were "very lively." We can best understand that statement by realizing that bones remain a constant in both life and death, and suggest potential movement between the two. As the gateway to life, the pelvic bone especially conveys this duality; in fact, this is one source of the connections so commonly made between mothers and the oceanic. Many groups share a belief in the power that resides in bones: that is why Asmat warriors, for instance, saved the skulls of their conquered enemies and beloved fathers (see the Introduction); that is why shamans in various cultures collect and use bones in their rituals. Gathered and arranged bones always suggest a certain spiritual power and the potential for the renewal of life.

O'Keeffe said of her bone and pelvis paintings that she wanted to paint the blue in the sky "that will always be there as it is now after all man's destruction is finished. I have tried to paint the Bones and the Blue."[36] In this statement, the equality of "Bones" and "Blue" puts her feelings before us starkly. Likewise, when O'Keeffe suggests in her letters that she would not mind if people were trees, one senses she is not being merely rhetorical. Her letters repeatedly offer greetings to the sun and wind and mountains evocative of animistic traditions. And there is evidence of an oceanic sensibility evolving before the Taos years: even as a young woman teaching in Texas, O'Keeffe recorded with pleasure her experiences of the land, such as being covered by dust, unable to perceive clearly the boundaries between her frame and the elements of nature.[37]

For O'Keeffe, the land is alive. Sky, people, trees, and bones are fully equivalent in her mind. Her renderings of the simple buildings and majestic landscape of New Mexico are as one with her late cloud pictures: everything she paints is both temporal and eternal, of this world and transcendent. Everything that is is secular and holy all at once. In a painting called *The Lawrence Tree*, for example, a rendering of D. H. Lawrence's favorite tree in Taos, O'Keeffe brilliantly creates a powerful visual equivalent of the oceanic emotions Lawrence gropingly expresses in his late fictions (see Chapter Two). In this painting, the tree is painted from below, in a dramatically foreshortened perspective.[38] The unusual perspective creates the impression that the tree is forcing the frame, surging, grasping, reaching upward. The tree is animated, snakelike, alive: it

looks like a gigantic squid, displaced from ocean to sky. It is also spiritually charged—appearing as a vivid, crooked highway from the human
world of the earth's surface to the cosmos full of stars.

If we compare O'Keeffe's art to that of Lawrence himself or of other
artists in New Mexico, perhaps the most startling feature of O'Keeffe's is
the absence of people. Photography was an influence on her work—how
could it not be, given the role of Stieglitz? But O'Keeffe never did portraits, and she never showed any interest in people as subjects. When
asked why, she claimed first that, having been a photographer's model
herself, she was unwilling to torture others. But she also claimed that
human life could be *inferred* from the places and things she painted. This
absence of the human except as inferred from places and things accounts
most, I believe, for the outrageous quality of her work. The traditional
hierarchy of creation one finds in European and American representa-
tional art is supplanted by a continuum of Being: earth, bone, and flower
exist at the same level as man, woman, and child. In her late paintings,
done following her first airplane trips, she renders rivers abstractly, from
above, as gigantic, liquid snakes, transposing mineral and organic forms
overtly now, as she had done covertly for so many years.

The vision of O'Keeffe's art challenges not only artistic convention
but also some axiomatic assumptions held by modern culture: Freud's
model of the mind as struggling away from id to ego, from oceanic feeling to the "reality principle"; science as conquering nature; cities as the
centers of culture; political history as the measure of progress. In her art,
and in her letters, which register a strong awareness of geological time,[39]
O'Keeffe faced the contrast between the short life of the individual and
the eternal life of the land unblinkingly, and without protest.

V

In O'Keeffe's old age, she allowed herself to be photographed against the
landscape of New Mexico by Todd Webb.[40] The experience recapitulated
her earlier collaboration with Stieglitz, but this time on her own terms.

Stieglitz had captured O'Keeffe as an image of what woman meant to him: young, beautiful, sexually alert, and (to be fair to Stieglitz' art) sly, austere, and partly androgynous. In these late photographs, O'Keeffe and Webb staged the second half of the female cycle, the sequel to Stieglitz' series: the woman as full androgyne, shaman, and crone. The photographs revise critics' perception of her as a "priestess of eternal womanhood"—for the woman herself is plainly no longer "eternal," especially not in her seductiveness. Nor is she forever young. She is in time and flowing with it all the way through the processes of old age and dissolution. The photographs sexualize everything around her—including the land. But O'Keeffe is no simple or idealized symbol of the sexual female.

In these black-and-white photos, O'Keeffe, clad in her own habitual blacks and whites, reinvents her relation to the land. In several photographs, O'Keeffe walks along a trickling stream, towards a pelvic-shaped rock formation. Often, light is the idiom of spiritual revelation, as in an image that places her in a cavern, as she looks up at a beam of light piercing the darkness. A mountain looms in the middle of another photograph, topped by a startling, reflective white cross; near the base of the mountain, tiny in scale, is a statue of the Virgin Mary, arms akimbo. O'Keeffe is stylized as a holy woman, often shot wearing what resembles a nun's headcloth. In striking contrast to the more conventional stare of the Stieglitz photos, O'Keeffe's eyes consistently look away. They are indifferent to the camera or beholder, but fixated upon the shapes, color, and light of the land around her. Outside, she holds skulls or antlers; indoors, they hover behind her, tacked to the wall or resplendent in her paintings. Suggestions of shamanism are pervasive: the bones, the flowers, the wrinkles. Webb frequently photographs her back in profile, its curve conforming to the contour of the background, as though to blend with the land she loved. The photographs bespeak a special relation to nature, the openness of inner to outer. If the imagery seems staged (and I think it was), it is nevertheless convincing as a somewhat more literal representation of the feelings evoked by O'Keeffe's paintings.

O'Keeffe's vision is bold. It is comprehensible only when we bracket, at least temporarily, values we have been taught to associate with civilization. O'Keeffe's art suggests ways of organizing and representing the cosmos that have been underemphasized in modern culture but are increasingly being uncovered and valued. O'Keeffe's art worships the land. It respects human life but looks beyond it to some more overarching source of spirit and energy. It provides a full range of positive female images. It allows alternative, accepting views of aging and death. This is why Georgia O'Keeffe has been so popular—almost a cult figure—in the urban, urbane, and fearful eighties and nineties. She offers a glimpse of something else, something different from the realities that structure everyday lives. Today, people are searching both for role models from the past and for contact with like-minded individuals. The next chapters will explore some other ideas to which people today have been drawn.

Tattoo by Vyvyn Lazonga
Photographer: Skip Williams

PART III

Trends and Movements

CHAPTER SIX

New American Indian/New American White

I N THE MIDWEST RECENTLY, I met a very dignified, almost strait-laced Anglo man whose name, as he pronounced it in syllables, had a distinctly Indian ring. The conversation worked its way around to his revealing that he was originally from Colorado, near the border with New Mexico. And without my having asked, he told me his suspicion that he had Indian blood.[1] There were tiny hints from his grandmother and mother: his grandfather's hair "had sure been long"; "that man was always on the move, like an eagle." The man hadn't understood these hints when he was younger—but now . . . his very eyebrows crinkled with pleasure at the thought.

My acquaintance was part of a growing trend. From 1970 to 1980, the number of Americans identifying themselves as Native Americans grew by a surprising 72 percent; then, from 1980 to 1990, it grew again by 38 percent.[2] The most dramatic rise was reported in Alabama, whose Indian population rose by a startling 118 percent. New births accounted for only a small fraction of the change. A larger percentage could be attributed to the Indian Self-Determination and Education Act of 1975, which allowed each tribe to set its own criteria for membership.[3] But even this new law cannot account for all the growth. Nor can generous adoption policies that do not require a specific "blood" quantum or other proof of Indian descent. For example, more than 308,000 Americans described themselves as Cherokee in 1990, some 163,000 more than those listed on the official tribal roll.

One Navajo spokesman attributed the rising numbers to "general awareness and pride," and to films like Kevin Costner's *Dances with Wolves*, discussed later in this chapter, which made many Americans eager to claim Indian blood.[4] Whatever the specific cause, the formerly common aversion to, even shame of, Indian roots has given way to an avid yearning for such genealogical connections. People are ferreting around in attics and questioning relatives, in search of Indian ancestors. Whenever the claim can be made plausibly, they increasingly choose to see themselves as Indians and to identify with Native values.

Throughout the history of encounters between Europeans and Indians in the Americas, views of Indians have varied substantially among whites, according to circumstances. The Indian as "noble savage" was a commonplace in eighteenth- and early nineteenth-century thought and was related to the earlier view of the New World as the Garden of Eden; historically, it also coincided with various political alliances between Indians, the French, and the British up through 1812.[5] But later in the nineteenth century, as Indians mounted wide-scale resistance to usurpation of their lands, particularly in the Plains states, any idealization was increasingly obscured by competing images of "murderous, rampaging Indians" who were deemed "good" only when "dead."[6] Around 1900, once the Indians were fully conquered, favorable views emerged once more, although prejudice and derogatory images persisted too. The resurgence of these favorable views coincided with America's and Europe's turn towards the primitive as a source of renewed health and power (see the Introduction).

What we are seeing now is the apotheosis of this process, as more and more Americans, both whites and Natives, are coming to value certain elements of traditional Indian life: close family ties, flexible and complementary gender roles, spirituality, and harmonious interdependence with animals and the land. This idealized, lyrical view of Indian life clearly represents for those who embrace it a cure for some of the ills of contemporary culture in the United States: the breakdown of families, environmental degradation, and a popular perception that the gulf separating the sexes is of an interplanetary magnitude—I allude to one best seller that locates men on Mars and women on Venus. The fear and loathing of the Indian have been supplanted by a growing fascination with and valuation of Indian ways.

If I had to set a single date for the full emergence of these lyrical views, it would probably be 1970, around the time of the Alcatraz uprising, the seizing of Wounded Knee, and the successful entry of Native Americans into courts of law.[7] At Wounded Knee, South Dakota, a small group of militant Indians seized control of a church in order to voice Indian grievances and urge that Indians work "outside the system" for Indian sovereignty rather than manipulate political structures that had been created by whites. They were armed only with hunting rifles. U.S. helicopters and troops encircled the church. Media images of the event recalled the murderous force that the federal government had marshalled against Indians in the past. The effect was to make Americans more aware of Indian versions of U.S. history—to feel, in a word, "guilty" for massacres like the one that had taken place at Wounded Knee in 1890, which now threatened to repeat itself.

At Alcatraz, a group of Indians seized control of the island in San Francisco Bay, once the site of a notorious prison. They issued a parodic Declaration of Independence and, wearing traditional headbands and blankets along with jeans and other "all-American" clothing, posed for photographs in front of signs that had been altered from "United States Property" to "United Indian Property."[8] Blurring tribal distinctions, the Indians were advancing a conglomerate, generalized idea of "Indianness"—and a single, unified political interest. By manipulating symbols of "Americanness" (the jeans) and "Indianness" (the headbands, the blankets), conflating the two, they were affirming both their Indianness and their entitlement to the rights and privileges enjoyed by other Americans. Such demonstrations allowed Indians to tap into the energies of youth movements and the civil rights struggle; they also constructed a common identity that could be shared by people across tribes and by people of mixed blood.

In general, the symbols chosen to represent "Indianness" (feathered headdresses, the Sun Dance, and so on) tended to be drawn from particular groups, like the Lakota Sioux and other Plains Indians. Others, like the Eastern Cherokee, might then, for strategic ends, adopt Plains Indian attributes that were not previously part of their cultures.[9] "Indianness" came to be regarded as a unified identity and a form of general property belonging to all Indians and part-Indians. Given the dynamics of American culture, it was perhaps only a matter of time before some would add, "Does it not, then, as part of U.S. culture, belong to *all* Americans?"

At the same time that Indianness was reclaiming its lost positive associations, whiteness was acquiring some rather undesirable ones. White America seemed a culpable actor in many national events around 1970; these included the civil rights movement; political assassinations; Attica; the women's movement; Vietnam; the proliferation of pesticides and other pollutants; the threat of nuclear accidents. But if I had to isolate a single concern that validated the Indian perspective and made the white perspective suspect, it would be, more than anything else, the spoliation of the earth. Changing attitudes towards the land was breeding deep ecological anxiety.[10] The United States, it seemed, was now leading the way down the wrong path. It needed to return to a more harmonious interdependence with nature, perceived to be typical in traditional Indian life. Nostalgia for Indians became an important part of a more generalized anxiety about survival itself.

In 1970, N. Scott Momaday published "An American Land Ethic" in the Sierra Club magazine.[11] It helped to crystallize an idea that had been gaining currency for some time in the United States: that Indians treat the land respectfully and that white America must begin to treat it that way too. Momaday personified the Indians' ecological energies in the figure of Ko-sahn, an aged female seer. Although Indian religions include many female deities (Earth, Sky, Water, and Corn Mothers), Momaday specifically and cannily built upon clichés of "Mother Earth."[12] "In Ko-sahn and in her people we have always had the example of a deep, ethical regard for the land," Momaday wrote. So "we Americans must come again to a moral comprehension of the earth and air. We must live according to the principle of a land ethic. The alternative is that we shall not live at all."[13] Within this constellation of ideas, the politics of Momaday's "we" is especially intriguing because it links Indians and whites together in the idea of a collective, environmentally responsible American.

The Navajo spokesman who credited Costner's film with raising the number of self-identifying Indians in the United States may have exaggerated a bit: the movies have reflected other causes of nostalgia for traditional ways. Nevertheless, media images of Indians have played an important role in the emergence of Indian pride and white sympathy for Indians. *Dances with Wolves* and other films, like the 1992 remake of *The Last of the Mohicans,* have mirrored changing cultural perspectives and contributed to the change. These two films have some telling similarities: they are both set in the context of wars that changed the course of American history (the aftermath of the Civil War in *Dances;* the French and Indian Wars in *Mohicans*); they both contain love plots but focus on male characters more than females; they both exist as published novels (*Dances with Wolves,* by Michael Blake; *The Last of the Mohicans,* James Fenimore Cooper's classic). Most of all, both are filmed in an "epic" style that emphasizes the gorgeous landscape and the white encounter with Indians as crucial to American identity. They are highly visible symbols of changing ideas about both Native Americans and American whites.

In these films, images of Indians and images of whites initially contrast, but not because the films emphasize the derogatory stereotypes of Indians once common in Westerns. Instead, by and large, it is the whites who are negatively stereotyped as being duplicitous and less attuned to natural harmony than the Indians. The films lovingly display nature as an eternal, boundaryless, oceanic phenomenon and show how Indians "intuitively" live in accord with the earth. Equally important for the films' overall effect, they also show that Indians know how to die with respect for and acceptance of the awesome power of oceanic nature. Indians mediate between the land and white people. Oceanic harmony with nature is a crucial theme positioning Indians as spiritual teachers and guides.

But as the films unfold, the categories of "Indian" and "white" get blurred in surprising ways. Both these films include white men and women who are coded "Indian," either by adoption and long acculturation, or else by their instinctive sympathies. These whites share the Native Americans' strong, empathetic response to nature. What's more, and very important, the whites are allowed to stand at the movie's end as the inheritors and perpetuators of Indian ways after the actual Indians are dead or as good as dead. The result is curious: the films initially define Indians as different from whites, but then show how the best among the whites think and feel like Indians. Bad white people usurp the Indians' physical space; but good whites move into their mental and spiritual space. And once whites occupy the space close to nature that has been coded as "Indian," actual Indians have nowhere to go but off into the proverbial sunset. The films operate, then, by sleight of hand. They seem to be entirely favorable to Natives, eschewing negative stereotypes. But the positive stereotypes they generate instead—about ecologically wise Indians who face death stoically—are surprisingly close to older, derogatory views: for example, General Sheridan's linking of "good Indians" and "death."

Dances was by far the more important and successful of these films, winner of the 1990 Academy Award for Best Motion Picture. But *Mohicans* is no less significant as the latest version of James Fenimore Cooper's novel, which, ever since its publication in 1826, has been a locus classicus of conflicting American attitudes towards Indians. Both these films and others on comparable themes are, then, important documents in relation to America's changing image of Indians and of the nation itself. I shall now take a closer look at how the patterns they share are realized in each, after which I will return to the more general issue of the new American Indian and new American white.

Dances with Wolves

In one of the most moving moments in *Dances with Wolves,* the female heroine is asked for the first time in many years to speak English. She remembers the last time she spoke it—at a picnic interrupted by some marauding Pawnee. English left her world as her father sank to the ground, an Indian hatchet buried in his back. The last thing she remembers is her mother crying "Christine," her name, never again uttered in the film since the Sioux call her Stands with a Fist. She responds, "Mommy," in her recollection, but perhaps not at the time. For at the actual moment, she was running away, out onto the prairie, a small child, not technically abandoned but in effect abandoned all the same.

That small body, singularly bereft, is a key image in *Dances with Wolves.* It signals the contrast between being alone, being lonely, and being with "the people," as the Sioux call themselves. "Christine" existed as part of a family that is now gone. As an isolated body running on the Plains, she is at a point of transition—scared and lonely, belonging to no one, no longer able to respond to her name. As Stands with a Fist, she is a brave and contented member of her tribe. I begin with "Christine's" history because it is important to the film as a whole: it echoes the main plot, in which the hero moves from isolation at Fort Cedric as Lt. John Dunbar to a new life with the Sioux as Dances with Wolves.

The first page of the novel *Dances with Wolves*, by Michael Blake, includes the words "This is religious."[14] That is Dunbar's response to "The great cloudless sky. The rolling ocean of grass." As he moves into the West, Dunbar compares prairie to ocean: he perceives nature in oceanic terms as vast and spiritual; disillusioned by "civilized" life, he is open to and eager for what he sees in the land.

The film is extremely effective in its evocation of nature as eternal. It is equally good at contrasting the expansiveness of nature—the meaning of the frontier in the film—with the white man's boxed-in life. Dunbar is looking for an escape from the box, but he mostly lacks positive human models until he glimpses the majestic Sioux.[15]

Riding white horses, hair fluttering in the breeze, the Sioux embody masculine, shamanic power. The first Lakota Sioux Dunbar befriends, Kicking Bird, is in fact a "holy man," revered as a thinker and seer by his people. Under the tutelage of Kicking Bird, Dunbar chooses a new future.

When Dunbar first witnesses scenes of Indian life, as the sun sets magnificently in the background, the hero says, in a voice-over, that whites are wrong about Indians. They are not "beggars and thieves." In fact, he says, he has never known a people so devoted "to family" and "to each other" as the Sioux. So devoted—he pauses, straining for the word—"to *harmony*." After the buffalo hunt, back at Fort Cedric, Dunbar builds a huge fire and dances around it, Indian style. Away from the Lakota, he feels a sense of loneliness he has never felt before.

More and more, Dunbar comes to recognize that the life he seeks exists among the Sioux, a people whose very existence is threatened by the advance of whiteness, of which he is the first wave. Dunbar is in a quandary: he loves the Sioux, but he knows that their civilization is doomed. He wants to share their last moments, to make them last. He will save the Sioux if he can (as it turns out, he can't). But he also decides to do the next best thing, something that is completely within his power: he decides to preserve the memory of the pre-contact Lakota Sioux in a detailed, illustrated journal. By 1865, when hideously brutal "reinforcements" have arrived at Fort Cedric, the handwriting is on the wall for the Plains Indians—and the message isn't good. Dunbar's journal bears witness to what we all know is about to end. It painstakingly records his early contacts with the Lakota, in the manner of early explorers and artists.

Men like Dunbar, who "went Indian" or who drew, wrote, or painted in the West, are not unknown in actual history. J. W. Powell is one example; Isak Dinesen's father is another. Some pioneers left journals in which their impressions of Indians were at odds with the typically negative views of settlers.[16] So it may not matter that "John Dunbar" did not exist in history; there were enough actual antecedents to make the journal a perfectly plausible plot element. The audience is asked to treat it as a "real" record of the Lakota world, written by someone of Dunbar's intelligence and goodness, before the white man came—although Dunbar is himself, of course, a white man.

Near the movie's end, Dunbar, who now refers to himself by his Indian name, Dances with Wolves, returns to the fort when he realizes he has forgotten his journal. Just at that moment, he is captured by brutal soldiers who see him as a traitor. The soldiers rip out the journal's pages and use them as toilet paper. They taunt Dunbar and beat him bloody. Finally, the Sioux rescue Dunbar at a river. His notebook floats downstream, but it reappears near the end of the movie, when a young Indian named Smiles a Lot returns it to its author, his friend: this good Indian has intuitively sensed the book's preciousness, its power to preserve a vanishing past.

The emphasis on the journal works well in the film, though it may sound overly contrived here, in isolation. That emphasis anticipates, I think, both the audience's faith in the written word and its intense desire to believe in the reality of a Lieutenant Dunbar and an alternative to the conventional white man's history of the West, in which Indians represent a terrifying Other. The film cultivates this desire through a prolonged suspension of the audience between the mad white world and the ordered world of the Sioux, between 1863 and the surrender of the last free Sioux in 1878. The suspension lasts some three hours, twice as long as the average movie. In that time, our assumptions and sensibilities are transformed along with Dunbar's. The movie plants Dunbar in what is at first a confusing paradise. Language, customs, and values are alien. It introduces him and the audience to the Lakota gradually, allowing both to know and love them.[17] We end with the threat of paradise being lost. Yet we remain suspended in a world of possibilities. Dunbar and Christine wend their solitary way back to the white world in the hope that reason and logic may appease the attackers.[18] The vengeful soldiers arrive at a camp—but which camp isn't clear: Dunbar's? One the Sioux made on the way to their home for the winter? The soldiers are on the trail. Will the Sioux village be destroyed within a matter of days? Or have the Sioux decided to move, at Dunbar's urging, to a safer place, one the soldiers won't be able to find? The ambiguity and the forestalling of catastrophe at the end of the movie are only slightly comforting, for the threat of bloody massacre looms, perhaps only ten minutes beyond the point in time at which the movie ends.

The last shots in the film are of Dunbar and his wife riding away, intercut with some of Pawnee scouts, working for the soldiers. Dances with Wolves and Stands with a Fist are tiny figures whose bodies blend into nature as they traverse it, suggesting many meanings. On the one hand, the couple, leaving a beloved place, evoke Adam and Eve. On the other, because they are fleeing enemies on horseback, they evoke Joseph and the pregnant Mary. Either way, Dances with Wolves and his wife, who is pregnant like Mary, have become an Ur-nuclear family unit, an "Indian" projectile into a "white" future.

But their tiny bodies also evoke a harmony with their surroundings. They represent everything that Indians experience, now endangered by the encroachment of whites. The final long shot ("the big picture") means to take the edge off the catastrophe that we know awaits the Sioux, despite the film's ambiguous ending. It means to suggest that all of the individual characters are insignificant in the context of the ongoing cycle of life and of nature: that's what Dances with Wolves, Stands with a Fist, and the Lakota understand; and that understanding is what makes the Indians so precious, so worthy of saving.

A caption tells us that thirteen years later the last free Sioux surrendered in South Dakota. Whether this camp was spared doesn't ultimately matter, though it matters a great deal to the audience now. The bloody end, even if avoided at this moment, is very near. The Sioux will survive only in patches, perhaps most decisively in the persons of Dunbar and Christine—Dances with Wolves and Stands with a Fist—and their heirs. The movie is entirely typical of how popular culture views the relationship between whites and Native Americans today. It wants to reimagine Indian history and to claim that whites are the true heirs to Indian culture, not just its destroyers.

The Last of the Mohicans

Michael Mann's *The Last of the Mohicans* (1992) reimagines the history of Indians and whites at a third or fourth remove from the reality it represents. It alters and retells Cooper's classic novel (itself completely fictional) and earlier filmed versions.[19] In a National Public Radio interview, Mann was very conscious of the need for fidelity to history and boasted of representing conditions on New York's frontier in 1757 more accurately than either Cooper or the earlier films had. He was especially proud of showing how whites and Indians "interacted" on the frontier—for example, playing a kind of "football" together in the marketplace. He also boasted about using actual Indians to play Chingachgook and Uncas, although one might argue that these two characters are less important in Mann's version of the story than in others.

In Mann's film, whites are not so much cruel and sinister as they are victims of their own culture. They are locked into self-destructive attitudes and hierarchies. Near the top of the heap are British and French officers like Munro and Montcalm. We sense that they are honorable men who would prefer to avoid wholesale slaughter but are forced to behave dishonorably by the need to win at any cost. Munro's commander, for example, has promised the frontiersmen that they can leave his army should they need to protect their families. But (as Munro knows when he refuses to release the men) the commander never intended to keep his word if it was inconvenient to do so. In the same way, Montcalm would never directly order the massacre of the British, who have been promised a safe retreat from the fort; but he tacitly allows Magua, the evil Huron who hates the British, to do the deed. Such slaughter not only allows the "savages" to collect booty and scalps; it guarantees that the British will not live to fight against the French another day. "The system," it seems, does not allow for honorable men.

Below Munro and Montcalm are junior officers, like Duncan. He too is an honorable man, as is clear from his gallantry towards Munro's daughters and his noble self-sacrifice near the end of the film, when he allows himself to suffer and die instead of Hawkeye. But while Duncan is in the fort, being ambitious, he doesn't hesitate to support his commanding officers' lies. Below them in the social hierarchy are the officers' women, then the ordinary soldiers, the frontiersmen, and their wives. Whites living on the frontier often came to the colonies as indentured servants; many are now free, but under colonial government are still subject to the officers' whims and power. The women are hemmed in and corseted: by hard work on the farm, if they are lower class; by fashion and convention, if their station is higher. Near the beginning of the film, Cora wears a wasp-waisted dress and a rigid hat, below which her eyes dart out, restlessly. She serves tea as a lady should, but her energy flashes through, although she can express it only in her willful insistence that she be free to choose her own mate.

These whites are not unsympathetic like those in *Dances with Wolves*. But they are prisoners, without knowing it—locked into codes of conduct and ways of life that are mercenary and repressive. Set apart from nature by their ridiculous clothing: "Redcoats" amid the glorious green of the North American forest. With few exceptions, the film registers them as petty markers and ciphers, interchangeable and unimportant. Other than Hawkeye and Cora, every white person in the film is bound for a gory death, but within the context of the film, this fact generates surprisingly little pathos. The deaths may be terrifying, but they are not in the least bit depressing. Their emotional potential is neutralized or aborted by the film's central preoccupation: nature. It is a reality Hawkeye understands from the start and Cora comes to appreciate. The audience is asked to identify almost totally with them.

In this film, Hawkeye is supposed to be James Fenimore Cooper's Natty Bumppo. But in the novel, Hawkeye is a middle-aged, craggy, Daniel Boone, bachelor type. Mann's Hawkeye looks and acts more like Uncas, the young Mohican brave who is Chingachgook's son in the novel. In fact, according to the film, Hawkeye, although white by birth, was adopted as a child by Chingachgook and raised as Uncas' brother.

He personifies and articulates the Indian point of view. He is a man of action capable, if provoked, of great violence. But Hawkeye also resembles Kicking Bird in *Dances with Wolves.* He embodies wisdom, thoughtfulness, and gentleness; most of all, he embodies the ideal of oneness with nature. These crucial changes in Hawkeye's character are not the only telling alterations Mann makes to Cooper's novel. But the film's strength is not fidelity to the book or even to history, as the director boasted. Instead, it is fidelity to a certain feeling about nature understood to be central to Indian culture.

Within the film's first few minutes, director Mann presents what I take to be the defining shot, one that encapsulates the story he wishes to tell. Three men—Hawkeye, Uncas, and Chingachgook—are running through a tall, dense forest, swift as the deer they are stalking. The men are quiet, surefooted, focused, intense. They negotiate the landscape intuitively; they read signs in the earth, in the sky, in the waters.

Among the characters, the Indians know nature's power from the beginning. They don't need to be reminded. As a result, they don't sentimentalize their lives or fear death—though they try to live as long as they can. The scene at the beginning in which Uncas, Chingachgook, and Hawkeye kill a deer is emblematic of this ethos, which whites today ascribe with deep admiration to Indians. The three men kill the animal but thank it for supplying food and honor it in prayer: the deer's death is seen as part of its destiny, appropriate to the natural course of things. The Indians and Indian-like characters (such as Hawkeye) know the inevitability of nature and death. Most of the whites have to learn this lesson gradually, if they learn it at all.

Of the European whites, Cora is the most able to learn. When she is first being transported to her father's fort, she glances with thrilled apprehension into the forest and, in a moment of subliminal suggestion, catches sight of the glowing eyes of a fox—a symbol of sexual awakening. The next moment, the forest erupts with the whoops of a war party, and the first of the massacres so central to the film takes place. Nature and violence are close-up and personal. Nature is indifferent to the violence. It is beautiful before violence erupts. It is equally beautiful once the muskets have stopped firing and the war clubs have stopped beating down on the hapless heads of the British soldiers—all dressed up to die, according to the film's logic.

The realism of the film's massacres has been singled out as the film's major accomplishment by reviewers apparently mesmerized by the clubbing, scalping, and gore. But the film's central preoccupation and true originality really have more to do with Hawkeye, who is a preternatural force and symbolizes the film's alliance of Indianness and nature. He whirls with mysterious intent through the chaos, invincible and in control. He is drawn to Cora almost *because* she is the focus of Magua's hatred, the lure for violence. Violence looses the erotic; both are powers of nature and manifestations of nature's majesty. Once Hawkeye protects Cora from violence, all his energy is directed towards her. They become a dyad in the film: dark long-haired man/dark long-haired woman. Meant for each other, like twins separated at birth, freed from the curse of incest. They reminded me of Cathy and Heathcliff in Emily Brontë's *Wuthering Heights*—but no longer star-crossed, no longer hemmed in by social conventions.

Cora and Hawkeye fall in love in a series of brief conversational exchanges, under the threat of violence and amid the lure of nature. They crouch in a graveyard, which as a sacred site affords them temporary protection from Magua's Hurons. They gaze at the sky and talk about how the stars are spirits of departed loved ones. They talk about social class and the perilous realities of life on the frontier as Hawkeye sees them, and as Cora is quickly coming to see them. She had not dreamed, Cora says throatily, how the frontier would stir her blood. Their relationship recalls Dunbar's with Stands with a Fist, except that in this film the male character does all the teaching.

Hawkeye encourages Cora's contempt for white social norms and her predilection for the Indians' law of nature. He tells her that the English and French officers treat the pioneers as badly as they treat Indians. In fact, he says, Indians and pioneers have had to learn to work together on the frontier in order to survive. That's why Chingachgook and Uncas speak English as well as Delaware, why they can sit at a pioneer family's table as easily as they pray to the departed spirit of a deer they have slain. The pioneers are poor whites willing to risk death for a piece of land and for a degree of independence they can't have in the towns; that's why Hawkeye has befriended them. Cora takes it all in. She becomes a class rebel.

The film's most dramatic love scene, while improbable, is dazzling all the same. Even in a frontier fort on the brink of destruction, a man of

Hawkeye's class would not likely be able simply to whisk the British colonel's daughter off into the shadows. But the darkly lit scene drips with an eroticism of surrender—hers to him, and his to her—that transcends social reality. Hawkeye meets Cora's eye, asks her permission silently; then he swoops in, kissing her lips and neck. Cora melts into his arms, is lifted up in them—the rest is left to our imagination. In an apparently postcoital embrace, the characters emerge from the love scene bonded. However unlikely within the confines of a British fort, this union is credible because the only bonds the film validates are those to nature.

At the climax of *The Last of the Mohicans,* towards which the film forcefully moves, nature once again provides the right, the only setting. We are out of the forest now, on a mountain, but not a green one that offers lofty, leafy vistas. It's a rocky place, a hard place, a ledge of death and daring. Hawkeye has rescued Cora from Magua once more—for good, this time. But Magua still has Alice, her younger sister, and Uncas, by now Alice's protector, is in hot pursuit. It may seem wrong that the audience is asked to focus on Alice and Uncas at the end of a film in which Hawkeye and Cora are the real show. But this version of the story, like Cooper's novel, depends heavily on the way it ends to establish its meanings. In this film, the shift to Alice and Uncas is important.

In *The Last of the Mohicans,* both the novel and the film, Alice represents pure "whiteness" and Uncas represents unalloyed "Indianness." The film needs to focus on them almost to exorcise the strict opposition they represent, before the stage is free for Hawkeye and Cora, who represent neither pure whiteness nor pure Indianness, but a synthesis. In the movie, Alice is not just young, conventional, and shy (as in the novel)—she's almost numb. After the first half hour, she says hardly anything at all and is increasingly debilitated by rough-and-tumble circumstances. Cora's soul is stirred by nature and violence and especially by the interplay of the two. Alice's is blasted by it. Although both women wear dresses throughout the film, by the end Cora looks large, strapping, and dishevelled, like an Amazon—or, more to the point, like an Indian. Alice looks proper and demure in a dimity print—as if she had been ripped away from the tea parties that are her native habitat. Once she enters the wilderness, Alice's eyes widen as she grows increasingly terrified, clinging ever more tightly to Cora. But after they leave Fort William Henry, Cora is in Hawkeye's arms, and no longer as available for Alice. Into this emotional void rushes the gentle Uncas. In the waterfall scene, when Magua has them trapped, it's Uncas who comforts the distraught Alice, freeing Cora to be with Hawkeye. By the time Uncas dashes off ahead of Chingachgook and Hawkeye to rescue Alice, I think we are to understand that he is in love— and that his attraction to Alice will quite literally be the death of him.

It's not clear that Alice is thinking about much of anything at this point. But she knows that Uncas is her new protector, a surrogate Cora. So when Uncas faces off alone against the Hurons, she believes that her rescue is imminent. Uncas kills one Huron, then another. But finally, as the action goes into slow motion, he grapples with Magua, who bloodies him, then slits his throat and pushes him off a precipice with casual indifference.

In the scuffle, Alice has moved to the edge of the cliff. Magua sees that his war prize is in danger and brusquely gestures Alice towards him. The camera focuses on Alice's face, the action still proceeding in slow motion. She looks at Magua, then looks back over her shoulder at the abyss into which Uncas was dropped, then back at Magua. In a flash, but with a lassitude that minimizes a sense of volition, she makes her choice, tossing herself into the abyss. The film shows a shot of her falling. Then Cora's horrified face as she watches from nearby. Then Magua, who doesn't even blink. A master of death, he wouldn't. He's as stony as the mountain—one side of nature, personified.

This is a spectacular moment. I say that even though—judged against Cooper's novel—Mann has gotten the wrong corpses into the abyss and totally corrupted the intended ending. In the novel, Uncas and Cora die. In this version, Uncas and Alice are sacrificed so that Cora and Hawkeye (who is, remember, partly based on the novel's Uncas) may survive. "Indianness" and "whiteness" are finished as pure, mutually exclusive cate gories. All that is left is a blending of the two. The film ends with Chingachgook, Hawkeye, and Cora performing an Indian funeral ablution against a gorgeous blue horizon. Chingachgook is the last of the Mohicans; but he's off to the side, waiting to die not far beyond the end point of the film's time frame. Still, the film has established a subversive logic according to which he's not really the last Mohican at all. Hawkeye, Chingachgook's adopted son, actually counts as a Mohican too. And as the movie makes clear, he is bound to go on and reproduce with Cora. Together, they will embody, and pass on, Indian ways. We end, then, with the same pattern as in *Dances with Wolves:* Indians are doomed;

whites become like Indians and inherit their culture—though they remain, biologically, "white." The film fully expects the audience to see this as an acceptable compromise, perhaps even as a fitting outcome.

In fact, the ending makes clear why Mann as director had to tinker so radically with the characters in Cooper's novel. Cooper follows Sir Walter Scott's formula for historical fiction. In Scott, the lackluster (usually blond and usually English) hero and heroine love each other and survive to reproduce the English bourgeois lifestyle; but the daring, exotic, dark hero and heroine (often, like the Munros, Scots) die off. In the novel, Uncas loves Cora and Duncan loves Alice. Hawkeye, as I've already said, isn't involved in the love plots at all. In the novel, there are hints that Cora is of mixed blood (her mother was West Indian, with some African ancestry), so that both she and Uncas represent a threat to emerging white Anglo-American identity. Cooper's formula via Scott decrees that Uncas and Cora, glamorous and attractive as they are, have to die. In Cooper's novel, only dull Alice and Duncan will survive to marry and reproduce the English middle way.

In the movie, both Duncan and Hawkeye love Cora. Cora's mixed blood is suppressed entirely as a theme. As the story develops, it becomes increasingly uncertain to readers of Cooper's novel who's going to be left alive at the end. But once Duncan, Alice, and Uncas die, Mann's logic becomes clear. Cooper's novel is a romance that flirts with miscegenation, but ultimately its logic requires that the race-crossed lovers must die. Mann's movie is a celebration not of the biological crossing of races (Hawkeye and Cora are both, after all, white) but of emotional and cultural crossing. Like *Dances with Wolves*, it shows how whites can be like Indians without actually being Indians. Indeed, it suggests that whites can inherit not only the Indians' land but their spiritual values as well.

Whose Culture Is It Anyhow?

The patterns I have been tracing extend beyond these two films. There have been many examples, especially since 1970, of lyricized views of Indians, and of whites who become heirs to Indian culture. In John

Boorman's *The Emerald Forest* (1985), for example, an engineer's son, kidnapped by Amazon Indians, grows up very happily to be a Jaguar shaman who no longer wants to live among whites. The "termite people" is what these Indians call whites, whom they see as unsmiling and destructive to the "universe" of the rain forest. Tomei, the engineer's son, becomes the leader of his group and is one of the few surviving males left to maintain Indian culture at the movie's end. He and his father destroy the dam the father helped build. Then Tomei (with his Amazon Indian wife) vanishes once more into the rain forest.

The twelve-part television miniseries of James A. Michener's *Centennial* (first broadcast in 1978 and shown several times since) similarly focuses on white men who understand Indian ways. These men speak up for Indians and for the environment. And, often, these champions of Indians either marry Indian women or are the offspring of mixed marriages. The series' plot suggests that, overall, whites threaten Indian culture. But some whites, especially these men, have an alternative value system, much like the Indians' own. What is more, only these white men are presented as effective spokespeople for Indian values in the modern world.

More recently, in Edward Zwick's *Legends of the Fall* (1995) the character Tristan (played by Brad Pitt) is more Indian than any of the actual Indians in the film. He wrestles with a bear who is his special totem; he takes the scalps of enemies; he has a rapport with nature and a hunger for "the primitive," a category that in this film includes not only Indians but Polynesians and Africans as well. Tristan is the only one of three young men in the film to reproduce, not surprisingly with a woman who is herself half Indian. The film tends to ignore his young daughter, and kills off his Indian wife, but it shows brief scenes of his son being educated into Indian ways by the wise old Indian who narrates the film. As in the other examples, the film *Legends* asserts that Indian values are most effectively perpetuated through white men. At the logical extreme, whites *are* Indians, either by adoption, by "blood," or by sufficiently strong sympathies.

There is no single "Indian" reaction to films like these. Indians always have been an extremely diverse group, in terms of languages and social customs.[20] Today, there is considerable variation with respect to extent of assimilation into white culture, level of formal education, and interest in pursuing traditional ways. But many Indians have voiced anxieties about white identification with Indian cultures such as these films express. While these dramas teach white Americans about genocide against Indians and generally encourage sympathy for Indians and support for environmental causes, they also raise questions of cultural appropriation analogous to those involved in the original seizure of Indian lands. Viewing these circumstances in the harshest light, John Lavelle, a Santee Sioux who directs the Center for Support and Protection of Indian Religions and Indigenous Traditions, says, "This is the final phase of genocide. First whites took the land and all that was physical. Now they're going after what is intangible."[21]

Media images of Indians these days tend to be overwhelmingly favorable. But they still raise questions about who should control Indian culture and its future. When movie whites become like Indians, everyone cheers what seems like an ennobling, spiritual transformation. But the new American white has chosen a model resembling a certain image of Indianness, a composite of stereotypes that are positive, but stereotypes all the same. It's a game of imitation that depends on actual Indians conforming to their assigned, if noble, image.

But what happens when real Indians see themselves differently from the way much of white America does? What happens when the lives of modern Indians differ substantially from the "oneness with earth" and mystical spirituality that films portray? What happens if Indians reject the role of this kind of American Indian? Doesn't the game end then for white and Indian alike?

Favorable Images/New Clichés

In late twentieth-century popular culture, Indians are commonly seen as ecologically wise and in touch with Mother Earth. They sell the best butter (for Land O' Lakes); they bemoan the pollution of the environment. Grandfathers instruct lads in the care of the countryside and its resources. This touching scene almost always takes place atop mountains or mesas, with shots of oceanic nature stretching into the distance. It is commonly believed that, like Chief Seattle, whose remarks were once widely cited by environmentalists, neither the grandfathers nor the lads would ever sell the land, the body of their Mother.

Most people see these attitudes as belonging to Native Americans by long and invariable cultural tradition. But it is extremely difficult, and perhaps impossible, to reconstruct the value systems of Indians from the remote past.[22] Records of ancient Indian cultures, when they exist at all, often are comprehensible only to experts, many of whom are more eager to bolster than to revise their models of Indian cultures. What is more, the whole issue of "change" with regard to Native Americans (and other so-called primitives) is extremely vexed. While it is true that traditional societies may resist the incursion of modern cultures in an act of self-preservation, there is also the cliché that "primitives" are people "without history" who "never change." This cliché has perpetuated ideas of European superiority to Others. Overturning it requires recognizing that over thousands of years, some change is likely within any group.

All of these factors complicate the process of evaluating specific evidence. Chief Seattle, for example, was supposed to have made his speech about not selling the body of his Mother in response to the encroachments of a railroad. By that time, Indians would have had ample evidence of what happened when whites sought their land; they would have known enough about whites to use their preconceptions to their own advantage. Chief Seattle's speech is as likely to have been a rhetorical, political tactic as much as a statement of Indian creed. But, in fact, it apparently never took place. In 1992, *The New York Times* reported that the speech was a hoax, written in the 1970s by a Texas environmentalist. Almost no one, Indian or white, wanted to believe that was true.[23]

Still, there is ample evidence that Indians did not always behave in ways that conform with current notions of ecology and balance. For example, fossils from the Pleistocene era, along the path Indians followed when they are thought to have migrated from Asia to Mexico, show that whole species of animals, including mastodons, became extinct around the time of the migrations. Whether overhunting, environmental change, or some combination was responsible remains in dispute. But some examples of species depredation are incontrovertible: at sites such as Smashed Buffalo Head in Canada, huge numbers of buffalo, far more than were needed for food or hides, were ritually lured to their death. Indians followed a system of rules and principles that was perhaps profoundly spiritual. But contemporary notions of ecology may have been foreign to many Indian systems of thought until contact with Europeans created new problems of scarcity (a classic example is the overhunting of beaver for the fur trade).[24] It seems likely that Indians learned how to treat nature through experience, by trial and error. They encountered bad effects from certain practices, such as overfarming and overhunting. Then, because they were dependent on the environment, they tended to alter their practices in a manner that today seems ecologically sound.[25] The idea of the Indian as ecologist is a good example of a cliché with some basis in truth which has been useful to both Indians and whites. Certainly, it has been a key factor in fostering the rehabilitation of white views of Indians.

Yet today the idea of the Indian as ecologist may suit some whites more than it does some Indians. It may even be a factor in whites' resistance to change and differences among Indians. Some whites expect Indians to remain models of specific "traditional" values. But not all Indians want perfect continuity with the past. To cite one recent instance, Indians now sometimes reclaim the land in order to build gambling casinos prohibited by state law outside of reservations. Sometimes, casinos are a response to decreased government funding—a way to maintain needed social services. But some casinos have made Indians more prosperous now "than at any time in generations, perhaps since whites arrived."[26] The idea of Indians owning valuable property—and using it to create a mini Las Vegas—has attracted an unusual amount of attention in the press, not much of it favorable. Some Indians see gambling as a means by which whites can dupe Indians and eventually disinherit them:[27] "the new buffalo economy," they call gambling, dismissively.

There is a hidden critique in much of the extensive media coverage of the casinos, an assumption that Indians should not be engaged in these kinds of activities, which are based on economic self-interest and participation in the life of the nation within which they seek separate, "sovereign" status. The attitude of white America seems to be this: if "they" (the Indians) want money, just like we do, why should we feel guilty, regard them as separate "nations," and give them special rights? Whites want to embrace the romantic images of Indians they see at the movies;

but they're as unwilling as ever for real Indians to step outside the territories whites designate for them.

As we approach the twenty-first century, the key issue for testing this question is likely to be not the casinos, but the storage of nuclear waste. The same Supreme Court ruling allowing Indians to ignore state gambling laws suggested that state environmental laws would be void on the land of "sovereign" Indian nations. In the West, where large tracts of land are still available to a few tribes (the Apache, the Navajo, and the Lakota, for example), some Indians are actively pursuing lucrative fees for the storage of nuclear waste. Other Indians protest the move, citing, for example, unexplained instances of cancer on the reservation from previous deposits. The issue has created an uproar, pitting white environmentalists against Native Americans and Natives against each other.[28]

At the movies, and in other popular phenomena today—including the mythopoetic men's movement and the New Age (the subjects of the next two chapters)—it seems ennobling for whites to become like Indians. This is so when "Indian" is equated with devotion to family, community, the land, and spirituality. But the reverse developmental pattern—one in which Indians might become interested in profit and otherwise become more and more like "whites"—seems substantially less appealing. The classic dynamic of defining the self through the Other requires that the Other remain a stable entity. Once, whites needed Indians as "savages" to justify the appropriation of their land. Now whites need Indians as "ecologists" to point the way to saving the land for the benefit of all Americans. When Indians refuse to be "ecologists," to conform to their refurbished positive stereotype, the basis for a new white American identity is undercut. The wars between whites and Indians may have ended in movies like *Dances with Wolves,* but there are still many border skirmishes ahead.

CHAPTER SEVEN

Of Drums and Men

A group of men sits around a fire, beating drums and singing in unison. African masks hang from surrounding trees. A man wearing a long feathered headdress dances around the fire. When he stops dancing, he begins to speak, telling what it is like to be a man, stressing his relationship to his father—what he learned from him, how his father had embodied the spirit of the grandfather and other male ancestors. Then he passes the speaking stick, topped with feathers, to the others around the circle, signalling to them to speak in turn. "I am standing here, at the fire, with my chest bare to the wind. A man enjoying the company of other men, as my father did," says the next man. When he finishes, the circle grunts its collective approval with a resounding "Ho!" and confirms the emotion with more beating of drums.

FIFTEEN YEARS AGO, such a description might have been found only in *National Geographic* or in the script of a B movie about "tribal" peoples. But in the 1990s, such scenes are being played out more commonly. This one might have been witnessed at a contemporary Wildmen's Retreat in Texas or at a meeting of the men's group I encountered in North Carolina. Both are part of the mythopoetic men's movement, which uses stories, myths, and Jungian psychology to define masculine norms and affirm male identity.[1] As a woman, I could not attend such a meeting, but this description is an accurate composite of one based on reported actions, audiotapes and videos of meetings, and the direct quotations of actual male participants.[2]

The meetings to which I had indirect access were attended almost entirely by college-educated, middle- to upper-middle-class white males over thirty. So are the vast majority of others within the mythopoetic men's movement. Yet these meetings draw extensively on Native American traditions (the feathered headdress, the talking stick, the drumming, the putatively Indian "Ho!")—with an occasional touch from Africa, such as the masks hanging from the trees. Other meetings draw more freely on African traditions, with songs sung in Swahili and storytelling by African men who serve as consultants to the movement in the United States. The agenda of men's movement meetings can vary considerably, including self-help sessions or poetry readings. But the evocation of "tribal" materials is pervasive, even when accompanied (as it sometimes is) by joking reminders that the men are not really Africans or Indians. Here, then, is one concrete manifestation of the current idealized, lyrical view of Native Americans (see Chapter Six). In this context, the positive stereotype emphasizes especially ideas about confident masculinity and harmonious relations between generations. Here are whites who want to think of themselves, at least in these particular respects, as being like "tribal" peoples.

I have indicated that these meetings are closed to females. Men, the logic goes, need a space of their own in order to do what the women's movement has done: encourage contact and communication among members of a sex that perceives itself as beleaguered. But the movement tends to go further than this in terms of its feelings towards women: a certain resentment often creeps in. Men, the movement seems to imply, have become overly dependent on women; women have made enormous strides in recent decades, getting ahead of men unfairly. So to learn about the men's movement, I had to rely largely on written descriptions of meetings and on the numerous books, audiotapes, and videos the movement has produced. I was also able to get firsthand reports from the participants I met, often when I gave early versions of this chapter in lecture form.[3]

On the basis of what I have learned, I have identified a certain structure common to mythopoetic men's events. The featured part of the meeting is almost always an inspirational talk by national leaders or, alternatively, statements about masculinity by individual participants who are in charge of that particular gathering (these men are often called "elders," regardless of age). The leader or elder typically begins by describing a problem he faced in life and then the steps he took to overcome it; Robert Bly, author of *Iron John*, for example, has been taped several times describing the shame he felt because of his father's alcoholism and his years of denial and compensation, followed by the need to embrace the father. Later in the program, members of the audience (or "nonelders") are invited to make brief statements or to talk about their own experiences. The format resembles the Twelve-Step method pioneered by Alcoholics Anonymous, a structural principle that informs many other phenomena loosely clustered under the label "New Age" (see Chapter Eight). But at men's movement meetings—and I found this quite significant—discussions of initiation and male identity always seem to be framed by physical activities aimed at promoting a sort of release. These activities include chanting, singing, drumming, and group dancing, and simulate what the men think of as the activities of African or Indian tribes.

Central though it may be to these activities, such communal release is not announced as the movement's most explicit goal. That distinction belongs to *initiation*, the key, as the movement sees it, to achieving male identity. All men's movement writers and organizers—Robert Bly, Michael Meade, Douglas Gillette, as well as the "elders" of small local groups—use or re-create some version of initiation. But only a few (like Malidoma Somé, a consultant to the movement who is from Burkina Faso) have experienced ritual initiation within their own cultures. In fact, whole books and whole conferences have been devoted to the subject and begin with the premise that initiation is what men in the United States need most. Writer Sam Keen (author of *Fire in the Belly*), for example, believes that tribal initiation had almost magical properties because it had

the virtue of being a social event. At a specific time a boy underwent a series of ceremonies after which he was pronounced a
man. Overnight his identification and social status changed. . . .
[T]raditional peoples knew who they were. They had a blueprint
of the world and a guidebook for their passage through time.
They didn't have the kinds of self-doubts we suffer. They didn't
have gender confusion.[4]

"They didn't have the kinds of self-doubts we suffer. They didn't
have gender confusion": the anxieties of men in the movement and their
desire for a healing balm could hardly be more clearly stated. In fact,
what modern society needs most, according to the Jungian psychologists
Robert Moore and Douglas Gillette, are rituals designed to assure male
identity. Society needs, they say,

> to take very seriously the disappearance of ritual processes for ini-
> tiating boys into manhood. In traditional societies there are stan-
> dard definitions of what makes up what we call Boy psychology
> and Man psychology. . . . [I]n tribal societies . . . [t]here are
> carefully constructed rituals for helping the boys of the tribe
> make the transition to manhood.[5]

One might debate the presence or absence of "initiation" rituals in
modern life; senior proms, first cars, military service, fraternities, and
events such as bar mitzvahs or confirmations have all been suggested as
possible correlatives. But it is impossible to deny the feeling on the part
of men that their manhood has never been properly achieved or recognized. Historical circumstance may have prevented one modern ritual
from operating for some. Many men in the movement were in college or
professional school (and hence draft-exempt) during the Vietnam era; as
a result, many never experienced boot camp and military service—two
potential, modern forms of initiation frequently mentioned, sometimes
with surprising longing. Some of these men may have been in college fraternities or joined other groups with restricted memberships (the Elks?
the Lions? It's curious how these men's groups often have animal
names). But if so, they do not mention it in their life histories. Whatever

the actual or missed opportunities, the mythopoetic men's movement voices an extremely strong nostalgia for initiation. Because mythopoetic men allude so frequently to "tribal" models, I want to compare current practices in the movement, at least provisionally, to initiation as it appears in ethnographic accounts of traditional peoples.

Initiations

Adolescent male circumcision; spiritual teaching in the wilderness; vision quests to discover one's totem; a first kill: these are some initiation rituals commonly described in ethnographic studies. Anthropologists have also recorded many other customs. On some Greek islands, for example, young men are expected to dive undersea without scuba equipment: youths who refuse are taunted; those who comply risk death or crippling. On Samoa, young men engage in drunken brawls on weekends and knife fights that begin with the conventionalized insult of referring to another man as a woman and threatening to slit the other's throat: the fights end by common agreement when one of the opponents has drawn a small amount of blood.[6]

These and other initiation structures share certain important features. They are operative for an age cohort somewhere between ten and twenty. They contain, indeed sometimes maximize, elements of fear and danger. They impose serious penalties for failure, such as a boy's permanent banishment or death, or a loss of status for the boy or his family if he fails to behave bravely. They are enacted (or, alternatively, their end results are displayed) before the community. In addition, they employ the symbolism of water and blood as the media through which initiation takes place—something about which I will want to say more shortly. But beyond these similarities, forms of initiation are subject to many variations. So many that it seems fair to say that there is no single, universal condition or gesture called "initiation." Yet the mythopoetic men's movement continually talks about "initiation" as though it were a universally understood experience. In addition, the movement seems to take for granted the power of initiation rituals to achieve "pure" and "authentic" manhood.

The evidence suggests that few cultures regard initiation as such a simple matter. In fact, it seems likely that initiation rituals grew out of a lack of certainty as to whether "manhood" coincides with biological growth and physical maturation at puberty. Ethnographers often note that although many groups have rituals to honor first menstruation, they think of womanhood as being conferred by the act of menstruation itself. In contrast, male initiation rituals seem to reflect not so much certainty about what makes a boy into a man as doubt that manhood can be recognized without initiation ceremonies.[7] In other words, the "magic" of initiation is little more than cultural consensus and placebo effect. There is no secret formula for manhood unless the culture agrees to agree on one. For the men's movement, that formula has evolved in terms of oppositions, mainly to womanhood and to homosexuality.

The men's movement was motivated by and has, to some extent, modelled itself on the women's movement. Yet it is suspicious of women and has completely eliminated them from its rituals. What is more, the men's movement is extremely squeamish about gender ambiguities and anxious about activities that sound like what the West calls homosexuality.[8] In fact, the movement almost uniformly defines a participant as one who is heterosexual, or at least who has the following relationships: a mother he needs to escape; a father he needs to embrace; and a girlfriend or wife who replicates the mother's role of interfering with the intimacy of men.[9] In effect, if not in intention, the movement tends to exclude men who did not grow up in nuclear families or who are not heterosexual.

It is easy to see why. The movement emphasizes pure manhood, a condition that finds its few objective qualifications—if any exist at all—in such social/biological roles as fatherhood. Homosexuality and bisexuality, while not excluding such roles, represent alternatives and thus diminish the power of those roles to define manhood. That's why the movement rarely mentions gay men and typically tries to avoid or finesse the issue. At men's movement meetings, a remark like "I was in the middle of all my men, who were my brothers, who were all men" will be greeted with an affirmative "Ho!" Images of being "breast to breast" with another man,[10] or enjoying some other physical closeness, are some-

times invoked but are understood to function within an idealized, frater-
nal culture that precludes homoeroticism.

Yet if manhood were a pure category, defined simply in terms of possession of a penis or the ability to ejaculate, the concept would be less
problematic, and the men's movement would have no logical purpose.
The category is inherently unstable, and this instability is particularly evident as the movement tries to maintain its opposition vis-à-vis womanhood and homosexuality while simultaneously embracing the initiation
rituals of cultures in which these oppositions do not necessarily obtain.

Consider, for example, the movement's praise for the New Guinean
practice of noisily abducting boys from their mothers.[11] In the Bill
Moyers' public television special that first brought the men's movement
to national attention, Robert Bly describes how women scream and wail
as men swoop through the village.[12] The women, Bly says, are "helping the men to scare 'the boy' out" of the initiates. Oddly, though, Bly
and other movement writers neglect to mention what follows the abduc-
tions in New Guinea: a prolonged period during which the boys live away
from their villages, fellating the men who have abducted them or being
anally penetrated to absorb what the culture calls "men's milk" (the male
ejaculate). "Men's milk" is thought to communicate, substantively, the
essence of manhood.[13] What the men's movement omits about the New
Guinean model is not, I think, at all trivial. Indeed, the omission points
up several fundamental problems with the how the movement is cur-
rently conceived and operates.

Likewise, and very important, initiation rituals of other cultures do
not really separate "maleness" from "femaleness." Many initiation rituals—including the one I have described from New Guinea—include
symbolic imitations of femaleness: menstruation is simulated in the circumcision of adolescent boys, for example, or in other rituals in which
blood is shed; the nursing of infants underlies the idea of "men's milk."
Indeed, in many traditional cultures, initiation includes symbolic reenact-
ments of birth: sojourns in caves, diving through water, jumping into
holes, crawling through tunnels, passing under and through their mother's
legs in a second "delivery."

Initiation rituals sometimes do physically separate males from females
by sending men into the wilderness. They sometimes even bar females

from the immediate arena of initiatory activities so that the boy's "birth" into manhood will be (as Nancy Jay says of ritual sacrifice) "birth done better," because done by men.[14] But many of those rituals retain imaginative links between male initiation and birth—and so between males and females. In fact, in many traditional groups, initiation is only one part of an ongoing ritual cycle in which men participate with women or even (as in some rituals performed after adolescence) dress and act like women. Indeed, in many traditional cultures, "initiation" is a rite reserved for adolescents, not for adults, and many ritual activities become available only *after* adolescent rites are completed—so that initiation is regarded as a means to an end and not an end in itself. As used by the mythopoetic men's movement, the metaphor of initiation more nearly makes men into boys rather than boys into men. It creates an illusion that forty- and fifty-year-olds can be Peter Pans or Eagle Scouts perpetually on the brink of initiation.

In the United States today, men often enter the men's movement when they experience a crisis at midlife. Often, it is a parent's death, an altered level of sexual desire, a first heart attack or other serious illness, a divorce, the loss of a job or career stagnation. There are many additional motivations—most notably, the desire to be a more "sensitive" or a more "nineties kind of guy," sometimes for the express purpose of pleasing women. But the need to cope with a sense of loss, often connected with aging, is the most commonly articulated reason for joining. Robert Bly, for example, helped found the men's movement in the wake of his father's death and a period of failure in his career as a poet. It is fascinating to note that earlier, during the 1970s, he had led a movement to revive the Great Mother Goddess and said repeatedly in interviews that "American humanity has gone as far as it's going to go in the direction of masculine consciousness."[15]

Yet the men's movement can be interpreted as reinscribing some particular forms of masculine consciousness, specifically the flirtation with boundary dissolution that we have seen men enact earlier in the twentieth century—which comes to an end under the perceived threat of the oceanic. I am struck, for example, by how the movement harps on the idea of initiation as the transformation of a boy into a man but scants the close association of that event, in many traditional cultures, both with submission to a community and with symbolic elements (water, blood, birth, death, femininity) that signal not just confirmed male identity but also potential boundary dissolution.

Consider, for example, Malidoma Somé's account of traditional initiation, in which village elders compel youths to experience how "everything that makes a human distinct from things and from other humans was gone."[16] In Somé's culture, the Dagara of Burkina Faso, initiates must jump into an opening in the earth where they encounter a sense of eternity but may (if they are careless) disappear forever; they must sleep alone without food or drink until they experience trees as appearing in feminine form and speaking in women's voices. Somé presents these phenomena not as supernatural or magical, as they might appear in the West, but as examples of how Dagara reality includes a belief in the interpenetration of the human and natural worlds. His account tallies with others of alternative realities within tribal cultures.[17]

As I have noted, Somé has served as a consultant to the Western men's movement and has led some of its national meetings. Yet in his book, he not only fails to identify himself as a member of the movement but also seems disillusioned by, even critical, of it. Westerners, he says, seek a " 'shortcut' to their own future . . . through their commitment to learning about indigenous cultures, non-Western spiritualities or, more recently, the Men's Movement." While Somé is not explicit on this point, part of his disillusionment may stem from the movement's extremely limited account of initiation. Somé describes initiation as the emergence of a mature male from a complex set of experiences consistent with (even dependent on) submission to the community, nature, and a sense of the sacred that is predicated on the interpenetration of the human and natural worlds. Instead, the movement's version of initiation picks and chooses from an à la carte menu. Respecting the original meanings of the rituals, the movement takes those it likes (for example, youth becoming manhood) and represses those it finds repugnant (for example, the feminine, the homosexual, and other confusions of boundaries).

Although I would not want to assert a strict, point-by-point analogy, the movement's uneasy relationship with women, homosexuals, and boundary dissolution replicates some of the conditions that Klaus Theweleit says existed among protofascist soldiers during the 1920s in Germany. Theweleit shows that these men recorded in their letters and diaries strong oceanic fantasies of merging (including, for example, the imagery of floods) which became distorted into violent misogyny and virulent homophobia (see the Bibliography under Introduction). The men's movement has not been the instrument of either violence or political repression, but it similarly promotes male bonding through the exclusion of women and gays. Does such exclusion have any connection to the distortion or repression of oceanic sensation? To address that question, I want to return to my description of the structure of movement meetings and highlight a feature that begins and ends the sessions: group activities intended to foster collectivity. My interest in such activities is their potential to bridge initiation as a phenomenon of individuation and ritual contexts of boundary dissolution.

Communitas

In my interviews, men often said that initially they found the dancing or drumming that precedes and follows discussions of male identity "silly" or "embarrassing" but that it ultimately helped them "really let go." According to movement participants, activities like drumming or dancing "somehow put [men] in touch with another center" and are valued because they lead to "powerful mystical experiences."[18] I consider these group activities important clues to understanding the men's movement. Indeed, in statements by mythopoetic men, they judge the success of their meetings on the basis of the strength of their connection to one another. One member of a mythopoetic group said: "The intensity of feelings I get when I go to gatherings and leave have [*sic*] always been special to me. They touch that inner nature that there's no room for anywhere else." For the men, a good meeting is one that creates a sense of deep connection. A bad meeting, on the other hand, leaves the men with the sense that "there's a deeper level we could get to." Metaphorically, the group activities seem to be the appetizer and dessert of the men's movement meal: they whet the appetite for self-revelation and connection and then cap off the experience with a sated feeling of release.

Despite the centrality of "initiation" and its related rhetoric, then, I believe that an even more fundamental goal of the contemporary mytho-poetic men's movement is joyful, transcendent experience—a feeling of intensity of life or complete "presentness" in the body that connects with others and with larger, cosmic forces. Although the movement claims to enact tribal initiation in order to confirm individual manhood, the more crucial purpose of imitating rituals within traditional cultures is some-thing less specific. The movement, I believe, also seeks the general sym-bolic richness, the ambiance or emotional surround, that a ritual like initiation can provide. More than the effect of a particular ritual (initia-tion), the men's movement seeks what has been described as the underly-ing spirit of ritual in general: a feeling of full, spontaneous participation that leads to the dissolution of the boundaries of individuality.

In this sense, the mythopoetic men seek not just initiation but what the anthropologist Victor Turner calls *communitas. Communitas* is the essence of what is meant by the concept of "community," but is nonethe-less so extreme that, according to Turner, it can only occur outside ordi-nary, quotidian social structures. To explain what he means, Turner quotes from Martin Buber. According to Buber, *communitas* is a feeling of radical, collective identity in which the participants experience "a turn-ing to, a dynamic facing of, the others, a flowing from *I* to *Thou*."[19] With respect to the men's movement, then, participants judge meetings "suc-cessful" if they produce a feeling of *communitas;* "failed," if they do not. Despite the hit-or-miss nature of the men's efforts, the chance to experi-ence something like *communitas* at least some of the time keeps men coming back to movement activities.[20]

But as I became convinced that the Holy Grail of the men's move-ment is *communitas,* I nevertheless wondered: Why do the men not ar-ticulate this goal more directly? Why all the rhetoric of sons, fathers, and male identity instead? The most likely answers concern the relationship between the men's movement and modern middle-class culture (whose norms make *communitas* an ambiguous goal at best), as well as certain paradoxes in the nature of *communitas* itself. Because similar relation-ships and paradoxes are also more broadly relevant to this book as a whole, a brief digression on the nature of *communitas* will be helpful at this point.

Victor Turner sees *communitas* as "a transformative experience that goes to the root of each person's being and finds in that root something profoundly communal and shared" (*The Ritual Process,* 138). Turner believes that no society can experience *communitas* all the time: hierarchy and the assignment of specific tasks to individuals undermine *communitas* but are necessary to make a society function. Indeed, he identifies the belief that primitive groups experience *communitas* all the time as a persistently romantic Western notion (130). Yet according to Turner, even though *communitas* takes place outside the quotidian activities of specific groups, it is still "normative" to cultures that engage in ritual processes leading to *communitas.* Indeed, *communitas* occurs between people who encounter each other at a different level during the course of ordinary life. I agree with Turner on these points.

But I would stress more strongly than Turner does the difference between groups that regularly choose to enact rituals which produce *communitas* and those that do not. Such a choice seems very likely to reflect or affect the nature of daily life in a society. Perhaps, for example, it mirrors or fosters a collective, rather than individualistic, social ethos or concepts of "family" somewhat different from either extended or nuclear families in the West.[21] Turner is surely right to say that *communitas* is outside quotidian life in all cultures. But one might argue that it is relatively normative (in the sense of welcome, and regularly invoked through ritual) among the African groups Turner studied and relatively scarce in the United States today.[22]

Turner's comparison of *communitas* to Buber's "I-Thou" introduces an additional level of ambiguity. Turner describes *communitas* as a "direct, immediate, and total confirmation of human identities." But for Buber, an animal or inanimate thing (like a rock) can also be a Thou in possession of a "direct, immediate, and total"—though clearly not human—identity. In fact, for Buber, the intense connections of *communitas* can and should occur across species and categories.[23] Thus, *communitas* would simultaneously be experienced as something intensely communal (similar to what Turner identifies in ritual process) and as something mystical, unboundaried, oceanic. For Buber, the two kinds of experience should ideally be fully consistent, one with the other.

Still, for Buber as for Turner, the relationship of *communitas* to quotidian existence was ultimately quite vexed. He struggled to find ways to reconcile the oceanic emotions of "I-Thou" with modern social or political life, looking to many varied social theories—Max Weber's *Gesellschaft* and *Gemeinschaft,* socialism, Hasidism, and Eastern and Christian mystical traditions—for an answer. Then, after World War II, he advocated a joint Arab-Jewish state in what is now Israel, a state that would illustrate the meaning of "I-Thou"; this idealistic position caused him to lose prestige in many Jewish communities. Yet Buber retained his conviction that "in the beginning"—in the earliest days of human society—*communitas* and connectedness were normative conditions, and that modern people must return to them.[24] In this regard, he fell into the trap Turner identifies of imagining primitives as engaged in a continuous experience of *communitas.* But, in turn, Buber's approach identifies the catch or "rub" in Turner's thinking: If *communitas* is such an essential and positive human experience, why should it be confined to ritual structures? Why should it not spill over into, or at least affect, other types of experience? Like most social scientists, Turner assumes that daily life must have secular structures; a spiritual thinker, Buber restlessly and continually asked, Why?

This brief digression cannot hope to represent Turner's and Buber's positions completely, much less to resolve the contradictions between them. Instead, it is designed to suggest that the relationship of *communitas* to ordinary workaday life is, and always has been, extremely vexed. Often, forms of *communitas* come to seem inappropriate to, or even come under the fire of, the groups that gave rise to them. For example, Francis of Assisi's radical brotherhood was both admired and resented by the Catholic church;[25] Martin Buber's intense ecumenicalism did not sit well with Orthodox rabbis. In a similar way, cults often run afoul of churches or governments.

The men's movement has to some extent tried to finesse these problems. But the very nature of *communitas* and the forms it has taken within existing cultures raise certain questions about the mythopoetic movement. Its members' lives come into contact only within the specific and limited context of movement meetings. By contrast, participants in tribal ritual also share daily lives. The men's movement bars women from its activities and even demonizes them; it provides no real place for men who are not heterosexual. In contrast, traditional rituals more flexibly engage, at least at the symbolic level, continuities between men and women and those between humans and nature. Do the isolation and exclusions practiced by the men's movement enhance *communitas,* or do they undercut its power?

From the start, the mythopoetic men's movement has expressed a desire to reverse social trends it dates from the beginning of the Industrial Revolution. It argues for a return to home, nature, and the primacy of father-son bonds, to a time when fathers worked at home and taught their skills to their boys.[26] It advocates a return to use-value as the paramount economic principle, a direct correspondence between things and human needs, and hence less emphasis on money and other phenomena contributing to what Georg Lukács called "reification"—the conversion of work and other relationships into abstract monetary values.[27] Loosely speaking, the movement's rhetoric has a Marxist ring to it.

But, ironically, the movement has reproduced many of the structures it wants to help its members escape. It questions how gender relations function in modern life but does not, by and large, question the cultural milieu responsible for making men feel estranged from their manhood. The movement lives, for example, in large part through its products—books, videos, and audiotapes for busy commuters. Men consume these books and tapes in the solitude of their dens or cars. Or they attend weekend workshops that do not conflict with the workweek. In other words, in the mythopoetic men's movement, there is little to contradict the entrepreneurial or bourgeois spirit of life since the Industrial Revolution. For this reason, it has been easy for writers like Tony Robbins to adapt the men's movement and other New Age or quasi-New Age philosophies to their rhetoric of "success," riches, and how-to-do-well-in-business. In the same way, businesses have naturally enlisted consultants steeped in the men's movement or other New Age philosophies in an effort to increase productivity and profitability. The men's movement is not at all inconsistent with such goals; indeed, it can be conceived as an opiate for these particular male, managerial masses.[28] Ultimately, the mythopoetic men's movement sells "male identity" as a property that every man must come to own.

In this regard, the mythopoetic men's movement strongly reminds me of the experiences of men like Gide, Jung, and Lawrence, the subjects of Part One of this book. Earlier in the twentieth century, these men travelled to Africa, the Pacific Rim, or the American Southwest because they felt ill at ease in the West and resisted certain conventional Western notions of manhood. In exotic locales, they felt the lure of the oceanic impulse towards the dissolution of boundaries—but ultimately they resisted it strongly as too threatening to the "mature European self." So it is no accident that Jung and Lawrence are two of the movement's cultural heroes, quoted frequently in its printed texts. Like Jung and Lawrence, men in the mythopoetic men's movement feel imprisoned in their modern lives and desperately want change. While Gide, Jung, and Lawrence travelled to "the primitive" in the flesh, their present-day counterparts travel via the imagination and what they believe to be faithful imitations of primitive ritual. The men are in search of connections with other men and with generations of maleness that they posit as existing in the primitive. They seek the joy that accompanies release from the confinements of selfhood. But like Gide, Jung, and Lawrence, they have trouble relinquishing the borders of masculine consciousness without reacting proactively to get them back. They organize and process experience so that everything remains safely contained: "differentiated," in Gide's terms, "preserved intact," in Jung's, punctuated by the "I," in Lawrence's.

I do not mean to end with so dismissive a statement as "boys will be boys." Indeed, I am reluctant, even averse, to assigning any trait or collection of traits either to males or females as biological destiny. Nor do I mean to imply that anyone, male or female, should wantonly surrender individuality—the relationship between individuality and the oceanic is a vexed question, to which I will return several times. But there does seem to be something especially resistant to the oceanic within traditional male Western sensibilities. At the surface level, stylistically, men today are notably open to the primitive and to various other expressions of spiritual life.[29] The quest for ecstasy has never been more socially acceptable, more open to public demonstration. Yet conditions in the United States today may not entirely permit transcendent experience, even as they foster aspirations to exceed the limitations of the body. Is masculine consciousness to blame? Or the product-laden conditions of modern life? Or is there some combination of limiting social factors at work? To answer these questions, I need to broaden my sample of contemporary phenomena and include some specifically practiced by women. The observations made in the next chapter—on the New Age, women, and evolving connections to traditional religious structures in the United States—will be consistent with, though they will not subsume, my more particular findings about mythopoetic men.

CHAPTER EIGHT

Medicine Wheels and Spirituality:
Primitivism in the New Age

New Age Odyssey

A S THE END of the millennium approaches, the New Age seems to be everywhere but continues to elude specific definition. The genealogy of New Age thinking can be traced to the sixties and the Age of Aquarius, and, much earlier, to Positive Thinking, Mind Cure, Christian Science, Theosophy, and spiritualism, and even further back, to Transcendentalism and the influence of Indian religions on American Protestantism. But the New Age cannot be accounted for in terms of a single root influence. It includes phenomena as diverse as Yoga and the Kabbalah, holistic healing and Wicca, veganism and acupuncture, contact with angels and spiritual computer interfaces, wilderness trips and tours of holy places, self-help and Jungian psychology, goddess revivals, and even the mythopoetic men's movement, the subject of the preceding chapter. It is a decidedly eclectic collection of phenomena, drawing from a variety of cultural and religious traditions, past and present, Western and Eastern, modern and primitive, familiar and exotically Other.

There are at least two ways of viewing this ferocious eclecticism. Supporters praise the New Age's freedom from dogma and capacity to acknowledge that many traditions offer valuable insight into how to integrate body, mind, and spirit with the powers of the universe. From this point of view, the New Age is the culmination of forces that have been developing throughout the millennium, and the movement's miscellaneous constitution is a strength, not a weakness. Skeptics counter that the New Age is a cluttered void tautologically defined by whatever happens to be featured in magazines or housed within bookstores on New Age shelves at any given moment. From this point of view, the movement's variety shows it to be rudderless, lacking in substance and direction.

When I began working on the New Age, I thought it would be easy to write about. New Age materials are all around us. They engage many of the same aspirations, ambivalences, and problems as the individual life histories I discussed earlier. What's more, the New Age provides concrete examples of how current lyrical views of Native Americans and other so-called primitives affect everyday life (see Chapter Six). But among the related phenomena I discuss, the New Age proved to be perhaps the most difficult for me to write about.

The New Age inspires passions that range from dithyrambic endorsement to withering contempt. Here, for example, is Marilyn Ferguson, in *The Aquarian Conspiracy,* describing how forces for change are gathering irresistibly and (despite the sinister connotations of her title) for the benefit of the earth: "A leaderless but powerful network is working to bring about radical change in the United States. Its members have broken with certain key elements of Western thought and they may even have broken continuity with history."[1] Like most people who have sought to describe the New Age, Ferguson writes from inside the movement and takes a stance of outright advocacy. James Redfield, author of *The Celestine Prophecy* and editor of *The Celestine Newsletter,* is another example, and there are many others.[2] But at the other extreme, in *The American Religion,* Harold Bloom aloofly declines to comment on the New Age, even though he thinks that its manifestations are both widespread and important: it is beneath his intellectual contempt. Similarly, Wendy Kaminer's *I'm Dysfunctional, You're Dysfunctional* blames New Age thinking for fostering psychologies of victimization that show up everywhere from Oprah to O.J.[3]

Between these polarized positions I found myself staking out a position of passionate ambivalence. Over a period of four years, I undertook a series of informal participant-observer exercises. I attended New Age conferences and meetings. I read books, listened to tapes, and talked with participants. At the end of the process, I found—to put it flat-footedly—that I liked some aspects of the New Age but disliked others. Some New Age tenets, such as the benefits of reducing stress and the need for greater ecological awareness, struck me as unequivocal common sense. Others, like astral projection and channelling, and some versions of angels and the transmigration of souls, seemed nonsensical. I have a personal as well as an intellectual interest in the questions towards which the New Age has gravitated: how to think about life and death, the self and the cosmos, harmonious relations between species and between the organic and the inorganic. But I believe that some New Age answers are profoundly mistaken, and that many others are either smug, superficial, or silly.

Yet it's not always possible to accept some New Age beliefs and reject others. Nor is it easy to reason with the followers. The New Age is not a church or even a fixed set of beliefs. In the words of one member, it is "even more universalist than the Unitarians."[4] Nevertheless, there are definite affinities between the New Age and organized religions.[5] Like more orthodox faiths, the New Age posits a unified power that orders the universe and the movement of individuals towards God or, to use a different vocabulary equally popular in the New Age, with "total cosmic force." Indeed, a belief in meaningful convergences between people and events is the New Age equivalent of religious faith. According to most New Agers, there are no accidents; events that appear accidental are actually meaningful coincidences whose accumulation brings into being states of altered awareness that are, in and of themselves, the New Age. New Agers truly believe this, and there is no arguing with true believers; one professor of religion, a self-described Christian, quipped, "If there is one thing that unites both Western Christians and New Agers, it is the absolute conviction that they are right and everyone else is wrong."[6] Such absolute conviction is one reason why the New Age gets under the skin of so many people—including me.

In fact, in the process of writing about the New Age, I felt more and more compelled to take a stand on theological issues. So while I would ordinarily not make disclosures of faith in nonautobiographical writing, here I go.

I was raised to follow Catholicism, a faith I have not practiced for a long time, but which always appealed to me at the level of symbol or metaphor. Although I have no trouble saying "God," I mean the word metaphorically to signify a nonanthropomorphized, genderless entity equivalent to the sum total of matter or energy in the universe. This part of my belief system is fairly close to that of many people in the New Age, although some New Agers prefer, as a corrective to Judeo-Christian and Islamic traditions, to feminize this force and call it the Goddess.[7]

In my view, this genderless force acts blindly with regard to individual lives—sometimes helping them, sometimes harming them. I believe that accidents and chance exist, as do unmotivated goodness and gratuitous evil. I have witnessed the stages leading to death, and what I have seen convinces me that Elisabeth Kübler-Ross' account of how the spirits of dead family members "guide" people into death has some validity.[8] I can easily imagine the body's conversion into different states of energy, and hence its "survival" and communion with "God" in this metaphoric sense. Yet I would be astonished to find after death that there was any kind of embodied afterlife.

My views are not, then, exactly secular. But they are also not in sync with those of many New Agers, who imagine God as a loving parent or good friend, and often believe in both reincarnation and the transmigration of souls.[9] The difference between my views and those typical of New Agers is, I think, much more than a matter of vocabulary, and it has affected my reactions to the New Age at almost every point.

Given that issues like these run deep, I decided that this chapter would have to begin with a frank confession of mixed feelings. Given the breadth of the New Age and the fact that it is continually developing, I also knew that anything I could write about it would be, by necessity, partial and highly selective—there would always be some hot new books or ideas that I had left out, some examples of New Age thinking I had failed to consider. To minimize that effect, I decided to restrict my discussion to one relatively straightforward use of the primitive in the New Age: certain rituals and ceremonies, often enacted by women, that approximate Native American spirituality.

Still, as I wrote, I could easily imagine readers whose own experiences of the New Age would contradict any claims I made. That risk, it seemed, comes with the territory. "Think of the New Age movement as a vacuum cleaner," one New Ager has been quoted as saying. "It picks up whatever is there. . . . If it had moved in a different direction it would have sucked all kinds of other things in. They would look quite unlike the first collection . . . but they would be New Age as well."[10] When I read such statements, I couldn't help but imagine this book—which uncovers traditions of oceanic thinking and asks how the primitive functions today as a medium for spiritual expression—drawn up into the vacuum cleaner. Read in a certain way, this book might even be viewed as advocating altered forms of consciousness that are part of the New Age. Once, when I was being interviewed for a job at a fundamentalist Christian university, one of the interviewers, upon learning that I was not a practicing Christian, asked me for my opinion of Jesus. I replied that I thought it would be presumptuous of me to have an opinion. He wagged a finger at me and said, "We'll get you yet." I could imagine a New Ager saying much the same thing.

Still, on the basis of what I have seen, heard, and read about the New Age, I believe that many of its participants are trapped in a rather moving contradiction. They adopt rituals and other aspects of cultures that depend fundamentally upon collective, communal experience—and sometimes on voiding or subordinating the autonomous self. Indeed, New Agers specifically and self-consciously choose traditions from a variety of cultures around the world, both past and present. They habitually attend meetings and join groups that they see as cornerstones of spiritual development. But New Agers almost invariably put these traditions and groups in the service of a thoroughly modern world view that takes the self as a thing to be owned, cultivated, and coddled—the veritable hub of the universe. My New Age odyssey begins at a conference attended largely by women. Then it circles back to the connection between the New Age, certain images of Native Americans, and the question of spirituality.

Nourishing the Soul

In 1992, I attended a New Age conference sponsored by a group called Common Boundary. The conference was entitled "Nourishing the Soul: Discovering the Spiritual in Everyday Life." Artifacts from Native American culture, regarded as promoting spirituality, were displayed everywhere. Medicine wheels, smudge sticks, feathers, flute music, and chants on tape were featured in the conference's workshops and available for purchase along an arcade of booths.

The people at the conference were overwhelmingly white (perhaps 99 percent), mostly female (perhaps 85 percent), and well educated. Almost all of the men present seemed to be with women, but the male-female couple was not really the norm. Most women had come with other women. Some appeared to be just friends, but there were also lesbian couples engaging in open displays of affection that attracted no special attention and caused no sign of discomfort in the group as a whole. With respect to social class and age, the composition of this group resembled that of the mythopoetic men's movement. Yet, in strong contrast to men's movement gatherings, it was mixed as to both gender and sexual orientation.

The conference began with a keynote talk by Clarissa Pinkola Estés. She spoke about the figure of La Muerte, a Mexican folkloric figure who represents both the life and death force.[11] Looking like an operatic diva, Pinkola Estés created a feeling of great intimacy in a crowded room. She described the need to recognize all the sides of La Muerte and to learn to let go of particular desires or relationships—even of life itself in the face of impending death. "How will you know when it's really time to let go?" Pinkola Estés asked the audience. "I can't tell you," she said. "You have to tell for yourself." But she could give us an image: "Is La Muerte standing at the foot or the head of the bed?" You have to recognize the figure of La Muerte and how close she is to the head of the bed. You cannot reason with her, Pinkola Estés said. "If she's at the head, it's time."

Pinkola Estés' talk addressed itself to small problems, like losing weight, as much as the most profound life questions. But most members of the audience responded to the talk in its loftier mode. At the end of the lecture, during the question period, a woman got up and described for the roughly two thousand people present the dreams she was having of being flayed alive—literally, like a rabbit. She was a troubled woman, experiencing pain, and she wanted relief right there and then—although Pinkola Estés (in my opinion, correctly) suggested she seek therapeutic help instead. This woman's dream was just the first of several startling public revelations that proved to be something of a norm at this conference.

At what was called a networking lunch, the couple to my right almost immediately shared with me their "psychic conviction" that I was meant to go on a vision quest. The couple, whom I will call Lynn and Don, believed (like most New Agers) in the meaningfulness of all coincidences. They were convinced that I had been brought to them for a purpose and proceeded to supply me with the intimate details of their lives, searching for a point of connection. Each had had an unhappy, abusive first marriage that ended in an ugly divorce. Then they had met two years ago on a vision quest that, they agreed, had done more "work" for both of them than "a decade of therapy."

Vision quests are adaptations of certain Native American rituals, generally practiced by males. Typically, the male is made to spend time alone in the wilderness, seeking a special rapport with some animal that assumes a role in his life similar to that of a totem or animal familiar. As is common before many rituals, prior to undertaking a vision quest, Native American participants often purify their bodies in a sweathouse. In the New Age, vision quests are open to men and women and sometimes function, as for Don and Lynn, as an occasion to meet other singles. Instead of being solitary trials, they tend to be group experiences of nature, with an emphasis on exercises designed to build trust between members of the group. Although some exercises, adapted from boot camp and Outward Bound-type programs, can be quite strenuous physically (rope climbing, crossing obstacle paths), others derived from therapies like EST present more of a psychological challenge, as when participants must trust the others to catch them when they fall, and so on. There were two "grand finales" to Don and Lynn's vision quest. First, each person had to spend a night alone in the wilderness. Then, everyone was packed into a sweathouse, where tears and emotional breakdowns were frequent, even expected.[12]

At the lunch, I said that I might be writing about things like vision quests but wasn't sure I'd want to go on one myself, whereupon Don and Lynn decided that the purpose of our meeting was to persuade me to do so. They offered many stories of people who had gone on vision quests unwillingly or by accident, only to have the experience change their lives. One doctor, for example, thought he was going to a Club Med for fishing. He spent the first few days complaining bitterly about the mistake that his secretary had made in sending him on this trip. Yet he was the first to break down in the sweat lodge, the couple said, and promised at the end to come back the following year. They were sure I'd have the same change of heart, and wouldn't stop until I had taken down the name and address of the company that had organized their vision quest. Then they beamed and assured me that I would go on that quest, and that we would meet again so that I could thank them.

But the most illuminating experience I had at the conference was in a workshop on creating ceremony in everyday life. The room was darkened. The 153 people present sat in three concentric circles—two on the floor and one in chairs around the perimeter of the room. At the center of the circles was what the speaker called a medicine wheel: a circular formation of items based on the circles of stones that mark Indian sacred places but are also more generally evocative of aspects of Native American life, including the roundness of tepees and the shape of many traditional encampments.[13] Circular forms allude to the harmony and unity ascribed to traditional Indian life. Symbolically, they are said to represent the four directions (north, south, east, and west) and the four seasons. This medicine wheel had been created from animal skulls, baskets, feathers, rattles, masks, and other props signifying particular aspects of Native American life. It also included a prayer bowl, plates of sage leaves, smudge sticks, and rocks. The speaker stood at the south pole of the medicine wheel, which she said symbolized innocence.[14]

At the beginning of the session, the leader talked for about twenty minutes. She told us about a period of invalidism in her past arising from no specific illness but marked by a persistent lack of energy and feeling of despair. This period came to an end when she introduced ceremony into her life and began to regard everyday activities (brushing her teeth was the example she gave) as having ceremonial value if done carefully and with attention.[15] Then she led the group through a series of exercises.

We beat the rocks to purify the room, to move energies. Each of us wished another person his or her "highest good" while grasping that person's knees or shoulders, then accepted that person's same wishes in return, silently, as the leader beat an Indian drum. We sang together, chewed the sage leaves, and then—in the final ceremonial gesture—spoke a word for what we needed most into the prayer bowl, which was passed from person to person around the circles. The most commonly uttered word was "healing" (not health—there is a difference); the next most commonly uttered were "clarity" and "voice." The reasons why the New Age looks so persistently to idealized versions of Native Americans and to other groups may be found, I believe, in the prayer bowl. They involve the words "healing," "clarity," and "voice."

One of the New Age's most substantial achievements has been its role in supporting the shift in psychoanalysis beyond Freud's theories and towards a variety of techniques and models based on interpersonal relations. Jung is an important resource for many New Age followers, who value his use of archetypes and techniques for self-realization, such as mandala drawings. Also important is D. W. Winnicott, although far fewer New Age adherents than one might expect seem to know his work by name. Winnicott studied infant-mother bonds as the prototype of what we might call interpersonal (or, a term I prefer, subject-subject) relations (as opposed to what Freud called subject-object relations).[16] In addition, many best-selling New Age materials have been written by practicing psychoanalysts or psychologists. In their books, they cite therapeutic experiences along with other examples from myth, literature, or film. To put it strongly, the new psychologies and the New Age are in a symbiotic relationship of theory and method. Women are especially attracted to New Age psychologies because they treat women and men on equal terms and share a core belief in women's status as subjects rather than objects (as in Freud's model of the mother-infant bond). In addition, these psychologies emphasize relationships and responsibilities along with self-realization—traditionally, "female" concerns.

But the New Age puts a particular spin on Jungian and Winnicottian materials. It stresses the self as something to be "realized," "helped," and "fulfilled." The way the leader of my session began by telling us about her own troubled history is typical. At New Age gatherings (as at men's movement meetings), confession and testimony are the norms. These gatherings combine elements of self-help groups, church services, and revival meetings. They can be highly theatrical and choreographed—for example, when members routinely applaud each person's statement or utterance. In fact, as Wendy Kaminer notes, many New Agers have a high tolerance for, and even cultivate and approve, public displays of personal trauma—hence the emphasis on "healing." This emphasis has a special significance for women, who, once again, constitute a majority at many New Age functions. The women often perceive themselves as having been wounded by patriarchal traditions, like the bourgeois nuclear family, Judaism, and Christianity.

Native American and other "exotic" cultural materials allow New Age participants access to alternative systems of spiritual belief. But because of the New Age's enormous assimilative capacity, followers can sample these systems under the New Age rubric without needing to accept fully the precepts of any particular system. That is why, for many New Age people, concepts like "Buddhism," "the Goddess," and "Native American" function similarly—despite their manifest differences. In fact, they signify much the same thing for New Agers: cultures that are ecologically sensitive, spiritually attuned to the universe, and woman-friendly.

In its appropriation of materials and practices from various traditions, the New Age shows little motivation to confront distasteful aspects of particular traditions, such as warfare among Native Americans. Nor does the New Age show much interest in verifying its images of the different cultures from which it borrows. Riane Eisler, author of *The Chalice and the Blade,* for example, describes prehistoric societies that worshipped the Goddess as having had "common ownership of the principal means of production and a perception of social power as responsibility or trusteeship for the benefit of all . . . a basically cooperative social organization. Both men and women worked cooperatively for the common good."[17] It scarcely seems to matter to Eisler and many New Agers that the evidence for any view of prehistory is bound to be extremely scanty. What matters for the New Age is not the historical accuracy of its images so much as their conformity to and reinforcement of the movement's general principles.

To take another example, in many New Age or New Age-friendly books, Native American culture is typically described as being matriarchal or matrifocal. The New Age tends to emphasize aspects of Indian life like the Corn Mothers (female deities) or governance institutions like the Iroquois female elders.[18] According to some writers, like Paula Gunn Allen, Indians are

> the carrier of the dream that most activist movements in the Americas claim to be seeking. The major difference . . . is that for millennia American Indians have based their social systems, however diverse, on ritual, spirit-centered, woman-focused worldviews.[19]

Gunn Allen further claims that Indians were respectful of lesbianism and woman-woman unions (*The Sacred Hoop*, 245–46), like those in evidence at the conference. She notes that "the physical and cultural genocide of American Indian tribes is and was mostly about patriarchal fear of gynocracy" (3). As in Eisler's description of prehistory, Gunn Allen isn't bothered by the absence of factual evidence that gynocracy and lesbianism were universally recognized and valued among traditional Indians. Instead, she sees the lack of evidence as the best proof that the "tribal lesbian" was a rich and vital figure. It was only natural, she argues, that Indians kept their most sacred customs hidden from whites. To put it mildly, it is extremely difficult to gauge the accuracy of such claims.

Yet I can say with some certainty that rumors or reports of female power among Native Americans have, since early in this century, attracted women to Native American groups, especially to the Pueblo and other cultures of the American Southwest. Women like Mary Austin, Elsie Clews Parsons, Mabel Dodge Luhan, Ruth Benedict, and many others worked in the Southwest as anthropologists, artists, and philanthropists.[20] Ruth Benedict, for example, studied Zuni Indians in *Patterns of Culture* in order to show, she said, that those whom the United States regards as "deviant" (like lesbians, a group to which she belonged and longed to declare public allegiance) might not be regarded in the same way in different cultures.[21] Mary Austin described Pueblo life as a "Mother hive" and noted that "peace and stability . . . are the first fruits of Mother-rule." She sought out pueblos as continuous with a vision she had had in childhood of "a warm lucent bubble of livingness," a unified force across species.[22] Pueblos and "livingness" were connected for Austin and others in this period by theologian Johann Bachofen's description of Mother Right as a time of "universal brotherhood . . . [and] undifferentiated unities" (see the end of Chapter One).[23] Among Indians, women often sought a world view similar to what Bachofen had described.

Mary Austin and Ruth Benedict predate the New Age by some fifty years. But some of the same assumptions and hopes for a society more accepting of a range of female identities underlie the primitivist aura of many New Age phenomena. Just as Africa or the American Southwest did for women who lived there, "the primitive" more abstractly understood and variously constituted provides New Age women with a space for alternative, positive images of what women can be and do. That is why after "healing" the two most popular words in the prayer bowl at the session I attended were "clarity" and "voice." In the New Age, these words are coded. "Clarity" refers to the goal of focusing female energies and getting women to recognize what they want; "voice" refers to speaking up and asserting female power.

The New Age conference I have described differed in some crucial ways from the men's movement gatherings I have treated. At the conference, "the primitive" represented a way of gaining access to strong, sure femininity within a broad vision of social progress and spiritual and ecological goals. In contrast, for the men, the primitive furnishes both access to "authentic" masculinity and a means of sublimating spiritual goals into nonverbal group activities. The groups' respective notions concerning what men and women should be like are frequently incompatible, even antithetical. In fact, participants in the men's groups and the "Nourishing the Soul" conference would probably not like to find themselves in the same room with one another.

Yet both groups lay claim, with equal confidence, to a version of traditional Native American life. What is more, each uses its particular version as a model of "the true," "the authentic," and "the desirable." It's hard to believe that traditional Native American culture could support *equally* and *accurately* the claims of both groups. Indeed, it's hard to believe that there ever was any such thing as "traditional Native American culture": there were always many cultures, organized differently and following very different lifeways—not all of which are likely to have conformed to current visions. But for the men's movement and the New Age, an often unspecific and inaccurate image called "Native American" speaks directly to current dilemmas and preoccupations; as another name for the primitive, it provides what people want or need most: a model of how to live a spiritual and harmonious life.

Secular Spirituality

The New Age critiques many problems associated with modern life, including confused or oppressive gender roles, cruelty to animals, and mutilation of the earth. It provides many people with solace and with a basis for altering some of the destructive patterns in their daily lives. It is by definition something new and revolutionary. But the New Age, like the men's movement, appears to operate well within the parameters of our cultural system. In fact, society tolerates the New Age quite easily and accepts it as a vehicle for spirituality that can work well with organized religions.

There is little doubt that spirituality is thriving, in many forms, in the United States today. Reports of God's death turn out to have been much exaggerated. In 1994, some 85 percent of the U.S. population declared a belief in some larger power called God and a full 20 percent felt they had received, during the last year, communication directly from God.[24] There are no statistics available, to my knowledge, concerning overlapping memberships between conventional churches and New Age groups. But it is fruitful to think about the New Age in a mutually influential connection with contemporary churches.

In fact, New Age thinking reflects certain modifications of traditional Judeo-Christian beliefs that show up in institutional religious settings as well. At Easter services I attended recently, for example, a Catholic priest supervised the lighting of a "pagan" bonfire. Later, he invited "anyone who shared" his belief that the Eucharist is the body and blood of Christ to partake of the sacrament—an acknowledgment I had never before heard at a Catholic mass that people present might not accept transubstantiation on faith. In the same way, a Reform rabbi invited me and my husband to use the words "Force that Moves the Universe" instead of "God" at my daughter's bat mitzvah "if it made us feel more comfortable." While much traditional dogma remains in place, similar accommodating forces are affecting traditional religions and the New Age, resulting in confluence between the two.[25] In the process, the image of a demanding and judgmental Judeo-Christian God is being eroded.

In 1994, the sociologist Robert Wuthnow published fascinating research in which he found that fully four out of ten Americans belonged to a "small group" that met regularly for purposes of self-help or for Bible study also aimed at self-help. Most of the groups Wuthnow studied, whether religious or secular, met within church buildings and often under church sponsorship. Membership in the groups was, like membership in the New Age, predominantly female, although there were some all-male groups as well.[26] Wuthnow's criteria for "small groups" excluded many New Age units, which are often larger, meet more aperiodically, and have shifting memberships; the four-out-of-ten figure might otherwise have been even higher. Still, many of his findings are directly applicable to the New Age.

The overarching belief guiding small groups, according to Wuthnow, is that the self comes first. In fact, he says, the need for members to support each other's sense of self-realization and self-fulfillment is so powerful that "to suggest that individual personal needs should be put in a secondary place runs against the ideology of many groups."[27] This belief is followed by a strong conviction that God is good and directly looks after the happiness of each individual. Wuthnow calls the ideology of small groups "secular spirituality," a form of religious expression suitable to modern life because, unlike some older forms of Judaic or Christian practice, it allows "people [to] go about their daily business without having to alter their lives very much because they are interested in spirituality" (*Sharing the Journey,* 7). It does not require individuals to engage in self-sacrifice or to subsume their desires in the interest of a group in the way that traditional families, communities, or religious orders typically do. It allows people to put themselves first.

What Wuthnow identifies as the essential appeal of secular spirituality holds true not only for the small groups he studied, but also for many aspects of the New Age. In fact, the ideology suggests a further motivation behind the New Age's affinity for Native American beliefs. In the contemporary imagination, the "tribal" primitive is posited as having a rich communal life. "I have never seen a people so devoted to family and to each other," says Kevin Costner's Lieutenant Dunbar in *Dances with Wolves*, in one typical expression of this view. But it is also posited as having a powerful, ecstatic, oceanic consciousness of the land.

In many of the life histories I have studied, achieving ecstatic consciousness required sacrifice, isolation from others, inner attunement to the eternal, and deviation from social norms—so much so that certain figures (like Gide and Lawrence) tended to back away, fearfully. For those who sustained their attraction to the oceanic—Dian Fossey and Georgia O'Keeffe, for example—closeness to animal life or the land seemed to necessitate giving up aspects of "ordinary" social and biological life. O'Keeffe cast off conventional marriage and motherhood; Fossey gave up not just marriage and motherhood but the preservation of her physical self. In a similar way, mystics within many Eastern and Western traditions—including Buddha, Ramakrishna, Francis of Assisi, Teresa of Avila, and others—felt the need to abandon property, reject marriage and sexuality, test the body, and surrender the self to the divine.[28] Historically, such mystical activity has often taken shape *within* traditional religions but then has proven disruptive enough to require cooptation and control—for example, when the Catholic church (a powerful property owner) compelled the Franciscan brotherhood to own property despite its founder's profound resistance, or when Spanish priests convinced Teresa that she must abandon her unconventional visions of a disembodied God. Mysticism often attracts unfavorable attention from social institutions because it has a radical, disruptive edge. This disruptive edge is something the New Age simply does not have.[29]

In fact, when one thinks about it, nothing particularly extreme is required for the exercise of spirituality through current, highly lyricized views of Native Americans or other "primitive" groups—as in today's New Age. Indeed, much that might ordinarily be jettisoned by the spiritual quester in other traditions—family, property, bodily health, good company, social acceptance, and comfort—can be preserved. Native Americans, after all, supposedly enjoyed *both* ideal family and community structures *and* a pervasive sense of access to the sacred, achieved effortlessly and expressed in daily life. Spirituality, we are asked to believe, *sim-*

ply happens for all good Indians and those who imitate them in ways they believe to be faithful.

Nor is anything special required of society in order to control or channel such spirituality. With regard to Indians, for example, the New Age typically imitates certain ceremonies, rituals, and attitudes; it does not, to sketch a different kind of possibility, support determined efforts to return the land of what is now the United States to its original owners—at which point, strong resistance from government or business might be expected. As a medium for spiritual expression, the New Age has no radical social consequences because it does not prevent anyone from enjoying a "normal" and comfortable existence. In the New Age, ecstatic impulses have come out of the closet, but they have also become curiously domesticated.

Now I need to be perfectly clear on this point: I do not mean to say that living a fairly ordinary life, socially and materially, is somehow inferior to casting off everything in spiritual fervor. Societies clearly depend for their continuation and good health on a certain number of people reproducing, working, and performing quotidian tasks. Nor do I mean to suggest that New Age participants are hypocritical or totally and utterly devoted to self (i.e., selfish). In fact, with regard to many individuals who participate in the New Age, I believe just the opposite to be true. People come to the movement—often, and I think significantly, in middle age—because they have experienced the limitations of autonomous individualism. They agree with William Wordsworth that in modern life, "getting and spending, we lay waste our powers." They want to connect to other people and to larger forces. In particular, they want to learn how to prepare for what comes after middle age: maturity, aging, the loss of gender and family roles that have anchored their lives, and ultimately death.[30] But in the most generalized history of the cultivation of spirituality, there are some essential tensions—between the worldly individual and the community, between self-consciousness and oceanic consciousness—that the New Age has found it possible to circumvent through its image of Native American life, its focus on self-help, and other means.

Have we arrived at a point where the ecstatic traditions of the past will converge? Are we really on the brink of a New Age? It seems likely instead that we may have moved beyond the point at which utopianism must conceive of itself as being at odds with society. Historian William

Leach sees ancestors of the New Age, like Mind Cure and Positive Thinking, as conditioned by the rise of the U.S. consumer culture.[31] I would make the same claim for the New Age, which has evolved through (and not just into) an elaborate network of businesses, with ties to publishing, psychological institutes, stores and clubs, the media, and other corporate entities, enjoying comfortable and lucrative niches within the very social structures it critiques. While it is true that many institutionalized churches also enjoy such comfortable niches, in the past they typically encountered considerable social resistance and grew *despite* persecution. Throughout this book, I have distinguished between religious emotions (spirituality) and their institutionalized forms within specific denominations. The New Age is not an institutionalized religion, but it has never existed outside organized, often commercial, social structures. Its commercial base explains, I believe, both its astonishing success and its greatest limitation.

In fact, the New Age demonstrates how the logic of our culture perceptibly demands that the impetus for change take shape within commercial enterprises and financial networks. Another way of putting this: many forms of fascination with the primitive today—New Age phenomena being good examples—are what we might call "tolerated transgression." Tolerated transgression allows discontents to surface and roil and circulate. It provides a continual windup towards change. But as to whether it ever allows for change, that remains to be seen.

CHAPTER NINE

Piercings

1990: The Video

THE PERFORMANCE ARTIST Monte Cazazza has made a video of his own genital piercing. There are no titles or credits. We go right to a close-up of a circumcised penis, totally flaccid, amid a tangle of pubic hair, lying against a white thigh. Electronic music erupts, punctuated by the word "Surgeon," repeated over and over in a robotic, heavily synthesized voice. The music increases in sound level and pace, but one ceases to notice it about twenty seconds into the three- to five-minute video.

The hand of an unseen operator holding a metallic needle-like device enters the scene. The needle pierces the head of the penis, leaving behind a single small gold stud, a rounded ball identical to those used to pierce ears in malls all over this country. The head of the penis, now adorned by the ball, is displayed to the camera for perhaps five seconds, then the penis is flipped over and an identical procedure is performed two to three times more, at the head and along the shaft.

Next, in a sequence that prompts a collective gasp in the audience, a tweezers-like device descends upon the head of the penis. It stretches the penis out like cotton candy, farther than anyone would have imagined the glans penis could be extended. The organ has been transformed into a visual object by now, only the awareness that it is actually still a penis prompts the deep collective gasp.

Now a broader needle, almost a lance, enters the amoeba-shaped, taffy-like, stretched and narrowed head of the penis. It makes a hole clear through, into which a metal bolt, perhaps ¼ inch thick, is inserted and secured at each end by a gleaming metal hemisphere. There is no blood visible, even though the video is in a grainy-textured color. The procedure completed, the penis is once again arranged on the thigh. For a few seconds, we are asked to admire the new adornments. Then the camera pans up to the performance artist's face. He's grinning and mouthing some words at us that are inaudible since the soundtrack consists only of chanted music. But he seems to be saying "It was great, man. Unbelievable."

• • •

THIS VIDEO was shown in 1990 at a conference held by jewelrymakers and craftspeople at the University of the Arts in Philadelphia. It was part of a quasi-underground phenomenon known as "piercing," which was then just emerging into public awareness and was on everybody's mind at this conference. Cazazza's video provided graphic evidence of genital piercing in contemporary culture. Before the 1990s, for many people the act did not exist outside certain books, like *The Story of O,* in which a woman wears rings and chains through her labia to signify her willingness to be a sexual slave. Such images—based loosely on the assumption that one form of penetration will lead to another—have been a standard convention in pornography for some time, and are especially featured with SM or related themes. They suggest how piercing is connected with sexuality in the modern imagination. But Cazazza's video shows that such acts are moving beyond the boundaries of pornography.

In fact, piercing has long had additional emotional overlays. It is associated with adolescent "gang" piercings of ears with needles (popularly at girls' sleep-overs). It is associated with gays and lesbians. It is connected with pirates and buccaneers, motorcycle gangs, and torturers. Piercing evokes associations along a continuum that ranges from adventuresomeness, roguishness, and travel, to rape, violence, and dismemberment. Both ends of this continuum are linked symbolically in the West to the idea of the primitive.

In addition, as decorative arts and social customs, piercing and tattooing are associated with "tribal" peoples. For these reasons, piercers today are sometimes called "modern primitives" after the title of a book published in 1989 by Re-Search. The book, *Modern Primitives,* is devoted to the contemporary arts of piercing, scarification, and tattooing, especially on or around the genitals. It includes a full panoply of penises and testicles, labia and clitorises, variously decked out. It also makes numerous allusions to "tribal" or indigenous cultures.

As one form of our contemporary fascination with the primitive, piercing is inspired by certain practices in parts of Africa, areas around the Indian Ocean, and the Americas. The Cazazza video, with its focus on the surgical alteration of male genitals (to the accompaniment of a repetitive chant) very loosely evokes rituals of adolescent male circumcision in Africa. More specifically, genital piercing borrows devices like ampellangs and other penile implants (such as tiny metal balls) from Bali and other places, where their purpose is typically the enhancement of sexual pleasure.[1] In addition, there are documented instances of tattooing, especially of female genitals, in the South Pacific, and of ritual bloodletting from the tongue or penis in ancient Mayan culture.[2]

But overall, and despite frequent allusions by the piercers themselves, it's misleading to compare contemporary piercing in the West too closely with documented instances from ancient or indigenous cultures. So far as I know, for example, no African group actually cuts or pierces the genitals solely for decorative purposes. Relatively few groups elsewhere are known to have decorated them with tattoos or scarification. In most traditional societies, piercing for decorative or ritual purposes, or both, while perhaps common, is usually confined to ears and noses; scarification and tattooing, to faces, chests, backs, and (in some cases) navels. What is more—and this is the angle from which I want to examine the topic—each of the non-Western examples functions within specific religious systems or within normative cultural contexts that make them quite different from genital piercing in the West. The current emphasis on genital piercing is first and foremost a postmodern phenomenon.

The Media, 1996

Since 1990, when I first saw the Cazazza video, piercing has emerged almost fully from the underground and become almost mainstream. In the early nineties, articles in *Newsday, Newsweek,* and other popular media have featured the practice. But—significantly—the discussion was minimally graphic and fairly sanitized. The articles described, for example, the kind of multiple ear and nose piercings that were already widely evident around the nation. A few publications, like *Newsweek,* showed tongue piercings as well, or mentioned genital piercings. But though procedures like Prince Alberts (in which hoops are inserted through the skin behind the head of the penis) were mentioned, they were not defined or even described as being done to the genitals.[3]

Meanwhile, specialized magazines devoted to the most extreme forms of genital piercing and tattooing were flooding alternative bookstores. Ads for "creative piercing" popped up in local newspapers and in the windows of shops frequented by the young or cool. A few, mostly arts-oriented periodicals ran pieces that frankly described genital piercing, often in connection with performance art. In *Art Journal,* Lonette Stinich published a version of the talk she'd given at the 1990 conference, when she showed Cazazza's video; among her interesting and valid suggestions was the idea that, as performance art, piercing has antecedents in Surrealism and Dada. In *Artforum International,* I published a short piece discussing both Cazazza's video and Stinich's lecture.[4]

But for the most part, readers of magazines and newspapers in general circulation were left free to imagine an ear or nose (or, occasionally, a brow, tongue, or navel) being pierced, instead of a penis or a clitoris. And that, I think, is what writers and editors had in mind: a two-tiered system of journalism, functioning differently for the uninitiated and for the cognoscenti. The uninitiated could get a vicarious thrill by being exposed to the idea of body piercing, without being seriously affronted by pictures or descriptions of breasts or genitals; the cognoscenti could get the additional charge of knowing what was "really" going on. These articles were classic teases, using one body part to stand in for another.

In 1992, Madonna's *Sex* introduced nipple piercing to a wide audience and reinforced its association with the imagery of pornography.[5] Alongside amateurish prose that read like Madonna's diary of sexual adventures, the book showed many nude images, among them both male and female nipples adorned with hoops. In some images, the rock star tugged at the nipple rings with her lips. The book assumed, fairly straightforwardly, that piercing was a sexual stimulant—like the garter belts or leather also shown in some of its images.[6]

By 1993, pierced lips, brows, and navels were all over alternative rock magazines and liner notes to rock CDs. Festivals like Lollapalooza were featured regularly in the national press and usually included, as standard stuff, booths for tattooing or piercing. In 1994, through the second Woodstock, moshing and raving became familiar terms and images. Almost overnight, they went from being code words known only in certain clubs and segments of rock culture for rough group dancing (sometimes done in mud or, at raves, with full primitivist regalia) to being buzzwords on MTV and in print journalism.[7] By the mid-nineties, perhaps predictably, a certain reverse chic had entered into the coverage. Lollapalooza, the word was, is just for kids. It had gone commercial, even mainstream. There was no alternative there anymore.

Around the same time, pierced brows, noses, lips, and navels became standard items on fashion runways and featured items in women's magazines. Even staid periodicals aimed at the well-heeled and mature, such as *Vogue,* ran spreads in which models wore nose or navel rings and dresses that simulated full body tattoos.[8] On the style page of *The New York Times,* photographs of seven fashionable men and women were grouped together. They grinned widely at the camera, overpowered by the joy of wearing their shirts—which looked for all the world like full-body Maori or Amazon Indian tattoos.[9]

By 1995, tattooed arms and pierced noses or lips began to appear, with some regularity, in ads for jeans and other casual clothing. For his perfume CK, Calvin Klein used male models wearing ear and nose rings, and a female wearing studs near her mouth, like metallic dimples. Even the normally "preppy," clean-cut Gap considered showing its clothes on tattooed or pierced models when its gear fell out of favor with people under thirty. If this comes to pass (it had not as this book went to press), CK and other brands will have beaten them to the punch.

Also in the mid-nineties, parents began to write about the trauma—or, as it often turned out, nontrauma—of having their adolescent children pierce their noses or navels.[10] One day during the summer of 1994, when I was swimming at a local pool in fairly placid Durham, North Carolina, a male sunbather proudly unveiled his large, thick gold nipple rings. People noticed (I could see the furtive glances; this is still not a common sight), but they tried their hardest not to be caught looking. A few years earlier, this man would have been likely to show his nipple rings only in certain, often gay, urban clubs. Now they had gone suburban.

As a topic, then, body piercing is a moving target; it is impossible to predict where it will be in a year's time. But in 1996, as this book went to press, the target still hovered just about at the navel; I took this fact to be significant, given the relative exposure, even domestication, of body piercing during the previous five years. When, for example, the title of an article in *The New York Times* asked "How Far Does Piercing Go?" I read with interest. I was intrigued to find that, once again, the article stopped rather chastely at midline. Coverage of piercing was moving lower. But by the mid-nineties, it hadn't gotten down as far as Cazazza's penis. Taboos on male frontal nudity were holding amazingly well. Allusions to genital piercing continued to be either coded or subliminal.

Despite all the quasi-exposure, discussions of piercing have been held in check. The limit, I believe, has been the boundary of pornography. The closest thing I've found to an up-front discussion of genital piercing was a very brief mention in Quentin Tarantino's film *Pulp Fiction* and a short section of Sallie Tisdale's *Talk Dirty to Me* (both 1994). In *Pulp Fiction*, a druggie named Jodie shows her tongue piercing and mentions a piercing in her "clit." The John Travolta character seems most interested in the tongue piercing. "It's a sex thing. For fellatio," says Jodie, putting piercing on familiar sexualized ground.[11] In a similar way, *Talk Dirty to Me* records "twenty-three 'traditional' sexual piercings," though it does not mention any quite as spectacular as Cazazza's ampellang. Tisdale speculates in an interesting way that "tattoos, scarification, and body piercing are normal among many people, perhaps among *most* people," and notes that they are no weirder than lifting "weights until your body becomes a new shape altogether" or inflating breasts with silicon—both fairly common in modern culture. Still, for Tisdale as for Madonna, genital piercing is primarily an erotic tool: piercing "increases sexual pleasure," pretty much like the sex toys Tisdale also mentions frequently in her book.[12]

In the late nineties, then, the context for discussing piercing is both different from and the same as that at the beginning of the decade. Different because the topic is "in the air"—both mentionable and mentioned. The same because it continues to be partially hidden or to get sublimated into discussions of sexuality, which is only part of what genital piercing is about. It isn't possible for me to feel as shocked about piercing in 1996 as in 1990; familiarity has bred familiarity. But with its uncompromising starkness, Cazazza's video would still, I believe, have the power to defamiliarize piercing and to evoke a gasp in the audience, fascination, a buzz. In fact, I suspect that the aura of sophistication surrounding the topic of piercing, and especially genital piercing, today is often feigned.[13]

I want to understand not just why and how piercing has entered the mainstream but also why and how it has not and probably cannot. These questions have a lot to do with the issues I have raised so far: how piercings are displayed and what they are allowed to mean to the viewer; the borders between the decorative, the sexual, and the pornographic. The questions also have a lot to do with the distinction between what I will call (following Lonette Stinich) "committed" and "casual" piercers. This distinction seems necessary and makes sense. I will use it repeatedly, even though I will ultimately want to claim that it is not an easy boundary to sustain because today seepage occurs in both directions. In fact, I will ultimately want to suggest that the act of piercing violates taboos ordinarily respected even by the pornographic text.

Committed Piercers

Committed piercers have been doing piercing for a while and have extensive piercings, sometimes also accompanied by large-scale tattoos or scarifications. Their bodies may appear normal when fully clothed, but they are noticeably different, even freakish, when undressed. The *Modern Primitives* volume, for example, shows fifty-two-year-old Fakir dressed for his job as an executive in Silicon Valley, wearing a three-piece suit and glasses. Then it shows Fakir with his many tattoos and piercings displayed both front and rear, or with his waist tightly bound in to nineteen inches. It's like Clark Kent, suddenly become Superman: Fakir reveals, beneath his mild-mannered exterior, the real him. Like Fakir, committed piercers identify themselves in a crucial way through their piercings and other body modifications and are likely to be from thirty on up in age. Often, they are celebrities among their peers and subscribe to philosophies they associate with and express through piercing. Although they may (like Fakir) be businessmen, they don't think of their piercings as part of everyday life or as things to be bought and sold. Instead, they typically think of their piercings as a protest against the commodification rampant in everyday life, and this makes sense to a point. Piercings are art in the body; they travel with the body and die with it. Except through the medium of photography or videos, after the initial act, piercings can no longer be bought or sold.[14]

Other, more casual piercers may have several ear or nose piercings, and perhaps also one or more eyebrow, tongue, lip, navel, or genital piercings. But they got pierced mostly because other people were doing it—out of a sense of style, fashion, fad, or curiosity. If they have a genital piercing, it is often with the straightforward expectation of enhanced sexual pleasure. While the piercing may be important to them and their image, they are usually much less involved with piercing as a philosophical issue, even an alternative lifestyle, than committed piercers. Often, although not always, these casual piercers are young, even teens still in high or middle school—too young to predict what direction (if any) piercing will take in their future lives.

Committed piercers, on the other hand, go pretty far and exert multiple pressures on their bodies. The frontispiece to *Modern Primitives,* for example, shows a white man enacting his version of the Plains Indian sun ritual. He hangs from a tree, suspended by metal hooks inserted through his chest tendons. His head lolls back in a way that clearly shows the thin, three-inch stick which has been inserted through the fleshy tip of his nose. He has some feathers stuck into (not, it appears, just onto) his legs and body, in a manner evocative of arrows. He has thick tattoos around his hips and abdomen and a few scattered tattoos on his chest. The hip and abdomen tattoos recall decorative Amazon or South Pacific styles and form a tight, unified girdle; the chest tattoos are less distinctive, more isolated, random tattoos of the kind common in the United States—"Mom," a heart, a dagger.

The man also has grass wrist- and anklebands and leather armbands (which also hold feathers). As he hangs, he crosses his hands gently, even fondly, directly above his penis, with the fingers pointing down in an annunciatory gesture. The image is strong stuff, drawing on a number of "primitive" and "modern" traditions. It is a fitting entrée to the book itself, which includes interviews with and photographs of famous piercers, tattooers, and body scarifiers, sometimes singly, sometimes in couples. It also includes multiple allusions to primitive cultures and source lists for further information.

Committed piercers claim detailed histories for their practices and matter-of-factly provide names, make distinctions, and trace genealogies. The Prince Albert, for example, was named after Victoria's spouse, who reportedly had one; the horizontal penis bolt shown in Cazazza's video is an ampellang similar to those used in areas surrounding the Indian Ocean. A guiche is a ring through the perineum. Mayans, Hindus, French legionnaires, and Europeans during the Middle Ages all practiced forms of genital piercing; which kinds and why they were used are discussed in a cool, historical tone in one section of the *Modern Primitives* volume.

In fact, all of the people represented in *Modern Primitives* have histories and philosophies that intersect in complicated ways with more main stream views. Several have travelled extensively in New Guinea or Polynesia. Some have lived in villages, learning and studying piercing and tattooing, much as ethnographers might do. Others have done extensive archival research and claim ancient precedents for their practices.

Wes Christensen, for example, sees piercing for men as a quasi-mystical experience. Christensen, who is described in *Modern Primitives* as a painter and scholar of Mayan history, says that through genital piercing "the Male expresses the desire to own the magically fertile menstrual flow by mimicking it." But, he adds, "the symbol seems less important than its function of linking the opposing forces of mother/father, sky/earth in one ritual practitioner" (88). Significantly, for Christensen, the piercing that remains in the body is relatively unimportant and whatever sexual pleasure it confers afterwards is not a motivation. For him, the motivation is access to the blood shed during the act of piercing. It represents access to "the female" and hence to a symbolic union of opposites.

The male piercer and performance artist Genesis P-Orridge invokes a similar mélange of Jungian principles and a desire for androgyny. P-Orridge says, "My nipples were a dead zone before they got pierced. Then they became a whole new discovery. It was nice—like being female as well" (*Modern Primitives*, 177). This pressure to share qualities of both sexes shows up again and again in testimonies by male piercers. It suggests that achieving gender mixtures within a single personality is often a psychological motivation for piercing, especially for men.[15]

This kind of gender difference makes sense in our culture. Pierced ears have been acceptable for women for a long time, even though they once, in some parts of Europe, were fashionable only among prostitutes. In the same way, in heterosexual pornography, it is usually the woman who gets pierced. Ear piercing became common for men only during the late 1970s and 1980s. Before that, it was assumed that only homosexuals did it. Ear piercing no longer implies very much about a man's straightness or gayness; the "is he or isn't he?" controversies of left ear versus right seem like a distant memory. But piercing retains a different ambiance for the two sexes. Ear piercing is a common and often communal act for women, with earrings circulating among women as loans and gifts. It is commonly done for female children in certain American ethnic cultures, such as Italian and Hispanic Americans. What is more, women who pierce their ears late in life often say that the act made them feel a certain connection to or sense of solidarity with other women. For men, piercing remains a relatively more isolated act. It bespeaks a certain impulse to adopt properties associated with the other sex. As Christensen and P-Orridge suggest, this impulse often functions for men as the symbol of even broader mergings or crossings.

Jungian images come up a lot in *Modern Primitives*. In fact, piercers and tattooers see their practices as points of entry to a universal, symbolic realm. For this reason, Carl Jung is a patron saint for tattooers and piercers, much as he is for the mythopoetic men and for many New Agers. The tattooer Ed Hardy, for example, developed an interest in tattooing at age twelve, when it struck him that tattooers "were like the Keepers of the Images. They'd have displayed the whole emotional gamut: love and hate and sex and death—all in codified designs that were bright and bold" (*Modern Primitives,* 52). He sees tattooing as a tribute to both the universal and the individual, as "an affirmation: you put it on yourself with the knowledge that this body is yours to have and enjoy" (51). The satanic cultist Anton LaVey agrees that control over the body is the goal of such practices, though his accent is less upbeat than Hardy's, stressing separation, not connection, as the point of tattooing: "If a person feels alienated . . . [and] they didn't happen to be *born* looking freaky or strange, then activities like getting a tattoo [or piercing] are a way of *stigmatizing one's self*" (LaVey's emphasis; *Modern Primitives,* 94). I want to stress the contrapuntal movement suggested by Hardy's comments and LaVey's: piercing and tattooing simultaneously connect piercers to "universal images" and others who are "freaky and strange," and separate them from their "ordinary" culture. In contemporary life, then, piercing enacts both a severing of the self from "mainstream" society and a joining with alternatives.

Raelyn Gallina, a jewelrymaker, articulates the same duality somewhat differently. She sees piercing and the related practice of scarification as ways to move from alienation to affirmation. "Piercing started at a time in my life when I was experiencing a lot of death, and grief, and transformation," Gallina says. "For a lot of people it's a rite of transformation, when they go from one state to the next"(*Modern Primitives,* 101). Gallina emphasizes that the emotions surrounding the experience must be devoid of violence and filled with trust and support. When that happens, she says, "a lot of times being cut [to produce the scars in scarification] is a very strengthening and powerful experience" (101).

Gallina's story typifies how, although one expects a certain amount of violence in these narratives, one does not find it. The volume emphasizes the good feelings piercing provides and entirely minimizes suggestions of violence outside the controlled and voluntary context of SM relationships. Piercings, then, enter the body but do not violate it. They have a different emotional surround from violent acts of penetration, such as rape, stabbing, or shooting. Yet the violent forms always hover around the edges of contemporary piercing.

In fact, the SM connection leaps to mind in connection with body piercing and comes up repeatedly in *Modern Primitives*. But it would be wrong to stress it too much. The *Modern Primitives* volume shows that committed piercers and tattooers are heterogeneous. Piercers include those who identify themselves as performance artists or simply as artists, as well as those who identify themselves by their sexual tastes: heterosexual, lesbian, gay, and bisexual; SM and not SM; in marriages or other long-term partnerships, and not; and various combinations. Educational levels and ways of making a living vary substantially. Stereotype associates tattooing and piercing with certain gay and lesbian subcultures, and these practices do in fact flourish there. Yet piercing and tattooing don't belong to any one group; they belong to a variety of self-defined groups within contemporary culture. The philosophies behind committed piercing suggest, in fact, that group definition is an important aspect of piercing, with the characteristics defining the group extending well beyond SM and other sexual expressions.

Ritual, Participation, and Display

The term "modern primitives" for committed piercers is both unfortunate and apt. When people allow themselves to be strung up by their chest tendons, they think of themselves as enacting Native American rituals. The actions are the same whether performed by Native Americans, now or in the past, or by men who are not Indians. Still, there must be gaps between the meanings of such actions when performed by different people in different contexts.

In a similar way, Cazazza's video very loosely evokes practices of genital cutting in some African cultures. Specifically, it evokes village rituals of adolescent male circumcision. These practices have held a special fascination for Western ethnographers and have been well documented. But the very form the documentation has taken helps to reveal an important difference between the indigenous models and the postmodern practice. I want to compare traditional and postmodern practices, not to judge the postmodern as "authentic" or "inauthentic," but to mark certain differences between piercers today and the groups they think of themselves as imitating.

In the "tribal" models, cutting is an activity in which everyone participates in ways that are clear and predetermined within each culture. This is true both in African male adolescent circumcision and in other, less pleasant group rituals in the past, such as torturing enemies among certain Indian tribes. The Indians had detailed etiquettes for which body parts would be cut first, and by which gender and age groups. The victims knew the etiquette too and what responses were expected of them. In "tribal" models, people see themselves as performing ritual functions, even if all they do is to stand and observe the cutting or admire the boy's or the enemy's stoicism in the face of pain. In other words (and this is one standard definition of ritual), "participation" takes place in many ways, but everyone who comes into contact with the ritual is a participant.

Today, cutting, piercing, and their aftermath are often secretive and done outside the public sphere. Or, if they are intended for display, they are displayed in front of audiences that may or may not share the belief systems of the piercer. In other words, spectatorship, rather than participation, is the norm. If acts like piercing have certain recognized, culturally defined meanings in indigenous cultures, they have arbitrary and unpredictable meanings today.

In ethnographic photos, especially those made in the nineteenth century or earlier in the twentieth century, Westerners held the camera. Africans or others participating in ritual regarded the camera as either irrelevant or as an outright intruder. We can see this in the ethnographic photographs taken by Marcel Mauss of male adolescent circumcision in Africa, photographs now displayed as part of the permanent collection at the Musée de l'Homme. In the photos, the boys about to be circumcised hang together, as if for support and protection, and share identical garb and ritual items. They peer out at the camera shyly, looking invaded and startled. When I see these photographs, I feel like a voyeur, someone who has violated the privacy of the boys and their culture.

It is even possible to say that the moment at which the camera becomes essential in the eyes of indigenous peoples, something important has been lost. When, for example, a group dances just for a fee or for the sake of being filmed, something has changed for the culture. It may be the sense that their ways of doing things are "natural" and "right." Or it may be the assumption that things will continue in the same way in the future. That may be why Pueblo Indian cultures in the Southwest strictly forbid photography, drawing, and taping (even audiotaping) at ritual dancing. That may be why we are haunted by photographs of Indians or others when they harbor an unwillingness to be photographed or seem ill at ease. I think, for example, of certain photographs of Filipinos at international "expositions" or of captured Indians whose hostility was just barely tamped down by the camera.

In contrast, the modern primitives in the Re-Search volume face the camera solo or in pairs and they almost always mug at the camera, play to it. They are comfortable with the camera, regard it as a friend and companion—something inevitable, perhaps even part of new and contemporary ritual structures (like wedding videos). For the modern primitives, being photographed or filmed is, in a sense, to really *be*. An action performed is somehow not enough; the trace, the record are needed too.

Photographs and videos make such records easy. They preserve the "ing" in piercing—a form of preservation to which traditional people were largely indifferent, and sometimes hostile. In addition, they solve the problem of how to show certain piercings, such as genital piercings, to the world. Modern primitives are like fans at a ball game (or even U.S. senators at the State of the Union address), tickled pink to catch a glimpse of themselves on TV monitors. Hi, Mom: once they have been on the monitor, they are somehow *more really there*, at the event, than ever. The camera is strictly incidental to the Africans whom Mauss photographed; it's a raison d'être, a reason for being, for the modern primitives.

The camera bespeaks a certain alienation from action as meaningful in itself. It even suggests acceptance of such alienation among modern primitives—and this is one reason that piercing exists in an ambiguous relationship to the concept called "reification," which deplores alienation in modern life.[16] But a counterimpulse is also at work. In indigenous cultures, scarification and tattoos often function to mark identity, profession, rank, or kinship affiliations. They are a way to affirm one's place in a normative communal structure. Contemporary piercing seeks new but transgressive forms of identity, community, and affiliation, based on holes and jewelry in various parts of the body. We who are pierced are one, the piercers seem to say. We are one as villagers are one. We recognize each other and are recognized as different from the American masses. We establish our difference from the norm—hint at it with the multiple pieces we wear in our ears and noses, confirm it with the pieces we wear in "private" zones we have willed into public speech.

In its extreme forms, especially its public forms like Cazazza's video, piercing presents itself as ritual. I mean here a stylized, repeatable action with a public dimension, an action designed to give order and meaning to the flux of experience, to draw disparate people into a whole. Cazazza's video and the testimony in the *Modern Primitives* volume make this point quite clear: piercers seek ritual itself, the essential things that will get to the essential.

In Extremis

Among people who know, teach, or parent casual piercers, one view comes up again and again. The piercing is like long hair and beards in the sixties; for the piercers, it's just a way of protesting, of marking themselves as different. It's as harmless as Woodstock. For the young, it's like green hair or shaved heads, a way of standing out, a generational style that, like all effective generational styles, has the ability to upset older people. Often, those advancing this view then trail off into a sense that something is different about piercing—though they can't say exactly what. But the comforting argument that it's just the sixties all over again, but in different terms, doesn't seem to work—at least, not exactly.

What makes piercing, tattooing, and scarification different from long hair, shaved heads, or beards? I think it has to do with irrevocability. A hole can close, but the sign or mark is always there, potentially to be reopened. A tattoo can be removed, but only by a process more arduous than creating the tattoo in the first place. A scarification will heal, but the smoothness of the skin can only be restored by further and different kinds of cutting in plastic surgery. Piercing, tattooing, and scarification are, and are intended to be, permanent—to mark a change of life and body, not just of appearance. What is more, unlike hair color or style, piercing (like tattooing and scarification) directly reaches flesh and blood. Piercing, even casual piercing, gets in there; it evokes core issues.

Onstage, Ron Athey, a performance artist, opens his skin or another man's with a scalpel and dapples paper towels with the blood released. Then he sends the towels out on clotheslines strung over the audience. In some performances, the blood is drawn from Athey himself, who is HIV-positive; in others, the blood is drawn from another artist, Darryl Carlton, who is HIV-negative. Either way, nothing at all harmful has happened to anyone looking on. The blood is up there on the clotheslines; it's not a possible source of contagion. But the acts are, and are intended to be, provocative, even aggressive. It's no accident that the conservative right is upset that the National Endowment for the Arts funded Athey.[17] Artists like Athey believe, and I agree, that art can legitimately, among many other possibilities, upset people. In fact, he means for anyone who sees or hears about his performance to feel uneasy. The actions tap into the audience's deepest fascinations and fears. That, I would suggest, is ultimately what piercing is and what piercing does.

Piercing, especially genital piercing, is an extreme bodily experience. It is thrilling and addictive, in touch with flesh and blood, life and death. This is true even when, as was the case in the Cazazza video, blood is not especially featured or visible. In fact, some genital piercings, like Cazazza's ampellang, must avoid blood-rich vessels or the man being pierced might literally bleed to death; that is why the head of Cazazza's penis was stretched out into a translucent amoeba-shape before the ampellang was inserted. Yet in Cazazza's video, the absence of blood serves to bespeak its possible and terrifying presence: *in getting an ampellang, a man risks bleeding to death.*

In fact, when modern primitives cease to celebrate the body, they tend to stress instead its fragility and utter mortality. The tattooer Ed Hardy, for example, added to his remark that "this body is yours to have and enjoy" the important codicil: "while you're here." In his interview, Genesis P-Orridge stressed, with an uneasy laugh, that death is "absolutely nothing, and do not kid yourself. It's the end: blank, black, gone, not even a mini-thought for a second." His partner and fellow piercer, Paula P-Orridge, added, "When you die you're just a piece of meat" (172). Such remarks percolate through *Modern Primitives.* They denote a crucial tension between decorating the body and recognizing its transience; between controlling and owning the self, demonstrated through piercing, and surrendering it. That is why, I believe, some people have proposed, as logical extensions of videos of one's body piercing, videos of one's own sterilization, or autopsy, or cremation. At this valence, clearly the death wish would be courted most. The owned body would be disowned and spectacularly, if morbidly, transformed into inorganic matter.

Piercing is the intersection or interpenetration of matter and flesh. It evokes crossings between bodies, blood, and minerals; sexuality, pleasure, and violence; life force and death force. It puts the inanimate and animate together in a tiny, controlled way, often with an accompanying desire for tableau, display, and witness. But it also evokes the possibility of more extensive, less controlled crossings from animate to inanimate, in which the witness can potentially become the victim too. It is, for example, a stretch—but not too great a stretch—to connect the impulses behind piercing with the need to revisit, in a controlled, minor key, the most terrible images of our time. Bodies or body parts piled in concentration camps, some awaiting transformation into soap or lampshades; bodies sprawled at Hiroshima or vaporized in the atomic blast; bodies plowed into mass graves in Kampuchea or Rwanda. In the Introduction, I claimed that these terrible events of our century have motivated, in part, the return to the primitive as a source of reinvigorating power. They simultaneously reveal how the impulse to merge can be either spiritual and harmonious, or connected with fearful destruction.

Piercing evokes the body in extremis. In a way, it is a willful, small-scale imitation of *sparagmos,* the dismemberment by hand of an animal or human body by an orgiastic, sacrificial mob. Piercing loosens a sense of promiscuous connection. There may well be something superficial about the way in which piercing and tattooing are being deployed in contemporary culture, and especially among casual piercers—I do not want to scant that fact. Indeed, the difference between committed piercers and casual, "Sunday" piercers epitomizes a fault line that runs throughout this book: between those who are open to transcendent experience—and, sometimes, achieve it—and those who are just dabbling or playing around. But the triviality of some piercing is a separate issue that should not obscure the core meanings of the act. Finally, there is nothing superficial or casual about the themes or the feelings to which piercing can furnish access.

Sacred Wounds

As the joining of mineral and flesh, piercing is almost a pure symbol of mergings and crossings. Lonette Stinich describes piercing as "a return to mystery, to the body, and to sensations" which "sanctifies blood and marks." I believe she is right. This image of piercing returns us once more to where we have been several times in this book. It returns us once again to the body in extremis as the body on the threshold of vision.

Neglect or abuse of the body and contempt for comfortable, bourgeois norms have been established parts of ecstatic practice in many religious traditions. With its imagery of penetration and blood, piercing seems especially related to Christian images of crucifixion, martyrdom, and abasement of the self before the divine: Christ's hands and feet, rent by stakes; Saint Sebastian, riddled with arrows; Saint Julian, crisscrossed by lances; Saint Teresa receiving the throes of divinity, kneeling at the feet of Bernini's spear-bearing, leering angel. Even outside Western traditions, the mystic's way seems to require mortification of the flesh. Legend has it that Buddha left his princely life and became an ascetic on his way to enlightenment; he had to reject his comely wife because he had to deny the pleasures of the flesh, the desire for immortality in or through the flesh. Centuries later, Gandhi practiced strict vegetarianism and hunger fasts, and eventually vowed sexual abstinence. The purpose of Plains Indian sun rituals, and of practices like sweat lodges or long hours of dancing, is to produce dehydration, hallucination, and vision.

Similar motifs and actions appear in mystical Christian traditions. Francis of Assisi left a comfortable merchant's home to sleep on straw among lepers, eating only what he could get from people in his town. He devoted his life to establishing a brotherhood that rejected all ownership of land and goods. The Church looked on with admiration, but also with extreme suspicion. It bided its time until it could impose rules and force property on Francis' brothers.[18] Teresa of Avila also rejected property. The nature of her visions aroused the suspicions of her church, specifically of the Inquisition.[19] Like many nuns, she experienced vague disorders affecting her bones and joints and was often unable to eat. Teresa's autobiography records again and again how she puked out her guts as a prelude to vision. It is easy to say that Teresa and some fellow nuns were bulimic and anorexic. But that statement is meaningless without understanding the symbolic content of the acts. Teresa and other mystics turned away from the body to achieve, through the body, sacred vision.

Renouncing certain pleasures is often perceived, in religious traditions, as inviting others. Often—and as a test or crucial case—property is rejected, as a metaphor for how ownership of the self is surrendered to the divine. "A feeling of the presence of God would come over me unexpectedly, so that I could in no wise doubt either that He was within me, or that I was wholly absorbed in Him," said Teresa. Through the female goddess Kali, whom he served, Ramakrishna experienced the sensation of being salt in "an ocean of ineffable joy." Amid the "ocean of the spirit, boundless, dazzling," Ramakrishna says, "It seemed as if nothing existed any more. . . . I was suffocated."[20] The body in extremis is the body on the threshold of vision. The body in extremis is on the threshold of merger with the divine.

The earlier, religious instances I have cited are widely regarded as images of transcendence. They are read as the assertion of spirit over body. Yet the body is the inevitable medium for spiritual experience. Religious emotions are registered in sexualized terms: Teresa's God within her; Ramakrishna's Mother as ocean to his salt. Contemporary piercing is, admittedly, colored by fashion and fad. Sometimes it is philosophically motivated, sometimes not. Its relationship to phenomena like "reification" is confused and vexed. Its ambiance gets sublimated (rather more directly than for Teresa and Ramakrishna) into sexuality. I do not want to sanctify committed piercers or to portray them as contemporary heroes: their practices are poised too precariously between internal transcendence and exhibitionism, eros and the death wish, for that to be a comfortable stance. But still, there is something about piercing that defamiliarizes the typical conditions of modern life and sets piercing apart from, for example, the New Age. And it is this spirit of questioning that I salute and even cherish. For some contemporary piercers, Prince Alberts and ampellangs are clearly a means to an end—like acrylics and oils for visionary artists; like chalices or communion hosts for practicing Catholics. Is it merely provocative, then—or only fair—to read some contemporary piercings as parables of transcendence too?

Storm over the Pedernal, Ghost Ranch, 1959
Photographer: Todd Webb
Courtesy of Todd Webb and Olaf Olaf

CONCLUSION

Why should we not also enjoy an original relation to the universe?

RALPH WALDO EMERSON, *Nature*

IN THE SUMMER of 1994, there was an official Native American protest against the New Age appropriation of Plains Indian spiritual traditions. A group of Lakota Sioux staged a sit-in at Bear Butte in the Black Hills of South Dakota, near the sites of the Little Bighorn and Wounded Knee massacres and Harney Peak, which is sacred to many Plains Indians (the visionary Black Elk called this spot "the center of the world"). The Black Hills also house Mount Rushmore, a twentieth-century monument to the U.S. presidents most responsible for expansion westward.

Recently, the Black Hills have been the subject of a prolonged and messy lawsuit. In the 1970s, the United States Supreme Court officially ruled that the land rightfully belonged to the Lakota and ordered that the federal government pay $105 million as compensation for wrongful seizure. But the court did not order legal transfer of the land. So far, the Lakota have refused to accept the monetary settlement, and today the Black Hills exist in a curious legal limbo.[1]

In 1994, the Native Americans' complaint was that New Age adherents were overrunning the site to perform their rituals. The New Agers saw themselves as imitating and honoring Native Americans, with some of the whites even dressing as and calling themselves shamans. But the Indians felt the rituals were bogus and disrespectful to the land. As one of them put it, the Sioux don't want white, "plastic medicine men." Such a feeling is widespread among those Native Americans interested in reviving traditional life. It might apply not just to New Age rituals at Bear Butte but to each of the contemporary phenomena chronicled in the last few chapters. Whites are trying hard to learn the lessons of Native spirituality and to re-create Native rituals. But Indians are not always flattered by these forms of imitation: "If whites want to be spiritual," said John Lavelle, director of a center for protecting Indian culture, "let them investigate their own religions" and look to their own "traditions."[2] *Let them look to their own traditions.* The attraction of the primitive in modern life results from both the desire and the difficulty of doing just that.

All of the figures and phenomena I have discussed are linked by a common identification of "tribal" or traditional peoples with oceanic experience. Often, Westerners seem like Adam and Eve banished from the Eden of the primitive, convinced that some ecstatic primal emotions have been lost, almost as a penalty for being Western. Yet from time to time in this book, I have suggested that what is now sought in the primitive is really a reflection or projection of something that could also be found in the West at many different times, in many different forms—and can even be found today. But recognizing the full range of sensations and emotions available within the West requires overturning long-held preconceptions about the essential differences of other cultures against which it defines itself.

We often hear, for example, that before contact with Europeans, Indians in the Americas had a different conception of time. For them, the present was simply the unravelling of the past in alternative, "branching" directions, a notion Europeans found mysteriously alien. But consider all the centuries of debate in the West concerning free will and its meaning—what were these inquiries but imaginings and reimaginings of the relationship between past, present, and future? Europeans were likewise fascinated by the Indians' belief in beings who were half animal and half human, and their imitation of such beings in their ritual dances. But what are the minotaur, the satyrs, and the mermaids if not Western versions of the half-animal/half-human beings who haunt many African and Native American traditions? Alchemy and trials involving animals as defendants were once fairly common in European life; their liberal investment of nature with supernatural powers closely resembles practices we would today call animism and attribute to "primitive" peoples. But to dissociate our contemporary Western selves from past Western impulses is to disown patterns of thought from Platonism through Transcendentalism that have assumed the existence of a spiritual realm at which our senses, limited to the material world, can only guess.

Even today, the Western creative imagination gravitates towards the supernatural. Popular culture is full of cyborgs, robots, and other futuristic phantasms that commingle organic and inorganic elements in a single being. Often, narratives featuring such beings include speculations about what the future will be like, speculations that sometimes posit—as in the *Terminator* series or *Planet of the Apes*—an apocalyptic return to prehistoric conditions of life. Similar impulses exist in modern literary forms such as magical realism, in which dead ancestors speak and the physical laws of the universe are suspended.[3]

But in searching for expressions of the collective Western fascination with the world beyond the senses, we need not limit ourselves to the past or to fictions for a sense of wonder. There are mainstream scientists who ponder the body and the brain, the cosmos and the dimensions of time, the properties of animals and viruses, as profound and often as extremely moving mysteries. I think, for example, of Sherwin Nuland's combination of technical mastery and awe in his descriptions of death in *How We Die*.[4] I think also of the scientific concept of an eventual, universal return to matter—a startling equivalent, in symbolic terms, of both the Christian afterlife (at the end of time, we become one with the eternal) and, in a rather different key, the Freudian death wish.[5] It requires only a change in accent to see continuities and not just differences between the posited unities of primitive cultures and the analytic modes of modern life.

As I was writing this book, I kept looking for ways of understanding how the process of effacing the oceanic in Western life had come to seem so natural. I also pondered how the oceanic had become entangled with the idea of the primitive and the feminine. At various points, I felt impelled to go to sources that seemed to me, at the time, mysterious: Euripides' *The Bacchae*, Western mystics like Francis of Assisi and Teresa of

Avila, European witchcraft trials, Martin Buber, Romain Rolland and Sigmund Freud, Claude Lévi-Strauss, even the counterculture of the 1960s.[6] I found in these seeming detours from the Western way a destination instead. Each represents a moment in the evolving drama of the civilized and the primitive, the masculine and the feminine, the secular and the spiritual, the self and some greater unity. Each is a point in the movement from ancient to modern times when the usual primacy of the first element in each pair over the second did not seem so inevitable.

Nevertheless, the question remains: How did we arrive at the illusion of utter separation between a primitive "them" and a civilized "us"?[7] I believe the answer to be this: Century by century, choice by choice, until by now the separation between "them" and "us," like the separation between the physical world and ourselves, appears to be inevitable. Bit by bit, thread by thread, the West has woven a tapestry in which the primitive, the oceanic, and the feminine have been banished to the margins in order to protect—or so the logic went—the primacy of civilization, masculinity, and the autonomous self.

The habit of imagining the oceanic as Other rather than as part of our own experience may have evolved, then, as a way of protecting the conditions which, in the West, now seem to ground the very idea of selfhood. These conditions include autonomy, hierarchy, gender, nation or ethnicity, family, and property. In fact, the West's aspirations to the permanence and efficacy of its social structures may well be the "rub," the difficulty, involved in embracing the oceanic fully. For the oceanic does not highlight individual human lives and genealogies, or specific societies and their particular values: these can only be a tiny and insignificant part of a greater totality. In the oceanic, "all can become nothing, even the living."[8] For these reasons, in a contemporary Western context, the oceanic can seem "counterintuitive" and to lack a space in which to unfold and develop.

But current conceptions of selfhood and the concomitant resistance to the oceanic did not emerge, like Athena, fully formed from the head of Western man. Instead, oceanic perceptions have been, at various times and places—including all those I have mentioned earlier—relatively close to the surface of Western life.[9] Even Sigmund Freud, that archenemy of the oceanic, in one of his most profound and moving paradoxical moments, described the death drive as resembling an "instinct towards perfection." But, he said, perfection is something "whose existence we [civilized beings, including Freud himself] cannot admit."[10] Freud surely understood the projected end of the universe as a form of transpersonal, inhuman "perfection"—similar in many ways to what certain scientists call the Omega Point and Eastern religions call the Tao.[11] But, as he said, he could never "admit" it. To do so would have been to undercut too radically the values by which he had chosen to live and work.

In the process by which the oceanic has been censored or effaced from the ordinary image of Western existence, two elements are particularly important and worth singling out. The first is organized religion; the second is the idea of ownership—for example, of land or property. I want to handle each in turn, beginning with the role of religion, which is complex and highly ambiguous.

On the one hand, Western religions have provided, and continue to provide, a home for oceanic emotions. Religions describe the intersection of the human and the divine, mortal existence and the ultimate meaning of the cosmos; they allow access to ecstatic experiences such as holy communion, speaking in tongues, and faith healing.[12] On the other hand, organized religions, as we have seen in the histories of Francis and Teresa, simultaneously work to police the oceanic—which by its very nature exceeds and overflows institutional bounds. Organized religions tend to channel ecstatic impulses into forms that are not threatening to the institutional church or the civil state, and may even serve them.[13]

In Matthew's Gospel, Christ says, "Render therefore unto Caesar the things which are Caesar's; and unto God the things that are God's." Christ is trying to evade the Pharisees' attempt to incriminate him in the eyes of Roman law. He responds by asserting that while spiritual interests and those of temporal authority do not always evolve together or serve the same goals, they can be kept apart and honored differently. But in practice, religion and the state have been extremely difficult to separate, as the recurrence of wars based on religious differences attests.

Christianity's treatment of Africans, Polynesians, Indians in the Americas, and others typifies another aspect of religion's effort to police the oceanic. The first wave of colonization in the New World and other territories was often religious, with the aim of eliminating what social science would come to call animism and the churches themselves often called heathenism. But that first wave was often accompanied or rapidly followed by mercantile systems with more pragmatic, profit-based motivations for wanting control of people and of land. Indigenous groups have sometimes successfully grafted Christianity onto the structure of traditional beliefs, so that, for example, Catholicism and animism coexist side by side within present-day Southwest Indian pueblos. But more often, Christianity has irrevocably altered the belief and social systems of indigenous cultures. Among many Native Americans, for example, Native languages were suppressed at mission schools, at which attendance was mandatory. Similar procedures were followed in parts of Africa and other sites of colonization. But equally striking and even more important to my argument here is the way in which Christianity and other institutionalized religions have operated in Europe and what is now the United States. Within European cultures, structures of thought and feeling similar to animism and magic have been purged or marginalized. In its early days, for example, the Catholic church openly tolerated practices it would later demonize as witchcraft. The cult of Mary, to take a salient instance, is widely agreed to have originated as an accommodation of pagan Mother cults. But by the fifteenth century, a church bloated with temporal power denounced Mother cults and their fertility rites, persecuting them ruthlessly.[14] The coincidence of the persecution of European witches and the "discovery" of the New World is, I believe, no accident. It is also no accident that most of those accused of witchcraft were female, and typically older females, past the age of reproduction.

The West undertook a grand program of parallel exorcisms: of witches at home, of heathenism and superstition abroad. The statistics relating to these purgations are fairly mind-boggling. From the fourteenth to the seventeenth century, for example, at least 250,000 people are thought to have been persecuted or executed as witches, with some estimates putting the figure as high as 2 million.[15] During the same historical epoch, and continuing into the nineteenth century, huge numbers of Indians in the Americas perished—by disease, warfare, or other effects of contact; Africans were routinely sold into slavery, solely on the basis of race. Western belief in an unbridgeable gap between the rational European and the Other may have been idle and fanciful, but it was not in the least bit ineffectual. It had dire consequences at home and abroad. Some of the cultures subject to colonization have never fully recovered. At the same time, in the witchcraft frenzy, Europe extirpated part of its own flesh, part of its living past.

The second key element in how the West developed its opposition between the civilized and the primitive, effacing the oceanic from Western life, is the idea of property ownership. Most often, "ownership" is applied to tangible goods or to land, but sometimes it may describe as well a relation to the self—so that the very fabric of our being is imagined in the terms of commercial culture. Descartes, for example, defined the individual existence in terms of possessing the ability to think: *Cogito, ergo sum* (I think, therefore I am). He also drew a crucial distinction between thinking things and perceived things, a distinction that, once fully assimilated in the West, formalized a chasm between humans and nature and, in a more vexed and permeable way, between humans and animals.[16] From this followed naturally the logic of the rational man's role as subjugator: the thinking thing has the right to control the inferior, nonthinking thing. Much of the West's intellectual energy—in the realm of philosophical thought, legal thought, linguistic thought, economic thought, and medical ethics—has flowed from that fundamental but vexed proposition.

In colonial history, primitives never seemed odder to people in the West than in their failure to accept the idea of individual ownership of the land. Many Africans and Native Americans found this plan incomprehensible, owing to long alternative traditions. The emerging U.S. government and commercial interests might conceivably have considered sharing land with Indians. But the uses of the land imagined by whites— accumulation, exclusive tillage or grazing, deeding to heirs—conflicted sharply with the Indians' conceptions of collective or overlapping ownership. In 1887, the U.S. government tried to solve the question of land ownership by simple fiat with the Dawes Act: 160 acres was to be allotted to every Indian family.[17] Some whites truly believed this to be a generous settlement that the Indians would eventually come to appreciate. But it was wholly inadequate in terms of its approach to traditional Indian ways of relating to the land. The immutable concept of ownership is thus at the root of one of the great dishonors of U.S. history: its unfair and cruel treatment of Indians. Significantly, it underlies another national dishonor of comparable magnitude: the claiming of Africans and their descendants as property during the long era of legal slavery.

It is easy to condemn the injustice of these and similar actions as constituting a Western heritage of guilt with regard to "primitive" peoples. Yet it is important to remember that these actions were conditioned by modes of political, social, and economic thought that affected the lives of Europeans too. Until relatively recent times, for example, voting rights were often keyed expressly to ownership of land. This was true even in what we imagine as bastions of democracy, like Great Britain, where, until 1918, suffrage for men depended on land ownership, the amount of rent paid on property, or similar requirements. Women with fathers or husbands were not allowed to own property in England (except under special conditions) until 1870. And they routinely were denied the vote until 1918.[18] In a sense, ownership served as the equivalent of tribal "initiation": to own was to be a full and mature member of the Western state.

Yet, as I have argued, the primacy of such philosophies of self and property, while in large part fundamental to the Western imagination, also wounded it. Alternative traditions within art and philosophy—including many of the forms of primitivism I have discussed in this book, even exploration itself—have sought to redress the effects of these assumptions. They have tried, I would suggest, to restore a sense of the self as part of a larger cosmos, a totality in which the very idea of ownership is irrelevant. Within the numerous instances of such alternative Western traditions, oceanic emotions thrive and shine. The German Romantic J. G. Herder, for example, articulated ideas that galvanized American Transcendentalists like Ralph Waldo Emerson. "The power, which thinks and acts in me," Herder wrote, "is, from its nature, as eternal as that which holds together the Sun and stars." Since this is so, Herder concludes, "the foundations of my being (not of my corporeal frame) are as fixed as the pillars of the universe."[19] A similar impulse runs through a variety of literary creations by novelists and poets such as William Blake, Emily Brontë, Emily Dickinson, Walt Whitman, Virginia Woolf, and Dylan Thomas.[20]

By cultivating its constitutive ideologies and metaphysics of self and property, it can be argued, the West has largely cut itself off, often to its detriment, from a fundamental mode of human experience. But I hasten to add that the most obvious antidote presents its own perils. To cultivate the intuition of the oceanic, as we have seen, is also to court complicated dangers, as various myths, life histories, and events from the recent past attest. When the Bacchae descended from the ecstatic mountaintop to the public square, ecstasy turned to ashes. When Dian Fossey married the primitive in her mind, she also flirted with an almost suicidal death. When the Nazis renewed a glorification of the primitive Folk and the primacy of Blood and Land, they unleashed a tidal wave of oceanic sentiment typified by the rallies at Nuremberg. They also produced the devastation of World War II and the horrors of the death camps. Even at the very point where the term "oceanic" enters the Western vocabulary to describe ecstatic experience—in Ramakrishna's utterances as transcribed in Romain Rolland's *The Life of Ramakrishna*—there are passages that evoke mass death. On the way to ecstasy, Ramakrishna is shown, and accepts unblinkingly, "heaps of human heads, mountain high."[21] Such passages have been notoriously literalized by events in our time. Whether these negative effects are avoidable no one can say for sure.

Do such experiences represent distortions or "misuses" of the oceanic—perhaps caused by initial repression? Or are they inevitable manifestations of its violent side? Is oceanic merging "safe" only in momentary doses or within prescribed boundaries, perhaps (as Victor Turner suggests is the case for *communitas* among the tribal peoples he studied) only within the boundaries of ritual?[22] Like Turner, I believe that no culture, "primitive" or modern, can experience oceanic sensations all the time: the oceanic always exists in a necessary tension with the structures of quotidian life. But by the same token, I see no reason to believe that any culture can deny oceanic sensations with impunity. The oceanic skates a razor's edge between ecstatic coexistence with others and inanimate things and a voiding of the self. Its suspension of social norms can lead as easily to transcendent states of consciousness as to violence or to violent forms of sexuality, misanthropy, and death. In pursuing the oceanic now, we cannot be sure that it will invariably lead to rich, harmonious connections between humans, the earth, and the cosmos. But the oceanic need not always lead to an untenable sense of self and to carelessness towards human life—let alone to the horrors of Nazism.[23]

The events leading up to World War II caused, without doubt, a crucial rupture in Western thinking about the oceanic. They dismayed even its strongest advocates, like Romain Rolland, who after 1931 turned away from his study of religion in order to concentrate on his fierce opposition to totalitarianism.[24] They seemed to confirm Sigmund Freud's fundamental pessimism about human aggressiveness, expressed in *Civilization and Its Discontents*. For a long time following the Second World War, it may have been impossible to think about the oceanic apart from its association with certain aspects of Nazism.[25] In fact, it may only now—some fifty years later—be possible to see the oceanic as linked to a great many other experiences in Western history rather than as the consequence of, or prelude to, totalitarianism. Only now may it be possible to give the oceanic its proper name and value. In any case, it is well to remember that there are distinctions to be made between the content of an idea and the effects of its historical applications and appropriations.

So today, we continue to face a crucial question: Can we find ways to think about self and nature, human culture and the surrounding cosmos—and ways to act on those thoughts—that honor both strong feelings of interconnectedness and the gains that have been made in the modern era?[26] The same question has been asked, in startlingly comparable terms, by Ralph Waldo Emerson, Martin Buber, and Georgia O'Keeffe, among others. Emerson said, "Why should we not also enjoy an original relation to the universe?" O'Keeffe asked: How can we not try to find "our own sense of balance with the world"?[27]

Significantly, each of these thinkers, and many others, welcomed oceanic experience but also maintained a strong sense of identity and self. In fact, Buber saw the experience of relatedness not as diminishing the self but as *strengthening* it through recognition of other selfhoods and communion with the eternal. The more one "selves" other beings and other elements, he believed, the more one "selves" oneself. This idea can seem like nonsense in the context of the usual subject-object divisions that structure so much Western thinking. Or it can seem among the greatest and most profound of paradoxes.[28] It may represent an ideal relationship between Western people and the oceanic—a way to acknowledge and accommodate moments of mystical or oceanic consciousness within a modern sense of self and society. It may even approximate the ways in which some traditional peoples understand the nets of Being-ness.

In fact, when all is said and done, texts or people that portray or embody the oceanic sensibility are as much a part of Western traditions as they are of any external primitive. The West has repeatedly tried to displace or dislodge the oceanic, severing it from the perceived self and projecting it outward. But the projection has never really worked. The time for denial seems to be long past. The recognition is overdue that primitivism is much more about "us" than about "them." In the same way, it is time to realize that the quest for ecstasy is as much a part of Western fears and desires as it is a part of the forest, the desert, or their people.

NOTES

INTRODUCTION

[1] In this paragraph, all the phrases in quotation marks come from Bronislaw Malinowski, *A Diary in the Strict Sense of the Term*, trans. Norbert Guterman (London: Routledge, 1967). The quotation about mastery and worry is on p. 175; that about women's bodies is on pp. 255–56; the phrases cited later about merging are on pp. 73 and 120, respectively. This diary was never intended for publication; it was found in Malinowski's desk after his sudden death from a heart attack in 1942 and published only in the changed moral climate of the late 1960s.

[2] In this book, "Western" refers to the sum total of European and European-American cultural traditions; "the West" to nations populated largely by people of Western European descent. "Indigenous" refers to the first-known or extremely long-term inhabitants of a particular region; "tribal" to groupings recognized in the West, which were sometimes the result of Western intervention.

[3] I take my definitions and chronological usages from the *Oxford English Dictionary*. See also Arthur O. Lovejoy and George Boas, *Primitivism and Related Ideas in Antiquity* (New York: Octagon, 1935) for early uses of the term.

[4] Marianna Torgovnick, *Gone Primitive: Savage Intellects, Modern Lives* (Chicago: Univ. of Chicago Press, 1990).

[5] Both homosexual and heterosexual experience can veer towards violence or towards overwhelming *eros*. There are abundant instances of sexual metaphors for spiritual experience in the Western tradition.

[6] See Peggy Reeves Sanday, *Divine Hunger: Cannibalism as Cultural System* (London: Cambridge Univ. Press, 1986).

[7] See Renato Rosaldo, *Ilongot Headhunting, 1883–1974: A Study in Society and History* (Stanford: Stanford Univ. Press, 1980).

[8] Tobias Schneebaum, *Where the Spirits Dwell* (New York: Grove, 1988). For typical expressions of fear, see Lawrence Blair and Lorne Blair, *Ring of Fire: Exploring the Last Remote Places of the World* (Toronto and New York: Bantam, 1988). See also an earlier book by Schneebaum about a group of Peruvian head-hunters, *Keep the River on Your Right* (New York: Grove, 1969).

⁹ There are some wonderful images in a documentary based on Swen Bergman's *My Father the Cannibal* (London: R. Hale, 1959).

¹⁰ The identification of human sacrifice with Christ's history may seem startling to some. But it was definitely a major implication of texts like Sir James Frazer's *The Golden Bough* (vol. 1, 1890), in which Christ was seen as a sacrificed god. A more radical connection between Christ's history and violence or cannibalism has suggested itself to many people working with the latter themes. See, for example, René Girard, *Violence and the Sacred* (Baltimore: Johns Hopkins Univ. Press, 1972), Maggie Kilgour, *From Communion to Cannibalism* (Princeton: Princeton Univ. Press, 1990), and Sanday, *Divine Hunger.*

¹¹ King James Version, Matthew 26:26–28. A great many motifs associated with the Last Supper and the Crucifixion recur in primitivism. The Grail, for example, has been sought as an object of spiritual bliss and mysterious powers in Western narratives from Parzival through the Arthurian cycle through *Indiana Jones and the Last Crusade.*

¹² For the figures on pre-contact Indians, see Chapter Six. On the colonial heritage in Rwanda, see Alex de Waal, "The Genocidal State," *TLS,* no. 4761 (1 July 1994): 3–4.

¹³ On the uses of primitive art by modern artists, see Robert J. Goldwater, *Primitivism in Modern Art* (1938; reprint, New York: Random House, 1967), originally published as *Primitivism in Modern Painting.* See also William Rubin, ed., *"Primitivism" in Twentieth-Century Art,* 2 vols. (New York: Museum of Modern Art, 1984). See also my own *Gone Primitive,* pt. 2. Roger Fry's *Vision and Design* (New York: Brentano's, 1920) argued for the formal greatness of primitive artists.

¹⁴ The first Tarzan novel appeared in 1912, followed by twenty-three others, most in the twenties and thirties; the first Tarzan film appeared in 1917, followed by roughly fifty films. See R. W. Fenton, *The Big Swingers* (Englewood Cliffs, N.J.: Prentice-Hall, 1967), and Irwin Porges, *Edgar Rice Burroughs: The Man Who Created Tarzan* (Provo, Utah: Brigham Young Univ. Press, 1975).

¹⁵ Sir James Frazer's *The Golden Bough,* a best seller from the 1890s through the 1920s, had paved the way, as had ballets like Nijinsky's *Le Sacre du printemps* (1913), in which men dressed in bear costumes strike down a maiden to ensure the fertility of the earth. Bronislaw Malinowski's *Argonauts of the Western Pacific* was published in 1922 (reprint, Prospect Heights, Ill.: Waveland Press, 1984); *The Sexual Life of Savages in North-Western Melanesia: An Ethnographic Account of Courtship, Marriage, and Family Life Among the Natives of the Trobriand Islands, British New Guinea* was published in 1929 (reprint, Boston: Beacon, 1988). Margaret Mead's *Coming of Age in Samoa* was published in 1928. Franz Boas published *Anthropology and Modern Life* in 1928, but was, of course, already a seminal figure in anthropology. Ruth Benedict's *Patterns of Culture* appeared in 1934; Marcel Mauss' *The Gift* was published in French as *Essai sur le don, forme archaïque de l'échange* in 1925.

¹⁶ See Robert Crawford, *The Savage and the City in the Work of T. S. Eliot* (Oxford: Clarendon, 1987).

¹⁷ Crawford suggests that Eliot's frustration in *Sweeney Agonistes* was a turning point in his life (*The Savage and the City,* 180).

¹⁸ Much of this thinking gave a new twist to the evolutionist premise that existing primitives mirrored modern Europe's past, a premise now largely discredited. See

Johannes Fabian, *Time and the Other: How Anthropology Makes Its Object* (New York: Columbia Univ. Press, 1983).

[19] Sigmund Freud, "Thoughts for the Time on War and Death," in Benjamin Nelson, ed., *On Creativity and the Unconscious* (New York: Harper, 1958).

[20] German philosophers of the previous century such as Nietzsche and Hegel had circulated various theories of master-slave relations; Buber clearly intended to offer an alternative.

[21] Martin Buber, *I and Thou*, trans. Ronald Gregor Smith (1923; New York: Collier, 1958), 16, 39, 18. Instead of the English "man," Buber often used "mensch," a gender-neutral word meaning "real person."

[22] See Martin Buber, *Ecstatic Confessions* (1909; San Francisco: Harper and Row, 1985). Buber collects statements from traditions as varied as Indian (Ramakrishna, Bayezid Bistami, and others), Sufi (Rabi'a), Gnostic (Valentius), Franciscan, Italian women (Catherine of Siena and others), Spanish women (Teresa de Jesus and others), and so on. Theosophy similarly looked both to Western religions and to Buddhism in the East.

[23] In Romain Rolland, *The Life of Ramakrishna* (Calcutta: Advaita Ashrama, 1929). Jeffrey Moussaieff Masson suggested these passages as the source for the term "oceanic" in *The Oceanic Feeling: The Origins of Religious Sentiment in Ancient India* (Boston: D. Reidel Publishing, 1980), 33–36.

[24] The exchange is preserved in collections of their letters: *Selected Letters of Romain Rolland,* ed. Francis Doré and Marie-Laure Prévost (translator not identified) (Bombay: Oxford Univ. Press, 1990), 86; *Letters of Sigmund Freud,* ed. Ernst L. Freud, trans. Tania Stern and James Stern (New York: Basic Books, 1960), 388–89.

As I was completing this book, a text detailing their relationship became available in French. It helped me dot some i's and cross some t's: *Sigmund Freud et Romain Rolland: Correspondance 1923–1936, De la sensation océanique au Trouble du souvenir sur l'Acropole,* ed. Henri Vermorel and Madeleine Vermorel (Paris: Presses Universitaires de France, 1993). I say more about these issues at the end of Chapter One.

[25] See Max Horkheimer and Theodor W. Adorno, *Dialectic of Enlightenment,* trans. John Cumming (1944; reprint, New York: Herder and Herder, 1972), chap. 1.

[26] It is unclear whether Horkheimer and Adorno would have agreed with the idea that this was a warped, demonic form of the oceanic or would have settled for the idea that Nazism represented a return to barbarism.

[27] Claude Lévi-Strauss, *Tristes Tropiques,* trans. John Weightman and Doreen Weightman (1955; New York: Atheneum, 1984), 38, 393.

[28] Rousseau's *Discourse* appears in *The Social Contract and Discourses* (1755; New York: Dutton, 1950); Montaigne's "Of Cannibals" in *The Complete Essays of Montaigne,* trans. Donald M. Frame (Stanford: Stanford Univ. Press, 1958).

[29] There are many indications of these interests in various parts of the world. See, for example, Tzvetan Todorov, *The Conquest of America* (1982; New York: Harper and Row, 1984), and J. M. Coetzee, *White Writing: On the Culture of Letters in South Africa* (New Haven: Yale Univ. Press, 1988).

[30] Adam Kuper, *The Invention of Primitive Society: Transformations of an Illusion* (London: Routledge, 1988), 13.

[31] Biographies of Francis and other mystics, such as Teresa of Avila, make it clear that they were both admired by the Church and regarded as disruptive threats. See the section of the Bibliography relating to Chapter Nine for some specific sources on these figures.

[32] There are, of course, equivalent bifurcations for women: the virgin and the whore, the angel in the house and the devouring mother. And there are equivalent bifurcations for collectivity: community versus mobs, congregations versus cults.

[33] The two most relevant texts by Freud are *Beyond the Pleasure Principle* (1922) and *Civilization and Its Discontents* (1930). Additional relevant texts are *Totem and Taboo* (1913) and *The Future of an Illusion* (1927). See also the final section of Chapter One and the Bibliography.

[34] In this book, I assume a distinction between sex as a biological category and gender as a cultural and constructed one. But the lines are never entirely crisp and clean. The section of the Bibliography relating to Chapter Three lists some sources on the debate between biology and culture and the nature of femininity.

[35] Many aspects of social change may be indicated: the civil rights struggle, the women's movement, environmentalism, new conceptions of masculinity, and gay and lesbian activism would be some.

[36] The quintessential primitive in the Western imagination was once Africa, which is now often viewed in the context of the third world and third world problems. Among Afrocentrists, though, "Africa" and concepts like *nommo* (communal patterns of call and response) continue to be idealized. See, for example, Molefi Kete Asante, *The Afrocentric Ideal* (Philadelphia: Temple Univ. Press, 1987).

CHAPTER ONE:
"WHAT AN ECSTASY IT WOULD HAVE BEEN!":
GIDE AND JUNG IN AFRICA

[1] *L'Immoraliste* was published in 1902 and is set, in part, in North Africa, which Gide had visited in 1893 and 1894.

[2] Gide's intimacy with Allegret had put considerable strain on his marriage since 1918, when Gide's wife dramatically burned all her husband's letters to her.

[3] These were published as a single volume in the United States, under the title *Travels in the Congo,* trans. Dorothy Bussy (1929; New York: Modern Age Books, 1937). I will use the French titles, but my citations are from Bussy's translation.

[4] See Albert Guérard, *André Gide* (Cambridge: Harvard Univ. Press, 1951). See also *The Journals of André Gide,* trans. and ed. Justin O'Brien (New York: Vintage, 1947), 2:33.

[5] In the visual arts, the continents were often represented as massive females: for example, the Albert Memorial in London.

[6] Here the French is better: "Indicible langueur. Heures sans contenu ni contour."

[7] The term "presymbolic" is associated with Jacques Lacan. Lacan's chief difference from Freud is that he stresses the role of language (associated with the father) in disrupting the mother-infant dyad.

[8] Joseph Conrad, *Heart of Darkness* (New York: Norton, 1988), 60.

⁹ See Gerhard Wehr, *Jung: A Biography* (Boston and London: Shambhala, 1987), 224.

¹⁰ Jung's biographers describe this period differently. Some see Jung as engaged in psychological experimentation between 1914 and 1918, with himself as subject; others see Jung as clinically ill, with a gradual recovery after 1918. They do not, however, doubt the traumatic nature of this period and the healing role of the journeys to Africa and the Southwest. See, for example, Vincent Brome, *Jung* (New York: Atheneum, 1978), and Anthony Stevens, *On Jung* (New York: Routledge, 1990).

¹¹ Carl G. Jung, *Memories, Dreams, Reflections*, ed. Aniela Jaffé, trans. Richard Winston and Clara Winston (1961; New York: Vintage, 1989), 90.

¹² See the amusing, but quite accurate, summary in Maggie Hyde and Michael McGuinness, *Jung for Beginners* (Cambridge: Icon Books, 1992), 3, 10.

¹³ Stevens, *On Jung*, 24. The imagery is, of course, associated with derogatory stereotypes of both Africans and women.

¹⁴ Ibid., 23.

¹⁵ Jung's disciples accept this dream as an appropriate warning that Jung had gone far enough into the primitive. Its oddity, it seems to me, is far more striking.

¹⁶ Preoccupied with marking differences between Freud and Jung, commentators have not paid enough attention to their similarities. Their mutual devotion to "ego" or "individuation" is one. It is quite interesting, for example, though outside the scope of this discussion, that Jung drew the line in his probing of what he called "Yoga" (Buddhism, Taoism, Hinduism, and the entire religious heritage of the East) at the possible loss of "ego-consciousness," which he felt to be absolutely basic to the Westerner. See Howard Coward, *Jung and Eastern Thought* (Albany: State Univ. of New York Press, 1985), and J. J. Clark, *Jung and Eastern Thought: A Dialogue with the Orient* (New York: Routledge, 1994).

¹⁷ Albert Guérard describes Gide as a "lay psychologist," for good reason. It is important to note that Gide's ideas emerged at roughly the same time as Freud's and Jung's, rather than being solely based on them.

¹⁸ Boas' comments are in a preface, reprinted in a 1967 selection of J. J. Bachofen's writings based on *Mutterrecht und Urreligion* called *Myth, Religion, and Mother Right: Selected Writings of J. J. Bachofen*, trans. Ralph Manheim, Bollingen series, vol. 84 (Princeton: Princeton Univ. Press, 1967). Quotations are from this edition.

¹⁹ Friedrich Engels, *The Origins of the Family, Private Property, and the State* (New York: International Publishers, 1972).

²⁰ There were countervailing voices in defense of female gods and the societies that worshipped them, defenders like Cambridge classicist Jane Harrison. There were also feminist rebuttals of Freud, for example, H.D.'s *Tribute to Freud* (New York: Pantheon, 1956), which is both a tribute and an act of one-upmanship.

²¹ For Jung, see the discussion that follows. Gide refers repeatedly to Nietzsche in *Si le grain ne meurt . . .* , almost always with great admiration. In fact, Gide perhaps absorbed Bachofen's ideas in part via Nietzsche.

²² Several editions of *The Bacchae* with German annotations were available when Bachofen wrote. Greek was, of course, a standard part of nineteenth-century university educations.

²³ Another classic example: *The Eumenides,* the final part of Aeschylus' trilogy, the *Oresteia.*

²⁴ The ending now printed with the play is reconstructed. It is impossible to say whether it is exactly the ending Euripides would have written. For some history on the play and its interpretation, see Donald Sutherland's "Critical Essay" accompanying a new translation of *The Bacchae* (Lincoln: Univ. of Nebraska Press, 1968), and Bernard Zimmerman, *Greek Tragedy: An Introduction,* trans. Thomas Marier (Baltimore: Johns Hopkins Univ. Press, 1986). See also studies of Greek religion, for example, Walter Burkert, *Greek Religion,* trans. John Raffan (Cambridge, Harvard Univ. Press, 1985).

²⁵ Carl Jung, *Psychology of the Unconscious,* trans. Beatrice M. Hinkle (1916; reprint, New York: Dodd, Mead, 1947), 427.

²⁶ As I discuss in the Introduction, the term "oceanic" was suggested by *The Life of Ramakrishna,* in which the saint experienced oneness via the goddess Kali. He addresses Kali as "Mother." Whether Freud conflated the divine Mother with human mothers is unclear—but highly likely.

Gide also had a strong intellectual relationship with Rolland. See *André Gide and Romain Rolland: Two Men Divided* (New Brunswick: Rutgers Univ. Press, 1973).

²⁷ A recent book in French devoted to the correspondence of Freud and Rolland speculates that Freud often resorted to maternal metaphors when faced with ideas that he feared. I agree. See *Sigmund Freud et Romain Rolland: Correspondance 1923–1936, De la sensation océanique au Trouble du souvenir sur l'Acropole,* ed. Henri Vermorel and Madeleine Vermorel (Paris: Presses Universitaires de France, 1993), 339.

²⁸ See the Conclusion for more on this issue.

²⁹ See D. W. Winnicott, *Playing and Reality* (New York: Basic, 1971), and Nancy Chodorow, *The Reproduction of Mothering: Psychoanalysis and the Sociology of Gender* (Berkeley: Univ. of California Press, 1978). See the Bibliography for more on this issue.

CHAPTER TWO:
"SOMETHING STOOD STILL IN MY SOUL":
D. H. LAWRENCE IN NEW MEXICO

¹ "New Mexico," in *Phoenix: The Posthumous Papers of D. H. Lawrence,* ed. Edward D. McDonald (New York: Viking, 1936), 142.

² D. H. Lawrence, *Women in Love,* ed. David Farmer, Lindeth Vasey, and John Worthen (1920; Cambridge: Cambridge Univ. Press, 1987), 479.

³ See Brenda Maddox, *D. H. Lawrence: The Story of a Marriage* (New York: Simon and Schuster, 1994), 295.

⁴ D. H. Lawrence, "Indians and Entertainment," in *Mornings in Mexico* (1927; London: Heinemann, 1956), 51–52.

⁵ Freud's most striking use of this image appears in *Civilization and Its Discontents,* published after Lawrence's death; hence I can only speculate on what Lawrence would have thought about Freud's argument. But he may well have been able to anticipate parts based on his reading of Freud's earlier works.

[6] Lawrence wrote two books both praising and modifying Freud: *Psychoanalysis and the Unconscious* (1921) and *Fantasia of the Unconscious* (1922).

[7] Mabel Dodge Luhan was married to Tony Luhan, a Taos Pueblo Indian, and worked on behalf of Indians, for example, in guaranteeing the Taos Pueblo exclusive access to sacred sites such as Blue Lake. But there is no evidence that the Luhans passed on specific knowledge to Lawrence. And, of course, Tony Luhan would hardly have been a reliable expert on all Indians.

[8] In "Morality and the Novel," collected in *Phoenix,* Lawrence says: "The business of art is to reveal the relation between man and his circumambient universe, at the living moment" (527).

[9] Lawrence's distinction resembles Jane Harrison's distinction between ritual and art (see the Bibliography and Chapter Seven). In fact, Lawrence very closely paraphrases her work on that subject.

[10] This is not an inclusive list; I have omitted, for example, *St. Mawr.*

[11] *The Plumed Serpent* (1926; New York: Vintage, 1959), 456. *The Plumed Serpent* is one of Lawrence's fictions that has been charged with protofascism; I return to the links between fascism and the oceanic in the Conclusion.

[12] The event never came off because of legal complications. See Roger Caillois, "The Collège de Sociologie: Paradox of an Active Sociology," *SubStance* 11–12 (1985): 61–64.

[13] D. H. Lawrence, *Lady Chatterley's Lover* (1928; New York: Signet, 1959), 195.

[14] Camille Paglia, *Sexual Personae* (1990; New York: Vintage, 1991), 47.

[15] D. H. Lawrence, *The Man Who Died,* with *St. Mawr* (New York: Vintage, 1953), 208.

CHAPTER THREE:

LOVING AFRICA:

MEMOIRS BY EUROPEAN WOMEN

[1] Meryl Streep delivers the lines in the 1985 film of *Out of Africa* (directed by Sydney Pollack) in a tone that suggests advanced age and in a setting like the one I have described. In reality, Dinesen wrote the book six years after leaving Africa, so she was still middle-aged; but the advanced decrepitude suggested by the film is still apt metaphorically. I used the Vintage edition for the quotations below (1937; New York: Random House, 1985).

[2] Her father travelled to the United States and spent several months living with Sioux, Pawnee, and Chippewa Indians. Later, Dinesen tended to see her father's experiences as redeemed by her own life in Africa. See Judith Thurman, *Isak Dinesen: The Life of a Storyteller* (New York: St. Martin's Press, 1982), 25.

[3] The term "Being-ness" is used in Jane Goodall's writing about chimpanzees (see Chapter Four).

[4] Since they are all writing about Kenya, we can assume that Gallmann read Markham and Dinesen and that Markham may have read Dinesen and De Watteville. Certain features of the narratives, such as episodic, discontinuous form, may derive from the earlier examples. But "tradition" would be too strong a word.

[5] See Dea Birkett, *Spinsters Abroad: Victorian Lady Explorers* (Oxford: Basil Blackwell, 1989), 187.

⁶ Mary Kingsley, *Travels in West Africa* (1897; London: Horace Marshall and Son, n.d.), 2.

⁷ After writing this chapter, I found additional support in Dea Birkett's book, *Spinsters Abroad*.

⁸ See Edward Said, *Culture and Imperialism* (New York: Knopf, 1992).

⁹ Birkett shows how Kingsley, like other female travellers, actually opposed feminism at home. They claimed the privileges they had found abroad as unique.

¹⁰ Keats, for example, in "To a Nightingale," contemplates the notion of "easeful death" in unison with the nightingale's song; but the poem famously records the poet's movement away from identification with the nightingale. Similarly, Wordsworth typically uses nature as a touchstone by which to measure human experience. And for Romantics like Shelley, nature provides metaphors for human emotions and poetic art.

¹¹ Vivienne de Watteville, *Speak to the Earth: Wanderings and Reflections Among Elephants and Mountains* (1935; New York: Penguin, 1988), 117–18.

¹² Markham does not mention her mother's desertion in *West with the Night* (1942; San Francisco: North Point Press, 1983). This information is from a biography of Markham by Mary S. Lovell, *Straight on Till Morning: The Biography of Beryl Markham* (New York: St. Martin's Press, 1987). All biographical information on Markham is based on Markham and Lovell.

¹³ The motif of naming is of interest in *West with the Night:* in the African childhood idyll, Beryl refers to herself simply as "girl."

¹⁴ On Markham's later life in Kenya, see the Lovell biography, *Straight on Till Morning*.

¹⁵ See Errol Trzebinski, *The Lives of Beryl Markham: Out of Africa's Hidden Seductress, Denys Finch Hatton's Last Great Love* (London: Heinemann, 1993).

¹⁶ Gallmann does not state the precise year of the accident in *I Dreamed of Africa* (New York: Viking, 1991). From those dates that are given, 1967 or 1968 would seem to be the year.

¹⁷ See Neil Hertz, *The End of the Line: Essays on Psychoanalysis and the Sublime* (New York: Columbia Univ. Press, 1985).

¹⁸ In *Isak Dinesen and the Engendering of Narrative* (Chicago: Univ. of Chicago Press, 1981), Susan Hardy Aiken claims that the discontinuous style of *Out of Africa* is the embodiment of Irigaray's *écriture féminine*. She also identifies Dinesen—whose pen name, Isak, means "laughter"—with Cixous' "The Laugh of the Medusa."

¹⁹ See, for example, Hélène Cixous, "Fiction and Its Phantoms: A Reading of Freud's *Das Unheimliche* (The 'Uncanny')," trans. Robert Denommé, in *New Literary History: A Journal of Theory and Interpretation* 7 (1976): 525–48; and Julia Kristeva, "Women's Time," trans. Alice Jardine and Harry Blake, *Signs: Journal of Women in Culture and Society* 7(1): 13–15.

²⁰ Dinesen's letters to her mother have been used as evidence. But Dinesen associates her mother with domesticated, cyclical nature and not with sublime, eternal nature. See, for example, Isak Dinesen, *Letters from Africa, 1914–31*, trans. Anne Born (Chicago: Univ. of Chicago Press, 1981).

²¹ Dea Birkett notes that this is a common pattern among female travellers to exotic sites.

[22] *The Question of Lay Analysis*, in *Standard Edition of the Complete Psychoanalytic Works of Sigmund Freud* (London: Hogarth, 1953–74), 20:212. Freud uses the phrase in English.

[23] The analogy with Agave both helps to explain and threatens to repeat male fears of women, connected with fears of the primitive (see Chapter One). That is why I give it an additional turn.

CHAPTER FOUR:
DIAN FOSSEY AMONG THE ANIMALS

[1] An image of this kind appears on the cover of Harold T. P. Hayes' *The Dark Romance of Dian Fossey* (New York: Simon and Schuster, 1990).

[2] In addition to the Hayes book, cited above, I refer to Alex Shoumatoff, *African Madness* (New York: Knopf, 1988), and Farley Mowat, *Woman in the Mists* (New York: Warner Books, 1987).

[3] See Donald Johanson and Maitland Edey, *Lucy: The Beginnings of Humankind* (New York: Simon and Schuster, 1981).

[4] As I was writing this book, a dazzling number of new discoveries concerning the origins of humankind were made. Clearly, this is a controversial and moving target.

[5] On the persistence of evolutionary modes of thinking, see Johannes Fabian, *Time and the Other* (New York: Columbia Univ. Press, 1983).

[6] See Sy Montgomery, *Walking with the Great Apes. June Goodall, Dian Fossey, Biruté Galdikas* (Boston: Houghton Mifflin, 1991), 142–47.

[7] See Hayes, *Dark Romance*, 312. At this point, many people, including Leakey, wanted Fossey away from Karisoke.

[8] There is a certain irony in Fossey's emphasis. Many paleontologists now believe that the various ape species were a "failed experiment in evolution" and would have reached extinction even without human encroachment on their lands. The apes' reproductive strategies, paleontologists say, proved less efficient than those of either nonprimate monkeys or early humans. See Johanson and Edey, *Lucy*.

[9] George B. Schaller, *The Year of the Gorilla* (Chicago: Univ. of Chicago Press, 1964), 3. Schaller's more academic report of his work with mountain gorillas is *The Mountain Gorilla: Ecology and Behavior* (Chicago: Univ. of Chicago Press, 1963).

[10] More recently, Schaller has had considerable success with *The Last Panda* (Chicago: Univ. of Chicago Press, 1993). Although this book reflects the current tendency among scientists to express more affection for animals than they once did, it also shows Schaller's concern, unlike Fossey's, with the sociological and political contexts surrounding issues of animal preservation.

[11] Dian Fossey, "Making Friends with Mountain Gorillas," photographs by Robert Campbell, *National Geographic* 137 (1970): 48–67, esp. 49, 52.

[12] The relevant volume and page numbers for "Making Friends with Mountain Gorillas" are given above. For "More Years with Mountain Gorillas," they are 140 (1971): 574–85; for "The Imperiled Mountain Gorilla," 159 (1981): 501–23.

[13] They corresponded sporadically during Fossey's years in Africa; but George Fossey committed suicide in 1969, just when Robert Campbell arrived in Karisoke.

See Mowat, *Woman in the Mists,* 69. The biographies differ on some details, such as the date when Fossey and her father renewed contact.

[14] Dian Fossey, *Gorillas in the Mist* (Boston: Houghton Mifflin, 1983), 70.

[15] Fossey had difficulty with long manuscripts, both the dissertation and *Gorillas in the Mist.*

[16] See Donna Haraway, *Primate Visions: Gender, Race, and Nature in the World of Modern Science* (New York: Routledge, 1989), 149–50.

[17] Sy Montgomery reproduces some of these photos in *Walking with the Great Apes,* 37. She also tells part of the story of the caged baby Grub, as does Goodall herself in Jane van Lawick Goodall, *In the Shadow of Man* (New York: Dell, 1971), 210–18, 261–62. The information about the cages needed for Grub appears in what is called a "Family Postscript" at the end of the book.

[18] See Jane Goodall, *Through a Window: My Thirty Years with the Chimpanzees at Gombe* (Boston: Houghton Mifflin, 1990).

[19] *In the Shadow of Man* was a book for general audiences. She also produced a book aimed at preteens, *My Life with the Chimpanzees* (New York: Minstrel, 1988), and a scholarly study based on her dissertation.

[20] The worker mentioned most by Fossey herself is Sanwecke. He may be the basis for the character in the film, but in reality Fossey had no African sidekicks.

[21] See Nancy Chodorow, *The Reproduction of Mothering: Psychoanalysis and the Sociology of Gender* (Berkeley: Univ. of California Press, 1978).

[22] Mircea Eliade has provided an analysis of the deep structures of shamanism. See *Shamanism,* trans. Willard Trask, Bollingen series, vol. 76 (New York: Pantheon, 1964).

[23] I found a gratifying confirmation of this interpretation in Biruté Galdikas' memoir, *Reflections of Eden: My Years with the Orangutans of Borneo* (Boston: Little, Brown, 1995), which appeared when I was doing final revisions on this book. Galdikas compares the experience of the primatologist accessing her subjects to that of a religious mystic, saying: "On occasion, fleetingly, just for a nanosecond, but with an intensity that is shocking in its profoundness, we recognize that there is no separation between ourselves and nature. We are allowed to see the eyes of God" (403).

[24] See Julia Kristeva, *Powers of Horror: An Essay on Abjection,* trans. Leon S. Roudiez (New York: Columbia Univ. Press, 1982), and Georges Bataille, *Visions of Excess: Selected Writings, 1927–1939,* ed. and trans. Allan Stoekl (Minneapolis: Univ. of Minnesota Press, 1985).

[25] According to E. M. Forster's *Aspects of the Novel,* this is the key element that makes narratives work (1927; New York: Harcourt, Brace, and World, 1954), 26–27.

[26] This comment was made by J. Daniélou, S.J., in *Sacramentum futuri,* quoted in Mircea Eliade, *Myths, Dreams, and Realities: The Encounter Between Contemporary Faiths and Archaic Realities,* trans. Philip Mairet (1957; New York: Harper, 1960), 67.

CHAPTER FIVE:
"THE BONES AND THE BLUE":
GEORGIA O'KEEFFE AND THE FEMALE PRIMITIVE

1 Mabel Dodge Luhan's remark is reproduced in Jack Cowart, Juan Hamilton, Sarah Greenough, eds., *Georgia O'Keeffe: Art and Letters,* letters selected and annotated by Sarah Greenough (Washington, D.C.: National Gallery of Art, 1987), 280. It originally appeared in an unpublished article on O'Keeffe called "The Art of Georgia O'Keeffe," now housed in the Beinecke Rare Book and Manuscript Library, Yale University. In context, the remark refers to O'Keeffe's work; but the article in which it appears also criticizes Stieglitz as a "showman" and "Camera-man" who exploited O'Keeffe. Citations to *Letters* refer to this volume, often to Greenough's excellent annotations.

2 See Roxana Robinson, *Georgia O'Keeffe: A Life* (New York: Harper and Row, 1989), 237–38. An exhibition of Stieglitz' photographs in 1921, which included some forty-five images of O'Keeffe, was "mobbed by an excited crowd."

3 Some of the photographs are reproduced in most biographies of O'Keeffe; a larger sampling can be found in Alfred Stieglitz, *Georgia O'Keeffe: A Portrait* (New York: Metropolitan Museum of Art, distributed by Viking Press, 1978).

4 Many critics note the uncanny effect of objects in O'Keeffe's art. In literary criticism, the aesthetic of defamiliarization says that art must reveal the "stoniness of the stone"—the essence of things—by portraying objects with a special vividness or from a special point of view. That aesthetic, named by and associated most with the Russian Formalists during the 1920s, was actually quite widespread in the period.

5 I consulted a number of biographies for facts about O'Keeffe's life. Interpretations taken from individual biographies are indicated in various notes below, and in the text. See also the Bibliography.

6 See Robert Pincus-Witten, introduction to *Georgia O'Keeffe: Selected Paintings and Works on Paper,* catalogue to exhibition at Hirschl and Adler Galleries, 1986.

7 See Laurie Lisle, *Portrait of an Artist: A Biography of Georgia O'Keeffe* (Albuquerque: Univ. of New Mexico Press, 1986), 107–108.

8 Benita Eisner stresses this interpretation in *O'Keeffe and Stieglitz: An American Romance* (New York: Doubleday, 1991).

9 Exhibition notes, "Two Lives: Georgia O'Keeffe and Alfred Stieglitz: A Conversation in Paintings and Photographs," Phillips Collection, 1992–93.

10 In the documentary, critic Barbara Rose describes the marriage as illustrating a harmonious blend of tastes and temperaments. While mostly true, the gloss misses O'Keeffe's tone. Compare also remarks like those quoted in the "Two Lives" exhibition, in which O'Keeffe says, "Before I put a brush to canvas, I question, Is this mine? or some photograph of an idea which I have acquired from a man?"

11 Oscar Bluemner, quoted in *Letters,* 139.

12 See, for example, Samuel M. Kootz, *Modern American Painters* (New York: Brewer and Warren, 1930), 49. Marsden Hartley took this line as early as 1920; see Lisle, *Portrait of an Artist,* 123.

13 This remark occurs in a catalogue for an exhibition at An American Place. Hartley's "takes" on O'Keeffe's art are collected in Marsden Hartley, *Adventures in*

Art: Informal Chapters on Painters, Vaudeville, and Poets (New York: Boni and Liveright, 1921). O'Keeffe's biographies indicate that, apart from a few favorites, her critics by turns upset and amused her.

14 Hunter's comment appeared in "A Note on Georgia O'Keeffe," *Contemporary Arts of the South and Southwest,* November–December 1932. Lewis Mumford made a similar comment in *The New Yorker,* 21 January 1933. Both are excerpted in Mitchell A. Wilder, ed., *Georgia O'Keeffe: An Exhibition of the Work of the Artist from 1915 to 1966* (Fort Worth, Tex.: Amon Carter Museum of Western Art, 1966), 14, 17.

Henry McBride compared O'Keeffe to Margaret Fuller and warned that she should flee to a nunnery (Ophelia style) lest other women besiege her for advice on how to live and paint. This comment apparently amused O'Keeffe rather than annoyed her: she selected it for a 1924 catalogue. See Lisle, *Portrait of an Artist,* 105, and Wilder, ed., *Georgia O'Keeffe: An Exhibition,* 13. Sarah Greenough notes that O'Keeffe liked McBride's wit and appreciated his downplaying of Freudian interpretations (*Letters,* 278).

15 The first uses date from around 1907; the fad continued in force through World War II and continues, in different forms, today. Several of O'Keeffe's critics dabbled in primitivism, in works such as Marsden Hartley's *Indian Fantasy* (1914).

16 See William Rubin, ed. *"Primitivism" in Twentieth-Century Art* (New York: Museum of Modern Art, 1984).

17 In a notable review as late as the mid-sixties, for example, the influential critic Clement Greenberg attacked O'Keeffe's work as "fetishes" (quoted in Lisle, *Portrait of an Artist,* 266).

18 In 1925, for example, she wrote to Mabel Dodge Luhan welcoming women's responses to her art (*Letters,* 130). On her later refusal to exhibit the flower paintings with other women's art, see Ann Sutherland and Linda Nochlin, *Women Artists, 1550–1950* (New York: Knopf, 1976), 11.

19 See Robinson, *Georgia O'Keeffe: A Life,* 351–53.

20 Art histories of the 1930s and 1940s make the conditions under which O'Keeffe labored startlingly clear. For example, Thomas Craven's survey, *Modern Art,* has the subtitle *The Men, The Movements, The Meaning* (New York: Simon and Schuster, 1940). Although he praises O'Keeffe, he mostly credits Stieglitz for her achievement: "Stieglitz discovered, developed, and married Georgia O'Keeffe, and first presented her in 1916" (314).

21 Judy Chicago, *Through the Flower: My Struggle as a Woman Artist* (Garden City, N.Y.: Doubleday, 1975), 182.

22 For celebration, see, for example, Judy Grahn, *Blood, Bread, and Roses: How Menstruation Created the World* (Boston: Beacon, 1993); for denigration, see Camille Paglia, *Sexual Personae* (1990; New York: Vintage, 1991).

23 Ernest Hemingway wrote the preface for the first English translation of the memoir called *Kiki's Memoirs* and published under the name of Alice Prin, trans. Samuel Putnam (Paris: At the Sign of the Black Manikin Press, 1930). For brief glimpses of Alice Prin, see Billy Klüver and Julie Martin, *Kiki's Paris: Artists and Lovers, 1900–1930* (New York: Abrams, 1989), and Shari Benstock, *Women of the Left Bank* (Austin: Univ. of Texas Press, 1986).

24 O'Keeffe's letters to McBride and Frank appear in *Letters,* 184–85; McBride's review appeared in the New York *Sun,* 15 January 1927; Waldo Frank's comments ap-

peared in *Time Exposures: By Search-Light* (New York: Boni and Liveright, 1926), published under a pseudonym. A volume called *The Flow of Art: Essays and Criticisms* by Henry McBride (New York: Atheneum, 1975) is also of interest.

[25] Kootz, *Modern American Painters,* 49.

[26] See, for example, *Letters,* 184, 189, 190.

[27] "Morality and the Novel," in *Phoenix: The Posthumous Writings of D. H. Lawrence,* ed. Edward D. McDonald (New York: Viking, 1936), 527.

[28] In this book, reissued under the title *Concerning the Spiritual in Art,* Wassily Kandinsky put it this way: "Art is the raising of the spiritual. . . . If the artist is the priest of beauty, nevertheless this beauty is to be sought only according to the principle of the inner need" (trans. M. T. H. Sadler [New York: Dover, 1977], 54–55). Abstractionists who articulated spiritual motivations include Mondrian, Malevich, and Brancusi.

Critics often recognized the religious dimension of O'Keeffe's work, sometimes rather dismissively. For example, Marsden Hartley: "A gallery is no place for it [O'Keeffe's art]. It ought to be viewed in a church. I should like Mae West to see it. It can only be properly understood, one feels, by someone who knows life thoroughly. On second thought I should like Mae West not to see it. It might disarrange her views. . . ." (from a review reprinted in Wilder, ed., *Georgia O'Keeffe: An Exhibition,* 14).

[29] As an art student, O'Keeffe read and valued Kandinsky's work, as well as Marius de Zaya on African art and Arthur W. Dow on Asian art. She worked with Arthur Dow's *Composition: A Series of Exercises Selected from a New System of Art Education,* which by 1913 was in its thirteenth edition (New York: Doubleday, Doran, 1913). Japanese, Buddhist, and African art, for all their differences, were usually imagined as variations of the primitive.

[30] Clive Bell, *Art* (London: Chatto and Windus, 1914), 91. O'Keeffe called this book "stupid stuff" in a letter written in 1917. See *Letters,* 159.

[31] Robert Hughes, "Golden Oldies, An Overambitious Survey of the Century's Distinctive Movement: Abstraction," *Time* 147 (2 March 1996): 60. Despite the potential value of "fossils," Hughes intends to be dismissive.

[32] She says as much in the Perry Miller Adato documentary and in a comment quoted in the brochure for the centenary exhibition: "It takes more than talent. It takes a kind of nerve." There are similar remarks in *Letters*—for example, 174–75.

[33] Her friendship with Tony Luhan did inspire rhapsodies about Indians. See *Letters,* 205.

[34] On Pueblo Indian religions, see Ramon A. Guttierrez' *When Jesus Came the Corn Mothers Went Away* (Albuquerque: Univ. of New Mexico Press, 1992); Vincent Scully, *Pueblo: Mountain, Village, Dance* (New York: Viking, 1975); and Erna Fergusson, *Dancing Gods: Indian Ceremonials of New Mexico and Arizona* (New York: Knopf, 1934).

[35] See, for one of many examples of O'Keeffe's views, *Letters,* 263.

[36] Georgia O'Keeffe, quoted by Henry McBride in "Miss O'Keeffe's Bones: An Artist of the Western Plains Just Misses Going Abstract," New York *Sun,* 15 January 1944, reprinted in Wilder, ed., *Georgia O'Keeffe, An Exhibition,* 19.

[37] See, for one of many examples, *Letters,* 156–57. O'Keeffe's letters continued to overflow with such comments. For a few other examples, see *Letters,* 201, 206, 232. We know that O'Keeffe knew and was impressed by Romain Rolland's writings (see

Robinson, *Georgia O'Keeffe: A Life,* 227). Her letters expressed an oceanic sensibility long before she read Rolland.

[38] O'Keeffe didn't care which way the painting was hung: with the trunk of the tree facing down or up.

[39] Indeed, her letters see various geological formations—ocean, plains, desert, and jungle—as equivalent to each other. They record an awareness that the fossils she collects prove that in the eons before human life, the desert lay under oceans.

[40] Todd Webb, *Georgia O'Keeffe: The Artist's Landscape* (Pasadena, Calif.: Twelvetrees Press, 1984).

CHAPTER SIX:
NEW AMERICAN INDIAN/
NEW AMERICAN WHITE

[1] I use four terms interchangeably in this chapter: Indian, American Indian, Native American, and Native. All four are used by members of the groups so designated.

[2] See Sam Roberts, *Who We Are: A Portrait of America Based on the Latest U.S. Census* (New York: Times Books/Random House, 1994), and Dennis McAuliffe, Jr., *The Deaths of Sybil Bolton: An American History* (New York: Times Books, 1994), 72.

[3] See Peter Nabokov, ed., *Native American Testimony: A Chronicle of Indian-White Relations from Prophecy to the Present, 1492–1992* (New York: Viking, 1991), 385; see also Philip J. De Loria, "Sovereignty," in *The Native Americans: An Illustrated History,* ed. Betty Ballantine and Ian Ballantine (Atlanta: Turner Publishing, 1993), 434.

[4] McAuliffe, *The Deaths of Sybil Bolton,* 72.

[5] On paradisal images, see Henri Baudet, *Paradise on Earth: Some Thoughts on and European Images of Non-European Man,* trans. Elizabeth Wentholt (1959; New Haven: Yale Univ. Press, 1965). On the end of French and British use of pan-Indian alliances to forestall expansion of the opposite power, see White, "Indian Rebellion," in *The Native Americans.*

[6] General Sheridan is notorious for saying, "The only good Indians I ever saw were dead."

[7] My thanks to Shep Kretch for pointing out the importance of events around 1970.

[8] *The Native Americans* refreshed my memory of events on Alcatraz; see De Loria, "What Indians Can Teach Us," 434–35.

[9] See *The Native Americans,* 399. In such cases, tourism is often involved.

[10] It is also important that racial categories as immutable entities were coming under scrutiny. See, for example, David Roediger, *The Wages of Whiteness: Race and the Making of the American Working Class* (London: Verso, 1991).

[11] John Muir, founder of the Sierra Club, coined the term "land ethic" when he called for the establishment of protected national parks.

[12] On the status of Mother Earth, see Sam Gill in *Mother Earth* (Chicago: Univ. of Chicago Press, 1987).

[13] N. Scott Momaday, "An American Land Ethic," *Sierra Club Bulletin* 55 (February 1970): 11.

[14] Michael Blake, *Dances with Wolves* (New York: Fawcett, 1988). Compare Willa Cather's *My Ántonia* and O'Keeffe's feelings for the desert, discussed in Chapter Five.

[15] One possible exception is the Union officer who saves Dunbar's leg and sends him west; but the film then negates this image of the good officer by showing the crazed one who sends Dunbar to Fort Cedric and the hapless one who occupies Fort Cedric at the end.

[16] For pioneer diaries, especially of women, see Annette Kolodny, *The Lay of the Land: Metaphor as Experience and History in American Life and Letters* (Chapel Hill: Univ. of North Carolina Press, 1975).

[17] The film thematizes the process of language acquisition through the relationship of Dunbar and Stands with a Fist. Once Dunbar becomes adept at the Lakota tongue, the subtitles that originally translate it disappear.

[18] I evoke the last lines of Milton's *Paradise Lost* deliberately, because the film does too.

[19] I know of four other versions made for movie theaters: 1920, director Maurice Tourneur; 1932, director Ford Beebe; 1936, director George B. Seitz; 1977, director James L. Conway.

[20] See *The Native Americans,* 466–67, for a helpful list of Indian groups by culture and language. As is true in many colonial encounters, the idea of "tribes" and tribal names were often originally imposed by whites.

[21] David Johnston, "Spiritual Seekers Borrow Indian Ways," *New York Times,* 27 December 1993, A1, A10.

[22] Sources for ideas about Native American religion were often transcribed by whites and may be worded in a way that reflects the preconceptions of the transcriber. This was apparently the case in a famous transcription *Black Elk Speaks*. Black Elk, for example, everyone's model of an Indian holy man, was apparently also a devout Christian and a missionary; see Michael F. Steltenkamp, *Black Elk: Holy Man of the Oglala* (Norman, Okla.: Univ. of Oklahoma Press, 1993).

[23] See *The Native Americans,* 461, for one highly ambiguous treatment of the facts. I heard the news on National Public Radio, in a report by Steven Smith called "Circle of Faith: Word of Seattle," 28 May 1992.

[24] Thanks to Shep Kretch for sharing with me the examples of Smashed Buffalo Head and the beaver trade, which are also discussed in *The Native Americans* and in William H. MacLeish, *The Day Before America* (Boston: Houghton Mifflin, 1994).

[25] This is the view advanced by David Hurst Thomas and Jay Miller in parts 1 and 2 of *The Native Americans*—and it makes good sense.

[26] Dirk Johnson, "Economies Come to Life on Indian Reservations," *New York Times,* 3 July 1994, A1.

[27] In 1987, only two states (Nevada and New Jersey) allowed legal gambling, so that Indian casinos in other states filled a void. As of this writing, some twenty states have passed laws permitting casinos off Indian land. And many casinos on Indian land are already managed by white-owned corporations that skim off some of the profits.

[28] As of this writing, the Indians' council first decided not to store the waste and then reversed itself.

CHAPTER SEVEN:
OF DRUMS AND MEN

[1] I want to stress the term "mythopoetic" in front of "men's movement" before moving to the more common usage, which is just "men's movement." Obviously, there are many other kinds of men's movements, some (like the militias) much more gun-oriented.

[2] The Texas meeting was described in Trip Gabriel, "Call of the Wildmen," *New York Times Magazine,* 14 October 1990, 36–49, esp. 47. The description of a local group comes from a book by Michael Schwalbe which I saw in manuscript form. Called *Unlocking the Iron Cage* (New York: Oxford, 1996), the book was published after my book was in press. I saw only chapter 4 of the manuscript.

[3] Two of my informants turned out to have been trained in social research and the participant-observer method: Steven Caton, an anthropologist at the University of California, Santa Cruz, and Michael Schwalbe, a sociologist at North Carolina State University. I am aware that my sample of interviewees, which included roughly six men in addition to these two, was highly selective.

[4] Sam Keen, *Fire in the Belly: On Being a Man* (New York: Bantam, 1991), 32.

[5] Robert Moore and Douglas Gillette, *King, Warrior, Magician, Lover: Rediscovering the Archetypes of the Mature Masculine* (San Francisco: Harper, 1990), xvi.

[6] All of these examples are cited in David Gilmore, *Manhood in the Making: Cultural Concepts of Masculinity* (New Haven: Yale Univ. Press, 1990), 92. They conform to anthropological sources.

[7] This is one of Gilmore's major points; I expand it somewhat.

[8] It is hard to define the status of male-male sexuality within other cultures. According to some accounts, sexual pleasure for the men is not the point of these activities. According to other accounts, many New Guinean and Bornean societies have institutions of male-male sex designed for pleasure.

[9] Despite the movement's Jungian roots, this formulation reverses and desexualizes gender roles in Freud's Oedipal triangle: sons need to eliminate one parent (in the men's movement, the mother) in order to chastely embrace the other (the father).

[10] Michael Schwalbe offers the two examples I cite in chapter 4 of his manuscript.

[11] Another favored moment: the fictional scene in John Boorman's *The Emerald Forest* (1985), when Tomei the boy is tormented by ants so that he will die and allow the birth of Tomei the man.

[12] *A Gathering of Men* was shown on PBS, then released as a video and an audiotape (Mystic Fire Video, 1990).

[13] Ethnographic reports on this custom are admittedly uneven. Some ethnographers do not mention it; others dwell on the events. For corroboration, see Gilmore, *Manhood in the Making,* and Tobias Schneebaum, *Where the Spirits Dwell: An Odyssey in New Guinea* (New York: Grove, 1987).

[14] Nancy Jay, *Throughout Your Generations Forever: Sacrifice, Religion, and Paternity* (Chicago: Univ. of Chicago Press, 1992), xiii. See also Bruno Bettel-

heim, *Symbolic Wounds: Puberty Rites and the Envious Male* (New York: Collier, 1962).

[15] Robert Bly, *Talking All Morning* (Ann Arbor: Univ. of Michigan Press, 1980), 208. Surprising as such views may be, all Bly has done, in a sense, is to shift parental metaphors.

[16] See Malidoma Somé, *Of Water and the Spirit: Ritual, Magic, and Initiation in the Life of an African Shaman* (New York: G. P. Putnam's Sons, 1994), 277. Despite the subtitle given his book, Somé does not claim to be a shaman.

[17] See, for example, Carlos Castenada's controversial books on Don Juan and Doucan Gersi's *Faces in the Smoke: An Eyewitness Experience of Voodoo, Shamanism, Psychic Healing, and Other Amazing Human Powers* (Los Angeles: Jeremy P. Tarcher, 1991). The resemblances between such accounts may result from what have become literary conventions for narrating non-Western experiences in the West. But even that would not prove that the accounts are false.

[18] This remark and the two that follow are quoted in chapter 4 of the manuscript by Michael Schwalbe.

[19] Martin Buber, *Between Man and Man,* quoted in Victor W. Turner, *The Ritual Process: Structure and Anti-Structure* (Ithaca: Cornell Univ. Press, 1969), 127.

[20] Schwalbe, manuscript, chap. 4, 30.

[21] In parts of Africa, for example, a child's family is defined as being whoever feeds the child.

[22] Written in 1969, Turner's book makes frequent comparisons between primitives and hippies. He was not (and at the time could not be) certain that the hippies would not actualize *communitas* in daily life.

[23] In the preface to *Ecstatic Confessions,* Buber writes: "Whether the soul meets a loved human being or a wild landscape of heaped-up stones—from this human being, this heap of stones, grace catches fire" (ed. Paul Mendes-Flohr, trans. Esther Cameron [1909; San Francisco: Harper and Row, 1985]).

[24] I used several biographies and studies of Buber in arriving at these views; see the Bibliography.

[25] For sources on Francis of Assisi, see the section of the Bibliography relating to Chapter Nine.

[26] A certain idealization of feudal structures often results, as in Bly's *Iron John.* Bly's idealization of the Arthurian court, for example, ignores the motifs of treachery and betrayal central to Arthurian narratives.

[27] Georg Lukács, "The Phenomenon of Reification" (part of "Reification and the Consciousness of the Proletariat" in *History and Class Consciousness: Studies in Marxist Dialectics,* trans. Rodney Livingstone (1922; Cambridge: MIT Press, 1988), 83–109.

[28] My line of argument suggests one additional reason why the men's movement has gravitated towards the metaphor of initiation: the metaphor harbors the implication of personal change, but only as one moves through traditional social structures; in other words, it is transformative at the personal level but conservative at the social level.

[29] It is not surprising, for example, that the mythopoetic men's movement has given rise to phenomena like the Promise Keepers and the Million Man March, which have more explicit connections to religion.

CHAPTER EIGHT:
MEDICINE WHEELS AND SPIRITUALITY:
PRIMITIVISM IN THE NEW AGE

[1] Marilyn Ferguson, *The Aquarian Conspiracy: Personal and Social Transformation in the 1980s* (Los Angeles: Jeremy P. Tarcher, 1980), 23.

[2] James Redfield, *The Celestine Prophecy* (New York: Time-Warner Books, 1994).

[3] Wendy Kaminer, *I'm Dysfunctional, You're Dysfunctional: The Recovery Movement and Other Self-Help Fashions* (Reading, Mass.: Addison-Wesley, 1992).

[4] The comment was made by an acquaintance.

[5] In fact, individual churches today sometimes describe themselves as New Age.

[6] John Drane, *What Is the New Age Saying to the Church?* (San Francisco: Marshall Pickering/HarperCollins, 1991), 11.

[7] I touch on the relationship between the New Age and some varieties of Goddess revival below; but it is outside the scope of this chapter. See the Bibliography for some relevant materials.

[8] Elisabeth Kübler-Ross' *On Death and Dying* (New York: Macmillan, 1981) is different from *On Life after Death* (Berkeley: Celestial Arts, 1991). On the transformation of her thought, see Jonathan Rosen, "Rewriting the End: Elisabeth Kübler-Ross," *New York Times Magazine*, 22 January 1995, 22–25.

[9] I borrow the image of God as "good parent" from Wendy Kaminer.

[10] Quoted in Drane, *What Is the New Age Saying to the Church?*, 15.

[11] Clarissa Pinkola Estés is best known as the author of *Women Who Run with the Wolves* (New York: Ballantine, 1992). The talk differed substantially in tone from the book.

[12] Although it was used as the "grand finale" at this New Age vision quest, purification in a sweathouse normally *precedes* ritual activity in Native American cultures.

[13] Emphasis on circular forms has become a common element in contemporary images of Native Americans. But many groups lived in structures other than rounded tepees, and not all Indians lived in circular encampments.

[14] In some sources, it symbolizes warmth or spring, but the speaker's identification is perhaps close enough. Since my point does not concern specific New Age practitioners, I will not be using the speaker's name.

[15] The leader of this workshop distinguished between ritual and ceremony. For her, ritual had an element of rote repetition that she wanted to avoid. Not all commentators would agree on the distinction.

[16] See the section of the Bibliography relating to Chapter One.

[17] Riane Eisler, *The Chalice and the Blade* (San Francisco: HarperCollins, 1987), 43.

[18] In this view, male chiefs and male dominance in tribal councils are somehow less important than these female institutions.

[19] Paula Gunn Allen, *The Sacred Hoop: Recovering the Feminine in American Indian Traditions* (1986; Boston: Beacon, 1992), 2.

[20] See Barbara A. Babcock and Nancy J. Parezo, *Daughters of the Desert: Women Anthropologists and the Native American Southwest, 1880–1980* (Albuquerque: Univ. of New Mexico Press, 1988).

²¹ See Margaret M. Caffrey, *Ruth Benedict: Stranger in This Land* (Austin: Univ. of Texas Press, 1989), and Judith Schachter Modell, *Ruth Benedict: Patterns of a Life* (Philadelphia: Univ. of Pennsylvania Press, 1983).

²² See Esther Stinemann, *Mary Austin: Story of a Maverick* (New Haven: Yale Univ. Press, 1989), 197, 18.

²³ J. J. Bachofen, *Myth, Religion, and Mother Right: Selected Writings of J. J. Bachofen*, trans. Ralph Manheim, Bollingen series, vol. 84 (Princeton: Princeton Univ. Press, 1967).

²⁴ These statistics are from "In Search of the Sacred," *Newsweek*, 28 November 1994, 54.

²⁵ There are, of course, many factors at work: reforms within American Catholicism (such as the change from masses in Latin to masses in English); increased instances of religious intermarriages, and so on.

²⁶ In U.S. church history, societies and groups that are allied with churches, as opposed to the priesthood or ministry, are often controlled by women.

²⁷ Robert Wuthnow, *Sharing the Journey: Support Groups and America's Quest for Community* (New York: Free Press, 1994), 12.

²⁸ The extremes represented by a Francis or a Teresa—especially their rejection of ownership and property—attracted considerable suspicion and were quietly coopted by the Church: in fact, during their lifetimes, Francis and Teresa were considered disruptive, problematic, even dangerous. See Chapter Nine and the section of the Bibliography relating to that chapter.

²⁹ I found it quite interesting that in a best-selling New Age text, *The Celestine Prophecy*, a modern government arrests and kills those who pursue New Age insights. In this book, persecution for their beliefs is a New Age fantasy.

³⁰ The New Age as a whole sometimes catapults over the question of death by gesturing towards solutions that are quite literally death-defying—as when it gravitates towards fairly positive and literal (not to mention extremely embodied) versions of reincarnation. In fact, there has been a curious transposition of ideas from Buddhism to the New Age. In most forms of Buddhism, nirvana is the escape from reincarnation; the more common Western take is that reincarnation is a positive thing and that "spiritual" people are aware of having had other lives.

³¹ See William Leach, *The Land of Desire: Merchants, Power, and the Rise of a New American Culture* (New York: Pantheon, 1993). It is worth noting that the decades Leach describes followed close upon the destruction of many forms of Indian life.

CHAPTER NINE:
PIERCINGS

¹ James Boon, *Affinities and Extremes: Crisscrossing the Bittersweet Ethnology of East Indies History, Hindu-Balinese Culture, and Indo-European Allure* (Chicago: Univ. of Chicago Press, 1990). In Bali, goats' eyelids are often used for this purpose.

² See the Bibliography for some relevant sources.

³ See, for example, Patrick Rogers with Rebecca Crandell, "Think of It as Therapy: Even the Suit and Tie Set Is into Body Piercing," *Newsweek*, 31 May 1993, 65.

⁴ Stinich generously shared a longer, written version of her talk with me. The citation for my own piece is Marianna Torgovnick, "Sticks and Bolts," *Artforum International* 31 (December 1992): 64–65.

⁵ Madonna, *Sex,* photographed by Steven Meisel, art directed by Fabian Baron, ed. Glenn O'Brien, produced by Callaway (New York: Warner Books, 1992).

⁶ Discussion of the book was curiously domestic, focusing on its high cost and shoddy workmanship.

⁷ See, for example, "Weirdstock: Rock's Wiggiest Road Show is Lollapalooza," *People,* 21 August 1992, 104–106, and Melissa Rossi, "Where Do We Go After the Rave?," *Newsweek,* 29 July 1993, 58.

⁸ See Suzy Menkes, "Body Piercing Moves into the Mainstream," *New York Times,* 23 November 1993, B4; *Vogue*'s piece ran in its March 1994 issue.

⁹ "Body Language," *New York Times,* 26 June 1994, 33 (Sunday "Styles" section).

¹⁰ Tom Singman, "Navel Maneuvers," *New York Times Magazine,* 20 January 1995, 20.

¹¹ Tarantino, of course, could show "Jodie's" tongue, as he could not have shown her nipple or clitoris, without tilting the film into the category of pornography.

¹² Sallie Tisdale, *Talk Dirty to Me: An Intimate Philosophy of Sex* (New York: Doubleday, 1994), 113–14.

¹³ At the 1995 Whitney Museum biennial exhibition, for example, photographs of a female artist and a man with extensive body tattoos, nipple piercings, and SM leather gear attracted special attention from the crowd and numerous (often disapproving) comments.

¹⁴ One performance artist recently "hung" himself at an exhibition: each day he would mount four pegs on the wall and remain in place until the exhibition closed for the day. Symbolically, this act demonstrated the difference between art as process (taking place in the artist) and as product (the completed work of art). The impulse has some affinities with piercing as performance art.

¹⁵ P-Orridge also describes how his Prince Albert affects urination, rejecting a traditional male prerogative: "The exit hole for Prince Alberts is underneath, so with that jet and the other one heading forward, you're bound to miss. Now I always sit down to piss. All men should sit anyway" (San Francisco: Re-Search, 1989), 175.

¹⁶ As, by definition, a crossing between the organic (bodies) and inorganic materials, piercing is a hyperbolic form of reification that can be read, alternatively, as a protest against reification or an example of it.

¹⁷ See William Grimes, "Performer's Pain Spreads to Arts Endowment," *New York Times,* 7 July 1994, B1, B2.

¹⁸ The Church had its chance when Francis travelled to the Holy Land. In his absence, his Franciscans were persuaded to adopt a "rule." See the Bibliography for materials on these religious figures.

¹⁹ Under the guidance of her confessors, Teresa increasingly recorded conventional visions of Christ and the saints in bodily form. Early on, she experienced divinity as energy or force.

²⁰ Teresa of Avila, *The Life of Teresa of Avila, Including the Relations of Her Spiritual State,* trans. David Lewis (1565; London: Burns and Oates, 1962), 60. Rama-

krishna's words are reproduced in Romain Rolland, *The Life of Ramakrishna* (1929; Calcutta: Advaita Ashrama, 1965), 33. For additional discussions of Rolland and the idea of the oceanic, see the Introduction and Chapter One.

CONCLUSION

[1] On the protest at Bear Butte, see "New Agers at Holy Places Arouse Protests by Indians," *New York Times*, 27 June 1993, A14. See also Phillip J. De Loria, "Termination," in *The Native Americans*, ed. Betty Ballantine and Ian Ballantine (Atlanta: Turner Publishing, 1993), 442.

[2] Lavelle is quoted in "Spiritual Seekers Borrow Indian Ways," *New York Times*, 27 December 1993, A1.

[3] It is likely to be no accident that magical realism flourished in Latin American fiction, in areas where Indian and Spanish culture have existed in close proximity. In her dissertation, "Dreamtime Fiction" (Duke University, 1993), Kathyrn West shows how such patterns also occur in African-American fiction, most notably in the fiction of Toni Morrison.

[4] Sherwin Nuland, *How We Die* (New York: Knopf, 1994).

[5] In January 1995, National Public Radio broadcast an interview with Frank J. Tipler, a physicist who, although an atheist, claims to have found proof of God's existence by using the Omega Point theory. Defining God as the matter left in the universe at the end of time, he concludes that because matter is omnipresent, omniscient, and omnipotent, "we" eventually will be absorbed in "God." See *The Physics of Immortality: Modern Cosmology, God, and the Resurrection of the Dead* (New York: Doubleday, 1994). I loved the interview but had some problems with the book.

[6] The sixties counterculture clearly had many oceanic impulses: Timothy Leary and other advocates of the 1960s drug culture, for example, programmatically sought ecstatic unities; the unofficial motto of the drug culture was the anticommercial "Turn on, Tune in, Drop Out." It is an interesting instance of wanting to make feelings of *communitas* and ecstatic oneness the basis of social life—to make them last and last.

[7] When I say "utter separation" I do not, of course, mean to deny the persistent efforts to trace modern humans back to their origins, a phenomenon frequently mentioned in this book, especially in Chapter Four. I refer here merely to the conceived difference between primitive and civilized beings with regard to the oceanic.

[8] From a conversation with Louise Fradenburg, professor of English at the University of California at Santa Barbara.

[9] The model I am proposing resembles that used by Mikhail Bakhtin in connection with the sporadic emergence of the novel as a genre at various points in literary history before it emerged for good and was named in the eighteenth century. I have found this model extremely supple and convincing. See *The Dialogic Imagination: Four Essays*, ed. Michael Holquist, trans. Caryl Emerson and Michael Holquist (Austin: Univ. of Texas Press, 1981).

[10] Sigmund Freud, *Beyond the Pleasure Principle*, trans. James Strachey (1920; New York: Norton, 1961), 37.

[11] Eastern religious texts are eloquent on this idea, for example, at the beginning of the *Tao Te Ching:*

> The Tao that can be talked about is not the true Tao
> The name that can be named
>   is not the eternal name.
> Everything in the universe comes out of Nothing.

Tao Te Ching, trans. Man-Ho Kwok, Martin Palmer, and Jay Ramsay (Shaftesbury, Dorset: Element Books, 1993).

[12] For this reason, my chapters on contemporary culture by and large omit religious fundamentalism, which projects ecstasy by routes that usually bypass primitivism. Still, as I noted in Chapters Seven and Eight, fundamentalism is beginning to interact with phenomena such as the men's movement and the New Age.

[13] Cults can dramatically increase oceanic potential and cause it to veer towards the death wish. They also can run headfirst against governmental authority: the mass suicides at Jonestown and Waco are recent examples.

[14] See Carlos Ginzberg, *Ecstasies: Deciphering the Witches' Sabbath* (New York: Pantheon, 1991).

[15] I agree with most experts that the latter figure is too high, except insofar as it may reflect the number of lives disrupted by the fear of witchcraft and, more especially, of being accused of witchcraft. See Anna Llewellyn Barstow, *Witchcraze: A New History of the European Witch Hunts* (San Francisco: Harper, 1993). In the Introduction, and Chapter One, I discuss some of the factors that contribute to accurate estimates.

[16] See René Descartes, *The Discourse on Method* (1637) and *Meditations* (1641).

[17] Sometimes the allotment was larger; land previously owned by Indians was sold in open "runs" or "rushes," like that in Oklahoma. See Peter Nabokov, "Closing In," in *The Native Americans,* 366–69.

[18] The major law on women's property in England was the Married Women's Property Act of 1870 (amended in 1874, and again in 1884). Even in the Representation of the People Act of 1918, age restrictions varied for men and women: universal suffrage for men over twenty-one, women over thirty. In 1928, twenty-one became the voting age for men and women.

[19] J. G. Herder, *Outline of a Philosophy of the History of Man.* This quotation, from an 1801 English translation by T. C. Churchill, is cited by Robert D. Richardson, Jr., in *Emerson: The Mind on Fire* (Berkeley: Univ. of California Press, 1995), 94.

[20] The first half of Brontë's *Wuthering Heights,* for example, is a fully oceanic text; the second half questions Cathy and Heathcliff's intuitions. The oceanic floats completely free in Brontë's poetry. Woolf's *The Waves* is a sustained meditation on the oceanic. Dylan Thomas' "The Force That Through the Green Fuse Drives the Flower" is one of many examples of oceanic verse.

[21] Jeffrey Moussaieff Masson points this out in *The Oceanic Feeling: The Origins of Religious Sentiment in Ancient India* (Boston: Reidel, 1980), 36.

[22] Victor W. Turner, *The Ritual Process: Structure and Anti-Structure* (Ithaca: Cornell Univ. Press, 1969); see Chapter Seven for a detailed discussion of Turner's ideas.

23 My argument is that specific combinations of factors can have different outcomes, depending on context and chance. A recent study of Nazis and ecology shows, for example, how ecological movements cropped up on both the left and the right after World War I—so that such impulses are inherently neither progressive nor conservative, democratic nor totalitarian. See Anna Bramwell, *Ecology in the Twentieth Century: A History* (New Haven: Yale Univ. Press, 1989).

24 See *Sigmund Freud et Romain Rolland: Correspondance, 1923–1936, De la sensation océanique au Trouble du souvenir sur l'Acrople*, ed. Henri Vermorel and Madeleine Vermorel (Paris: Presses Universitaires de France, 1993), 383–99.

25 The Nazis were attracted not just to oceanic rituals but to an ideology of land ecology and also to the protection of animals. See Simon Schama, *Landscape and Memory* (New York: Knopf, 1995), chap. 2, and Luc Ferry, *The New Ecological Order*, trans. Carol Volk (Chicago: Univ. of Chicago Press, 1995), chap. 5.

I take it to be significant that both these books, published in 1995, treat Nazism in contexts other than the social or military history of World War II. But by the same token, they seem uncertain about how to proceed. Schama overlooks how the example of Nazism problematizes the message of hope he derives from the history of human veneration for landscape; Ferry tends to assume too much that ecological interests necessarily veer away from humanism and towards totalitarianism.

26 Almost all attempts to think about these concepts together have foundered on questions of definition. Freud, for example, defined maturity and civilization as constitutively dependent on the suppression of human instincts. In a recent book about the dangers of "deep ecology," Luc Ferry defines human beings as "antinatural" in *The New Ecological Order* (xxviii). He sees deep ecology, animal rights, and ecofeminism as potentially eroding humanism and democracy—two of the gains in modern life. This Conclusion, and the book as a whole, includes many definitions of humans as something other than "antinatural."

27 The quotation from Emerson is from *Nature*. O'Keeffe's remark occurs in her letters (see Chapter Five).

28 The concept also resembles Mikhail Bakhtin's radical rethinking of Christianity. See also my discussion in *Closure in the Novel* of Virginia Woolf's *The Waves* (Princeton: Princeton Univ. Press, 1981), in which Woolf depicts a range of characters' relationships to the balance of self and the oceanic.

BIBLIOGRAPHY

For primary sources, see the notes and the references in individual chapters.

INTRODUCTION

All work on the topic of primitivism is indebted to classic rebuttals of the idea of a singular or simple "primitive." Franz Boas' *The Mind of Primitive Man* (1911; rev. ed., 1938; New York: Collier, 1963) represents the historicizing, particularizing dimension of ethnographic research; ethnographies that put Boas' principles into practice are too numerous to cite here. Equally important to anyone working with the history of anthropology is the more universalizing, structuralist tendency, represented best, perhaps, by Claude Lévi-Strauss in *The Savage Mind* (Chicago: Univ. of Chicago Press, 1966) and his four-part *Mythologiques*, of which the best-known volume is *The Raw and the Cooked*, trans. John Weightman and Doreen Weightman (New York: Harper, 1969).

Attention to Western images of other cultures has been inspired in a very profound way by Edward Said's *Orientalism* (New York: Pantheon, 1978) and *Culture and Imperialism* (New York: Knopf, 1992). Among books on this general subject, James Clifford's *The Predicament of Culture* (Cambridge: Harvard Univ. Press, 1988) is especially interesting on crossings between "exotic" and Western cultures. With George Marcus, Clifford has also edited a collection of essays that helped to raise questions about the factuality of ethnographic findings called *Writing Culture: The Poetics and Politics of Ethnography* (Berkeley: Univ. of California Press, 1986).

Henry Louis Gates, Jr., edited a collection of essays called *"Race," Writing, and Difference* (Chicago: Univ. of Chicago Press, 1986) that brought close reading to bear on debates concerning race and postcolonialism. Sander Gilman provides fascinating information from medical history in *Difference and Pathology: Stereotypes of Sexuality, Race, and Madness* (Ithaca: Cornell Univ. Press, 1986).

On more general images of primitive peoples, I am indebted to Stanley Diamond, *In Search of the Primitive: A Critique of Civilization* (New Brunswick: Transaction, 1974); Philip Curtin, *The Image of Africa: British Ideas and Action, 1780–1850* (Madison: Univ. of Wisconsin Press, 1964); Dorothy Hammond and Alta Jablow, *The Myth of Africa* (New York: Library of Social Science, 1977); and Lois

/ 245

Whitney, *Primitivism and the Idea of Progress in English Popular Literature of the Eighteenth Century* (New York: Octagon, 1965).

On male attitudes towards the primitive, in addition to working with primary texts, I found inspiring Jessica Benjamin's *The Bonds of Love* (New York: Pantheon, 1988). Klaus Theweleit's *Male Fantasies*, vol. 1, *Women, Floods, Bodies, History* helped to sharpen my sense of how certain aspects of Nazism were also a perverse variation on primitivism (trans. Stephen Conway, in collaboration with Erica Carter and Chris Turner [Minneapolis: Univ. of Minnesota Press, 1987]).

Several exciting recent books have explored ecological aspects of Western traditions. I see these traditions as parallel to, and sometimes, as intersecting with, those I have examined. Robert Pogue Harrison's *Forests* (Chicago: Univ. of Chicago Press, 1992) is a meditation on sylvan themes. Matt Cartmill's *A View to a Death in the Morning: Hunting and Nature Through History* (Cambridge: Harvard Univ. Press, 1993) reconstructs the West's shifting attitudes towards animals. Simon Schama's *Landscape and Memory* (New York: Knopf, 1995) surveys Western attitudes towards forests, rivers, and mountains. All document complexities and contradictions in Western thought in a way that I found extremely helpful and suggestive, although in some cases, notably Schama's, the books appeared too late to be reflected in more than late revisions. Still, these books confirmed my intuition that primitivism today involves much more than the condition of indigenous peoples—vast and important as that subject is.

On the oceanic, my interest was first piqued many years ago by Virginia Woolf's *The Waves* (1930), which I discussed in chapter 9 of *Closure in the Novel* (Princeton: Princeton Univ. Press, 1981). Surprisingly, there are few formal bibliographies of writings on the subject, which tend to cross many fields and many levels of culture. One of the fullest bibliographies I found was in a self-help book on interpersonal relations: Harville Hendrix, *Getting the Love You Want: A Guide for Couples* (1988; San Francisco: Harper, 1990).

The primary texts cited in the notes, including especially Martin Buber's *I and Thou* and the correspondence between Romain Rolland and Sigmund Freud, clinched my sense that the oceanic is a great repressed force in modern culture. Buber's *Ecstatic Confessions*, a collection of writings by mystics, provided firsthand examples including personal testimonies (trans. Esther Cameron, ed. Paul Mendes-Flohr [1909; New York: Harper and Row, 1985]).

I read Mircea Eliade's *Myths, Dreams, and Mysteries: The Encounter Between Contemporary Faiths and Archaic Realities* at a crucial point in the writing of this book; it helped me to think about primitivism today as a form of spiritual questing and pointed me towards certain similarities between contemporary religions and the beliefs of archaic peoples (trans. Philip Mairet [1957; New York: Harper, 1975]).

On images of "natives" at the point of their first encounters with Europeans, the literature is vast, and growing. Among the striking contributions not included in the notes is Jonathan Goldberg, "Discovering America," chapter 6 of *Sodometries: Renaissance Texts, Modern Sexualities* (Stanford: Stanford Univ. Press, 1992). See also the materials listed in the section of the Bibliography relating to Chapter Six.

Accounts of specific groups and their beliefs are legion in both classic and contemporary anthropological texts, and are too numerous to cite here. I benefited especially from the literature on Native American cultures and that on ritual, cited in the sections of the Bibliography relating to Chapters Six and Seven, respectively; I also benefited from the literature on potlatch. One unusual and distinctive book reconstructing indigenous points of view is Doucan Gersi's *Faces in the Smoke: An Eyewitness Experience of Voodoo, Shamanism, Psychic Healing, and Other Amazing Human Powers* (Los Angeles: Jeremy P. Tarcher, 1991). It documents various phenomena associated with beliefs that "everything in nature, every single bit of matter, is alive." There are many European and American accounts of becoming a shaman's apprentice which support Gersi's contentions, the most famous being Carlos Castaneda's controversial series of books on Don Juan (New York: Simon and Schuster, 1971–87); among the more recent is Mark J. Plotkin, *Tales of a Shaman's Apprentice: An Ethnobotanist Searches for New Medicines in the Amazon Rain Forest* (New York: Viking, 1993).

At a more abstract, less experiential level, Jean-François Lyotard posits "tribal" unity between generations as the antithesis of the postmodern condition in *The Postmodern Condition: A Report on Knowledge*, trans. Geoff Bennington and Brian Massumi, Theory and History of Literature series, vol. 10 (1979; Minneapolis: Univ. of Minnesota Press, 1984). On the needs of postmodern people, I found Lyotard and the following texts suggestive as both symptoms and diagnoses of the problem: Rollo May, *The Cry for Myth* (New York: Norton, 1991); Christopher Lasch, *The Culture of Narcissism: American Life in an Age of Diminishing Expectations* (New York: Norton, 1979); Herbert Marcuse, *Eros and Civilization* (1966; Boston: Beacon, 1979), Norman O. Brown, *Love's Body* (New York: Random House, 1966).

CHAPTER ONE:
"WHAT AN ECSTASY IT WOULD HAVE BEEN!":
GIDE AND JUNG IN AFRICA

For Gide, I have attempted only a close reading of *Voyage au Congo* and *Le Retour du Tchad* and not an interpretation of his long and protean career. Among critical studies consulted for Gide in Africa, I would single out five in English: Justin O'Brien, *Portrait of André Gide: A Critical Biography* (New York: Knopf, 1953); Germaine Brée, *André Gide* (New Brunswick: Rutgers Univ. Press, 1963): George Painter, *André Gide* (New York: Atheneum, 1968); Wallace Fowlie, *André Gide: His Life and Art* (New York: Collier, 1965); and Albert Guérard, *André Gide* (Cambridge: Harvard Univ. Press, 1951). It is worth noting that all of these books were published before postcolonial approaches came to be regarded as a "literary" issue. They thus have almost nothing to say about Gide's African materials. In addition, two books in French deal directly with Gide in Africa, providing factual information: Gabriel Michaud, *Gide et Afrique* (Paris: Collection Alternance, 1961), and Jacqueline M. Chadourne, *André Gide et l'Afrique: Le Rôle de l'Afrique dans la vie et l'œuvre de l'écrivain* (Paris: A. G. Nizet, 1968).

My attention to Jung was similarly focused on the African experience. I was aided considerably by Jung's late autobiography, *Memories, Dreams, Reflections* (see notes). This book was, admittedly, staged by Jung and his followers late in the psychologist's life in an effort to perpetuate the growing Jung myth. But it remains an elegant and indispensable source; much of the material in it has yet to be mined.

In contrast to recent work on Freud, almost all of the writing on Jung has been done by devoted disciples. In addition to the biographies cited in the notes, several other books deserve mention: Laurens van der Post, *Jung and the Story of Our Time* (New York: Pantheon, 1975); Barbara Hanna, *Jung: His Life and Work* (New York: G. P. Putnam's Sons, 1976); Marie-Louise van Franz, *C. G. Jung: His Myth in Our Time,* trans. William H. Kennedy (New York: G. P. Putnam's Sons for the C. G. Jung Foundation for Analytical Psychology, 1975); and Gerhard Wehr, *An Illustrated Biography of C. G. Jung* (Boston: Shambhala, 1989).

Debunkers of Jung, though comparatively few, include Richard Noll in *The Jung Cult: Origins of a Charismatic Movement* (Princeton: Princeton Univ. Press, 1994), which provides an abundance of historical background information placing Jung in the context of traditions of his time. An additional, useful source is Peter Homans' *Jung in Context: Modernity and the Making of a Psychology* (Chicago: Univ. of Chicago Press, 1979), which discusses the interrelationship of religion and psychoanalysis during this period.

Critical literature on Bachofen is surprisingly scanty in English. Boas' preface to *Myth, Religion, and Mother Right: Selected Writings of J. J. Bachofen* (see notes) remains among the more extensive pieces, as does Joan Bamberger's "The Myth of Matriarchy: Why Men Rule in Primitive Societies," in *Women, Culture, and Society,* ed. Michelle Zimbalist Rosaldo and Louise Lamphere (Stanford: Stanford Univ. Press, 1974). There is also an unpublished dissertation by Jonathan Fishbane, "Mother-Right, Myth and Renewal: The Thought of Johann Jakob Bachofen and Its Relationship to the Perception of Cultural Decadence in the Nineteenth Century" (Univ. of Michigan Press, 1981), which stresses Bachofen's work as part of the emerging critique of modernity.

Jane Harrison's classic texts, *Prolegomena to the Study of Greek Religion* (Cambridge: Cambridge Univ. Press, 1908) and *Mythology* (Boston: Marshall Jones, 1924), helped me to understand how the irrational was a part of Greek culture. Nietzsche's *The Birth of Tragedy* (New York: Doubleday, 1956) remains an indispensable introduction to these patterns of thought. Wole Soyinka's translation and reinterpretation of the text of *The Bacchae,* subtitled *A Communion Rite,* is stunning and suggestive (New York: Norton, 1974).

The number of books reading Freud as a writer of fictions rather than as a scientist is growing and too large to cite here. These may ultimately prove to be more than simply debunking: they may allow us to understand the extremely moving contours of Freud's life and career. For an early and still highly readable example, see Stanley Edgar Hyman, *The Tangled Bank: Darwin, Marx, Frazer, and Freud as Imaginative Writers* (New York: Atheneum, 1962).

Freud's ideas about primitive peoples and the idea of the primitive evolved over a number of years, most clearly in *Totem and Taboo: Resemblances Between the Psychic Lives of Savages and Neurotics* (1913) and *Civilization and Its Discontents* (1930). But it's a mistake not to bring many other Freudian texts to bear, among them *Beyond the Pleasure Principle* (1922), *The Future of an Illusion* (1927), Freud's various exchanges with Romain Rolland (see the Introduction and notes), "Female Sexuality" (1931), "Femininity" (1933), and "A Disturbance of Vision on Visiting the Acropolis" (1937). Many biographies and studies of Freud also provide fascinating information concerning his relationships with his father, his mother, and his working-class nurse.

I single out two: Peter Gay, *Freud: A Life for Our Time* (New York: Norton, 1988), and Anne McClintock's chapter on Freud in *Imperial Leather: Race, Gender, and Sexuality in the Colonial Conquest* (New York: Routledge, 1995).

James W. Jones' *Contemporary Psychoanalysis and Religion* (New Haven: Yale Univ. Press, 1991) helped me to work out connections between Freud's denunciation of religion as illusion and his rejection of relatedness as a model of human experience. On the same complex subject, the following books were also helpful: W. W. Meissner's *Psychoanalysis and Religious Experience* (New Haven: Yale Univ. Press, 1984); Sudhir Kakar's *The Analyst and the Mystic: Psychoanalytic Reflections on Religion and Mysticism* (Chicago: Univ. of Chicago Press, 1991); Hans Kung's *Freud and the Problem of God*, trans. Edward Quinn (New Haven: Yale Univ. Press, 1979); and Sander Gilman, *Jewish Self-Hatred: Anti-Semitism and the Hidden Language of the Jews* (Baltimore: Johns Hopkins Univ. Press, 1986).

Useful in understanding Freud's influence on females and psychoanalysis are Helene Deutsch, *The Psychology of Women: A Psychoanalytic Interpretation*, vol. 1 (New York: Grune and Stratton, 1944); Juliet Mitchell, *Psychoanalysis and Feminism* (New York: Pantheon, 1974); Simone de Beauvoir, *The Second Sex*, trans. H. M. Parshley (New York: Knopf, 1953); and Jean Baker Miller, ed., *Psychoanalysis and Women* (Baltimore: Penguin, 1973).

Jacques Lacan's extremely influential theories also deal with the relationship between mothers and infants; see *Feminine Sexuality*, ed. Juliet Mitchell and Jacqueline Rose, trans. Jacqueline Rose (New York: Norton, 1982). Other important work after 1970 offers suggestive sidelights on these themes: for example, Julia Kristeva, *Powers of Horror: An Essay on Abjection*, trans. Leon S. Roudiez, European Perspectives series (New York: Columbia Univ. Press, 1982), and *Tales of Love*, trans. Leon S. Roudiez (New York: Columbia Univ. Press, 1987).

In the area of psychological theory on interpersonal relations there are several landmark texts. D. W. Winnicott (see notes) introduced the concept of the "good enough mother" as one who helps infants combine a sense of self and a sense of relatedness. Additional works on interpersonal relations that I found useful are Margaret S. Mahler, Fred Pine, and Anni Bergman, *The Psychological Birth of the Human Infant: Symbiosis and Identification* (New York: Basic Books, 1975), and Shirley Nelson Garner, Claire Kahane, and Madelon Sprengnether, *The (M)other Tongue: Essays in Feminist Psychoanalytic Interpretation* (Ithaca: Cornell Univ. Press, 1985).

Two extreme, and polar, texts that take for granted the identification of women with nature are Susan Griffin's *Women and Nature: The Roaring Within Her* (New York: Harper and Row, 1978), which idealizes women on this basis; and Camille Paglia's *Sexual Personae*, which revisits certain stereotypes derived from Nietzsche. Speculation on male fear of women is a theme that crosses several chapters in my book. Bibliographical references can also be found in the books listed below on female versus male psychology (Chapter Four), the figure of the crone (Chapter Five), ritual (Chapter Seven), and goddesses (Chapter Eight).

CHAPTER TWO:
"SOMETHING STOOD STILL IN MY SOUL":
D. H. LAWRENCE IN NEW MEXICO

Two classic biographies of D. H. Lawrence are by Harry Moore, *The Intelligent Heart* (New York: Farrar, Straus, and Young, 1956), and Frank Kermode, *D. H. Lawrence* (New York: Viking, 1973). But there has been a recent spate of biographies—for example, John Worthen's *Lawrence: A Literary Life* (New York: St. Martin's Press, 1993). Many stress Lawrence's relationship with his wife, Frieda. Elaine Feinstein's *Lawrence's Women: The Intimate Life of D. H. Lawrence* (New York: HarperCollins, 1993) sees Lawrence's marriage as one of several formative relationships he had with women. Brenda Maddox, *D. H. Lawrence: Story of a Marriage* (New York: Simon and Schuster, 1994), has provided fascinating information, especially about Frieda's early involvement with Otto Gross and with the cult of the Magna Mater.

Frieda comes in for biographies of her own in Robert Lucas, *Frieda Lawrence: The Story of Frieda von Richthofen and D. H. Lawrence,* trans. Geoffrey Skeleton (New York: Viking, 1973), and Martin Green, *The Von Richthofen Sisters: The Triumphant and the Tragic Modes of Love* (New York: Basic, 1974). Frieda speaks for herself in *Not I, but the Wind* (New York: Viking, 1934). Many other memoirs dealing with Lawrence during his Taos years survive, among them Mabel Dodge Luhan, *Lorenzo in Taos* (London: M. Secker, 1933), and Witter Bynner, *Journey with Genius: Recollections and Reflections Concerning the D. H. Lawrences* (New York: J. Day, 1951).

Lawrence criticism has never fully recovered from Kate Millett's indictment of the author's hostile attitudes towards clitoral orgasm in *Sexual Politics* (New York: Doubleday, 1970). Still, there are signs of life in recent criticism, including Tony Pinckney, *D. H. Lawrence and Modernism* (Iowa City: Univ. of Iowa Press, 1990), and Robert M. Polhemus, *Erotic Faith: Being in Love from Jane Austen to D. H. Lawrence* (Chicago: Univ. of Chicago Press, 1990). Some books directly relevant to the themes I develop here are *A Descriptive Bibliography of Lady Chatterley's Lover, with Essays Towards a Publishing History of the Novel,* ed. Jay A. Gertzman (Westport, Conn.: Greenwood, 1989); Cornelia Nixon, *Lawrence's Leadership Politics* (Berkeley: Univ. of California Press, 1986); Judith Ruderman, *D. H. Lawrence and the Devouring Mother: The Search for a Patriarchal Ideal of Leadership* (Durham, N.C.: Duke Univ. Press, 1984); and Charles Rossman, "D. H. Lawrence and Mexico," in *D. H. Lawrence: A Centenary Consideration,* ed. Peter Balbert and Phillip L. Marcus (Ithaca: Cornell Univ. Press, 1985).

I have myself written on Lawrence in two previous books: *The Visual Arts, Pictorialism, and the Novel: James, Lawrence, and Woolf* (Princeton: Princeton Univ. Press, 1985) and *Gone Primitive: Savage Intellects, Modern Lives* (Chicago: Univ. of Chicago, 1990).

CHAPTER THREE:
LOVING AFRICA:
MEMOIRS BY EUROPEAN WOMEN

The biographies of women in Africa cited in the notes were invaluable sources of information. Yet of the women treated in this chapter, only Isak Dinesen has received substantial critical attention—and even she has received relatively little. Among useful discussions, in addition to those cited in the notes, are: Robert Langbaum, *The Gayety of Vision: A Study of Isak Dinesen's Art* (New York: Random House, 1964) and Stephen Dwynn, *The Life of Mary Kingsley* (London: Macmillan, 1933).

Interest in women's travels in "exotic" places and encounters with primitive peoples has been stimulated by postcolonial approaches to literature. In addition to the volumes cited in the notes, I consulted Mary Louise Pratt's *Imperial Eyes: Travel Writing and Transculturation* (London: Routledge, 1992) and Marion Tinling's *Women into the Unknown: A Sourcebook on Women Explorers and Adventurers* (New York: Greenwood, 1989).

My observations about women in Africa were confirmed by books I had no space to include within this chapter: for example, Elspeth Huxley's *The Flame Trees of Thika* (New York: Penguin, 1974). Other books on women in remote locales appeared after I had written my own materials: for example, Julia Blackburn's *Daisy Bates in the Desert* (New York: Pantheon, 1994). Because it has been so long neglected in the past, women's writing is likely to be an active area of research; I suspect other books will have appeared too late to be acknowledged here.

Also of interest to me in writing this chapter was women's nature writing, which frequently shows patterns of oceanic experience. See, for example, Diana Kappel-Smith, *Desert Time: A Journey Through the American Southwest* (Boston: Little, Brown, 1992), and Terry Tempest Williams, *An Unspoken Hunger: Stories from the Field* (New York: Pantheon Books, 1994). I also used the following recent women's writing: Kathleen Norris, *Dakota: A Spiritual Geography* (New York: Ticknor and Fields, 1993), and Gretel Ehrlich, *The Solace of Open Spaces* (New York: Viking, 1985).

There is a large and important literature on female differences from males and the controversial question of whether they are biologically based, culturally based, or both, depending on the individual, the specific traits at issue, and context. The latter is my own position. Speaking eloquently on various aspects and sides of the issue are: Nancy Chodorow, *The Reproduction of Mothering: Psychoanalysis and the Sociology of Gender* (Berkeley: Univ. of California Press, 1978); Carol Gilligan, *In a Different Voice* (Cambridge: Harvard Univ. Press, 1982); Mary Field Belenky, Blythe McVicker Clinchy, Nancy Rule Goldberger, and Jill Mattuck Tannile, *Women's Ways of Knowing: The Development of Self, Voice, and Mind* (New York: Basic, 1986); Sherry Ruth Anderson and Patricia Hopkins, *The Feminine Face of God: The Unfolding of the Sacred in Women* (New York: Bantam, 1991); Hester Eisenstein and Alice Jardine, eds., *The Future of Difference* (Boston: G. K. Hall, 1980); Hélène Cixous and Catherine Clément, *The Newly Born Woman*, Theory and History of Literature series, vol. 24 (Minneapolis: Univ. of Minnesota Press, 1986).

CHAPTER FOUR:
DIAN FOSSEY AMONG THE ANIMALS

I relied heavily in this chapter on Dian Fossey's own writings and on biographies of her. These are cited in the text, along with writings by and about other female primatologists. Donna Haraway's *Primate Visions: Gender, Race, and Nature in the World of Modern Science* (see notes) provides a fascinating history of primatology in light of current debates about culture and science, but much remains to be done in this area.

Numerous books on paleoanthropology, human origins, and the controversial issue of animal language also influenced my thinking about Fossey's career and its meaning. I mention just a few that are not cited elsewhere: Dale Peterson and Jane Goodall, *Visions of Caliban: On Chimpanzees and People* (New York: Houghton Mifflin, 1993); Dorothy L. Cheney and Robert M. Seyfarth, *How Monkeys See the World: Inside the Mind of Another Species* (Chicago: Univ. of Chicago Press, 1990); and Vicki Hearne, *Adam's Task: Calling Animals by Name* (New York: Knopf, 1986).

Additional books about humans and animals which I consulted as I wrote this chapter include highly sympathetic renderings in Joy Adamson, *Born Free: The Incredible Story of Elsa the Lioness* (New York: Bantam, 1960); Elizabeth Marshall Thomas, *The Hidden Life of Dogs* (New York: Pocket Books, 1995); and Jeffrey Moussaieff Masson and Susan McCarthy, *When Elephants Weep: The Emotional Lives of Animals* (London: Cape, 1994).

Mircea Eliade (see notes) can be credited with circulating the concept of shamanism. Numerous books from Lynn Andrews' fictions to Jean Auel's *The Clan of the Cave Bear* (New York: Bantam, 1980), and its sequels, testify to current interest in shamanism as a theme, and its association with women.

CHAPTER FIVE:
''THE BONES AND THE BLUE'':
GEORGIA O'KEEFFE AND THE FEMALE PRIMITIVE

In addition to the important biographies of O'Keeffe cited in the notes, several others provided useful information concerning her life and career: Katherine Hoffman, *An Enduring Spirit: The Art of Georgia O'Keeffe* (Metuchen, N.J.: Scarecrow Press, 1984); Jan Garden Castro, *The Art and Life of Georgia O'Keeffe* (New York: Crown, 1985); and Jeffrey Hogrefe, *O'Keeffe: The Life of an American Legend* (New York: Bantam, 1992).

I was fortunate to have access to O'Keeffe's selected letters via *Georgia O'Keeffe: Art and Letters* (see notes). The centenary exhibit was a resource for me, as were several other illuminating exhibitions that appeared in the late eighties and early nineties; in addition to those cited in the notes, I learned from "Alfred Stieglitz in the Darkroom" at the National Gallery of Art in Washington, D.C. (4 October 1992–14 February 1993).

Attention to how modern culture uses tribal art was sparked by a 1984 exhibition at the Museum of Modern Art, "'Primitivism' in Twentieth-Century Art." The exhibition provoked numerous responses, among them Hal Foster, "The 'Primitive' Unconscious of Modern Art," *October* 34 (Fall 1985): 45–70; James Clifford, "Histories of the Tribal and the Modern," in *The Predicament of Culture* (Cambridge: Harvard Univ. Press, 1988); and Arthur C. Danto, "African Art and Artifacts," in *Encounters and Reflections* (New York: Farrar, Straus, and Giroux, 1990). Earlier scholarly work on tribal art dates back to the 1920s with studies by Roger Fry in *Vision and Design* (New York: Brentano's, 1920) and Robert Goldwater in *Primitivism in Modern Art* (1938; New York: Random House, 1967).

On Taos artists, see Patricia Janis Broder, *Taos: A Painter's Dream* (Boston: New York Graphic Society, 1980), and Mabel Dodge Luhan, *Taos and Its Artists* (New York: Duell, Sloan, and Pearce, 1947). On what I call the menstrual primitive, see Judy Grahn, *Blood, Bread, and Roses: How Menstruation Created the World* (Boston: Beacon, 1993). For the imagery of the crone, much of it relevant to O'Keeffe, see Barbara G. Walker, *The Crone: Woman of Age, Wisdom, and Power* (San Francisco: Harper and Row, 1985).

CHAPTER SIX:
NEW AMERICAN INDIAN/
NEW AMERICAN WHITE

For accounts of traditional Indian religions, I relied on a variety of sources, among them *Black Elk Speaks: Being the Life Story of a Holy Man of the Oglala Sioux,* as told through John G. Neihardt (1932; Lincoln: Univ. of Nebraska Press, 1979); *Growing Up Native American,* ed. Patricia Riley (New York: Morrow, 1993); *Native American Testimony: A Chronicle of Indian-White Relations from Prophecy to the Present, 1492–1992,* ed. Peter Nabokov (1978; New York: Viking, 1991); *American Indian Myths and Legends,* selected and edited by Richard Erdoes and Alfonso Ortiz (New York: Pantheon, 1984); and Ramon A. Guttierez, *When Jesus Came the Corn Mothers Went Away: Marriage, Sexuality, and Power in New Mexico, 1500–1846* (Stanford: Stanford Univ. Press, 1991). Some of the difficulties connected with working on this topic are indicated in the chapter and the notes.

Additional important sources on Indian/white relations are: Vine Deloria, *God Is Red* (New York: Gosset and Dunlap, 1973); Daniel Francis, *The Imaginary Indian: The Image of the Indian in Canadian Culture* (Vancouver, B.C.: Arsenal, 1992); and Jack Weatherford, *Indian Givers: How the Indians of the Americas Transformed the World* (New York: Crown, 1988).

First Images of America: The Impact of the New World on the Old collects classic essays on early European perceptions of Indians from a variety of disciplines (ed. Michael J. B. Allen and Robert L. Benson [Berkeley: Univ. of California Press, 1975]). German Arciniegas' *America in Europe: A History of the New World in Reverse,* trans. Gabriela Arciniegas and R. Victoria Arana (1975; San Diego: Harcourt Brace Jovanovich, 1986), provides a spirited and personal view, as do Tzvetan Todorov's *The Conquest of America* (see the Introduction and notes) and Arthur Quinn's *A New World: An Epic of Colonial America from the Founding of Jamestown to the Fall of Quebec* (Boston: Faber and Faber, 1994).

On Indian perceptions of whites, the following texts (in addition to sources listed in the first paragraph) are recommended: *Violence, Resistance, and Survival in the Americas: Native Americans and the Legacy of Conquest* (Washington: Smithsonian Institution Press, 1994) and Ronald Wright, *Stolen Continent: Through Indian Eyes Since 1492* (Boston: Houghton Mifflin, 1992).

I also relied on newspaper and magazine articles to chart what is often rapidly changing territory—for example, on casinos.

CHAPTER SEVEN:
OF DRUMS AND MEN

Accounts of the men's movement too often begin and end with Robert Bly's *Iron John* (Reading, Mass.: Addison-Wesley, 1990). This is too bad. Authors like Keen, Moore and Gillette, Somé, Meade, and others provide additional and important perspectives.

Whenever possible, I turned to earlier work by men's movement authors to chart their trajectory. For example, Sam Keen's profile as a men's movement leader is enriched if one looks at some of his earlier books: *A Dancing God* (New York: Harper and Row, 1970), on educational reform; and *Your Mythic Journey: Finding Meaning in Your Life Through Writing and Storytelling* (New York: Jeremy P. Tarcher, 1989), a Jungian self-help book. Similarly, Robert Bly has been involved with Jungian theory and has written eloquently about Mother goddesses in *Sleepers Joining Hands* (New York: Harper and Row, 1973). An Ur-text for images of women is Robert Graves' *The White Goddess: A Historical Grammar of Poetic Myth* (New York: Creative Age Press, 1948).

For this chapter, I also used videos and audiotapes actively: for example, *Images of Initiation,* by James Hillman, Michael Meade, and Malidoma Somé—a tape made of a conference. Several of John Boorman's films are useful in understanding the men's movement, especially *Deliverance* (1972) and *The Emerald Forest* (1985).

I would also refer readers to the work of Paul Monette, *Becoming a Man: Half a Life Story* (1992; San Francisco: HarperCollins, 1993), and Edmund White, *The Burning Library* (New York: Knopf, 1994). These books, on gay male identity, provide a useful supplement to men's movement views.

From the huge literature on ritual and ancient or tribal peoples, I used especially, in addition to material in the notes, Jane Harrison's *Ancient Art and Ritual* (New York: Henry Holt, 1913), which provides a fascinating, elegant description of ritual that seems very much connected with evolving definitions of the oceanic. Victor Turner's ideas in *The Ritual Process: Structure and Anti-Structure* (Ithaca: Cornell Univ. Press, 1969) were clarified for me by a later essay, "Passages, Margins, and Poverty: Religious Symbols of Communitas," in *Dramas, Fields, and Metaphors* (Ithaca: Cornell Univ. Press, 1974). I am indebted at many points to Turner's insights and speculations.

On the idea of *communitas,* studies of Martin Buber clarify both the biographical and intellectual basis of his thinking. I used especially Bernard Susser, *Existence and Utopia: the Social and Political Thought of Martin Buber* (Rutherford, N.J.: Fairleigh Dickinson Univ. Press, 1989); Lawrence J. Silberstein, *Martin Buber's Social and Religious Thought: Alienation and the Question of Meaning* (New York: NYU Press, 1989); Maurice Friedman, *Encounter on a Narrow Ridge: A Life of Martin Buber* (New York: Paragon, 1991); and Ronald C. Arnett, *Communication and Com-*

munity: Implications of Martin Buber's Dialogue (Carbondale and Edwardsville: Southern Illinois Univ. Press, 1986).

Critiques of the men's movement can be found in Susan Faludi, *Backlash: The Undeclared War Against American Women* (New York: Anchor Doubleday, 1991), and *Women Respond to the Men's Movement,* ed. Kay Leigh Hagan (New York: HarperCollins, 1992).

CHAPTER EIGHT:
MEDICINE WHEELS AND SPIRITUALITY:
PRIMITIVISM IN THE NEW AGE

To learn more about how antecedents of the New Age often drew on Eastern religions, I went to books like H. P. Blavatsky's *The Key to Theosophy: Being a Clear Exposition in the Form of Question and Answer of the Ethics, Science, and Philosophy for the Study of which the Theosophical Society Has been Founded* (Los Angeles: United Lodge of Theosophists, 1920). I also found intriguing the following studies of the evolution of religion in the United States: Harold Bloom, *The American Religion: The Emergence of the Post-Christian Nation* (New York: Simon and Schuster, 1992), and Catherine N. Albanese, *Nature Religion in America: From the Algonkian Indians to the New Age* (Chicago: Univ. of Chicago Press, 1990). Charles Strozier's *Apocalypse: On the Psychology of Fundamentalism in America* (Boston: Beacon, 1994) provided case studies of "endism"; it helped me understand the confluence now taking place between at least some fundamentalist groups and some aspects of the New Age.

I investigated additional branches of New Age thinking that affected the overall argument presented in this chapter. On Wicca (witchcraft), I was especially informed by Starhawk, *The Spiral Dance: A Rebirth of the Ancient Religion of the Great Goddess* (1979; San Francisco: Harper and Row, 1989), and Margot Adler, *Drawing Down the Moon: Witches, Druids, Goddess-Worshippers, and Other Pagans in America Today* (Boston: Beacon, 1979).

Goddess materials, on which the literature is vast, were also valuable in shaping my thinking about the relationship between the New Age and women. Noteworthy materials include scholarly books like Gerda Lerner's *The Creation of Patriarchy* (New York: Oxford Univ. Press, 1986) and relatively scholarly books like Erich Neumann, *The Great Mother,* trans. Ralph Manheim, Bollingen series, vol. 47 (New York: Pantheon, 1955); Merlin Stone, *When God Was a Woman* (New York: Dial Press, 1976); Riane Eisler, *The Chalice and the Blade: Our History, Our Future* (San Francisco: HarperCollins, 1988); and Carol Ochs, *Beyond the Sex of God: Towards a New Consciousness—Transcending Matriarchy and Patriarchy* (New York: Beacon, 1977). They include as well popularizing texts like Jean Shinoda Boden's *Goddesses in Everywoman: A New Psychology of Women* (New York: Colophon Books, 1984), Marilyn Woolger's *The Goddess Within: A Guide to the Eternal Myths That Shape Women's Lives* (New York: Fawcett Columbine, 1987), and Marianne Williamson's *A Return to Love: Reflections on the Principles of a Course in Miracles* (New York: HarperCollins, 1992).

Work on the poet H.D. (Hilda Dolittle) was also important to me as I wrote this section; I would single out H.D.'s trilogy of long poems (especially *The Walls Do Not*

Fall) and Diane Chisholm, *H.D.'s Freudian Poetics: Psychoanalysis in Translation* (Ithaca: Cornell Univ. Press, 1992).

A number of books written from theological perspectives address some basic issues concerning the New Age. Some consider the New Age a fad; some see it as a cult; some see it as a valid form of spiritual activity. See Rachel Storn, *In Search of Heaven on Earth* (London: Bloomsbury Reference, 1991); Dave Hunt, *America, The Sorcerer's New Apprentice: The Rise of New Age Shamanism* (Eugene, Oreg.: Harvest House, 1988); Edward F. Heenan, *Mystery, Magic, and Miracle: Religion in a Post-Aquarian Age* (Englewood Cliffs, N.J.: Prentice-Hall, 1973); and Russell Chandler, *Understanding the New Age* (Dallas: World Publishing, 1988).

In thinking about "safety valves" in contemporary culture, I found helpful Michel Foucault's *The History of Sexuality*, vol. 1, *An Introduction*, trans. Robert Hurley (1978; New York: Vintage, 1980).

CHAPTER NINE:

PIERCINGS

On Mayan bloodletting, see Linda Schele and Mary Ellen Miller, *The Blood of Kings* (New York: George Braziller in association with the Kimbell Art Museum, Fort Worth, 1986). Malinowski makes passing references to genital tattooing of women in his ethnographies; see Bronislaw Malinowski, *The Sexual Life of Savages in North-Western Melanesia* (1929; Boston: Beacon, 1988). For more bibliographical information on Balinese penile implants than is given in the notes, see Donald E. Brown, James W. Edwards, and Ruth P. Moore, *The Penis Inserts of Southeast Asia: An Annotated Bibliography with an Overview and Comparative Perspectives*, Occasional Paper Series, no. 15 (Berkeley: Center for South and Southeast Asia Studies, 1988).

On contemporary piercing, the 1989 Re-Search volume, *Modern Primitives*, remains the best overall source. See also Frances E. Mascia-Lees and Patricia Sharpe, eds., *Tattoo, Torture, Mutilation, and Adornment* (Albany: State Univ. of New York Press, 1992).

The stories of the Hindu mystics told by Gananath Obeyeskere in *Medusa's Hair: An Essay on Personal Symbols and Religious Experience* (Chicago: Univ. of Chicago Press, 1981) helped me to understand how a point of personal crisis (often a parent's death or a marital crisis) can serve as the point of initiation into trance experiences and body piercing.

From time to time in this book, but most extensively here, I have drawn on several biographies of Francis of Assisi and Teresa of Avila. My special interest has been in how their societies had difficulty accommodating them and even persecuted them. A chapter on piercings may seem like a strange place to list saints' lives, but, as the chapter suggests, maybe not. I relied especially on Anthony Mockler, *Francis of Assisi: The Wandering Years* (New York: Dutton, 1976); E. M. Almedingen, *Francis of Assisi: A Portrait* (London: Bodley Head, 1967); *St. Francis of Assisi: The Legends and Lauds*, edited, selected, and annotated by Otto Karrer, trans. N. Wydenbruck (New York: Sheed and Ward, 1948). Francis' "Canticle of the Sun" is especially interesting in terms of the oceanic emotion, as is his association in iconography with birds, animals, and mountains.

Teresa's autobiography, especially the first half, is extremely eloquent: *The Life of Teresa of Avila: Including the Relations of her Spiritual State*, trans. David Lewis (1565; London: Burns and Oates, 1962). Alison Weber in *Teresa of Avila and the Rhetoric of Femininity* (Princeton: Princeton Univ. Press, 1990) offers a striking reading of Teresa as negotiating, among other things, the ancestry of her Jewish-convert paternal grandfather and the needs of a woman within a male power structure.

CONCLUSION

Books on the history of religion are too numerous to mention. I cite two that raise interesting questions about the relationship between religion and the modern state: Thomas Luckmann, *The Invisible Religion: The Problem of Religion in Modern Society* (New York: Macmillan, 1967), and Jonathan Z. Smith, *Imagining Religion: From Babylon to Jonestown* (Chicago: Univ. of Chicago Press, 1982). Elaine Pagels' *Adam, Eve, and the Serpent* (New York: Random House, 1988) got me thinking about what Christianity has cast off during its long history, especially with regard to women.

Hans Peter Duerr's *Dreamtime: Concerning the Boundary Between Wilderness and Civilization* (London: Basil Blackwell, 1985) helped me to think about the connections between alternative conceptions of reality and what has been repressed in the West. Michael Taussig works in a very different register on questions of the self and the Other: *Shamanism, Colonialism, and the Wild Man: A Study in Terror and Healing* (Chicago: Univ. of Chicago Press, 1987) describes "going to the Indians for their healing power and killing them for their wildness." *Mimesis and Alterity: A Particular History of the Senses* (New York: Routledge, 1993) is stimulating on issues of alterity, mimesis (imitation), and violence.

The connection between Nazism and the oceanic, when it has been noted, has too often been quickly passed over, or, alternatively, the oceanic has been seen as destined to lead to totalitarian or other undesirable outcomes. An exception is Klaus Theweleit's very suggestive book *Male Fantasies*, vol. 1, *Women, Floods, Bodies, History* (see the section of the Bibliography relating to the Introduction). Late encounters with the following books helped to shape this Conclusion: Simon Schama's *Landscape and Memory* (see the section of the Bibliography relating to the Introduction), Luc Ferry's *The New Ecological Order*, and Robert D. Richardson, *Emerson: The Mind on Fire* (see notes). I was also stimulated by rereading Lévi-Strauss' *Tristes Tropiques*, which elaborates a suspect, but suggestive, theory that Buddhism represents a "feminine" component lost to the West, potentially to be regained through "savages and exploration."

Numerous newspaper and magazine stories during the 1990s suggested to me that the era dominated by images of the two world wars, which initiated current relationships to the idea of the primitive, may now be coming to an end.

ACKNOWLEDGMENTS

Primitive Passions was an exhilarating book to discuss with friends and colleagues, many of whom provided special help. Cathy Davidson, Alice Kaplan, Jan Radway, Betsy Cox, Julie Tetel, Nancy Hewitt, and Jane Tompkins all read significant portions of the manuscript, sometimes more than once. Their insights and writing tips as members of my writing groups (one ongoing, the other ad hoc), not to mention their friendship, are warmly acknowledged.

David Paletz and Syd Nathans, fellow members of a long-term lunch group, provided conversations over several years that greatly enriched this study; Shep Kretch, Steven Caton, and Margery Wolfe were a few of our guests who provided insightful conversation based on special forms of expertise. Alicia Ostriker, Natalie Zemon Davis, Elaine Showalter, Joyce Carol Oates, Susan Wolfson, Barbara Herrnstein Smith, Chris Herbert, Richard Ohmann, Reynolds Price, Thomas Pfau, and others all provided food for thought during the writing of this book. Thomas Ferraro and Martin Hipsky provided late readings of the Introduction and Conclusion that reassured an anxious author.

Audiences at the University of the Arts in Philadelphia, the Whitney Museum in New York, Duke University, Wesleyan University, Northwestern University, the University of North Carolina, Princeton University, the American Anthropological Association, the Modern Language Association, a symposium at Site Santa Fe and other places, asked good questions and sometimes affected the course of my argument. In seminars on Modernism, students at Duke and Princeton—both graduate and undergraduate—were superbly responsive. Dan Blanton, my research assistant for most of the project, deserves special thanks for his ingenuity, insights, and speed. Jed Esty, Sara Willburn, Alexi Murdoch, and others gave of their native intelligence in informal discussions.

Portions of *Primitive Passions* appeared in earlier versions in *American Literary History* and *Art Forum International;* my thanks to those publications for providing the opportunity to write and think things through. Duke University provided grants through its Research Council and several semesters of leave during which this book was written and seen through press: I am grateful to the University's administrators—Roy Weintraub, Bill Chafe, John Strohbehn, and Nan Keohane—for having faith in unusual projects and for making Duke an exciting, adventurous place to work.

George Andreou, my editor at Knopf, was a joy to work with—providing everything that an author could want. His rigorous, intelligent comments were infused with generosity, understanding, and praise; they served as good friends throughout the process of revision. Geri Thoma, my agent, was always available for helpful advice. My thanks also to Iris Weinstein, Susan Carroll, and others who helped bring the book into physical being.

Todd Webb showed exemplary kindness in allowing me to use his magnificent photographs of New Mexico. They reflected for me important aspects of the spirit of my book; I would have felt much poorer without them. My acknowledgment also of Betsy Evans Hunt and Olaf for making possible the inclusion of these photographs. My thanks also to Saki Karavas, Esq., and to the Museum of Fine Arts, part of the Museum of New Mexico, in Santa Fe, for providing photographs.

Finally, and closest to home, I thank my husband, Stuart, who had faith in the book and provided reminders, when necessary, of the usual vicissitudes of my writing process. My gratitude also to him for tip-toeing around my time for work. My daughters, Kate and Elizabeth, were alert, curious, and helpful about the project from the start. As I vetted titles and cover, Elizabeth was especially enthusiastic and supportive. Kate, a budding writer, helped refine the catalogue and jacket copy. I owe my family thanks for all this and much more.

INDEX

abject, the, 110
Abraham, 7
Adams, Ansel, 118
Adato, Perry Miller, 119
Adorno, Theodor, 12
Africa
   de Watteville's experiences, 69–73
   Dinesen's experiences, 61–2
   Gallmann's experiences, 76–82
   Gide's experiences, 25–9
   Goodall's experiences, 101–4
   Jung's experiences, 33–6
   Kingsley's experiences, 64–9
   landscape, women identified with,
      27, 86–7
   Markham's experiences, 73–6
   missionaries in, 68
   mythopoetic men's movement and,
      157
   women's experience of, 62–4
   see also Fossey, Dian
African Madness (Shoumatoff), 106
Afrocentrism, 224n36
Albert, Prince, 197
Alcatraz seizure by Indians, 137
Allegret, Marc, 25
Allen, Paula Gunn, 182
"American Land Ethic, An" (Momaday),
   138
American Religion, The (Bloom), 173–4
Anderson, Sherwood, 125

animism, 71, 79, 211, 214
anthropology, 9–10, 13–14, 37–8
Anthropology and Modern Life (Boas), 9
Aquarian Conspiracy, The (Ferguson),
   173
Arab Ruta (Kibbii), 73, 74
Argonauts of the Western Pacific
   (Malinowski), 9
Artaud, Antonin, 23, 51
Artforum International, 192
Art Journal, 192
Art of Spiritual Harmony, The
   (Kandinsky), 125, 233n28
Asmat people, 4, 6
Athey, Ron, 203–4
At the Rodeo (O'Keeffe), 127
Austin, Mary, 182–3
Aztec people, 4, 7, 51

Bacchae, The (Euripides), 39, 87, 226n24
Bachofen, Johann, 37–9, 183
Baker, Josephine, 9
Bakhtin, Mikhail, 241n9, 243n28
Bataille, Georges, 51
"Beating of a Drum, The" (Eliot), 10
Being-ness, 15, 109, 112, 218
Bell, Clive, 125
Benedict, Ruth, 9–10, 182
Bernays, Minna, 30
Berninghaus, Oscar E., 127
Beyond the Pleasure Principle (Freud), 41

A NOTE ABOUT THE AUTHOR

*Marianna Torgovnick is a professor
in the English department of Duke
University. Her previous books include* Gone
Primitive: Savage Intellects, Modern Lives
and Crossing Ocean Parkway: Readings by
an Italian American Daughter, *which won
the American Book Award in 1995.*